YO-CCH-971

THE ENGLISH GENIUS

THE ENGLISH GENIUS

BY

HUGH KINGSMILL *Lunn.*

KENNIKAT PRESS
Port Washington, N. Y./London

THE ENGLISH GENIUS

First published in 1939
Reissued in 1971 by Kennikat Press
Library of Congress Catalog Card No: 73-105799
ISBN 0-8046-1359-1

Manufactured by Taylor Publishing Company   Dallas, Texas

CONTENTS

INTRODUCTION
BY
HUGH KINGSMILL

INTRODUCTION

SOME years ago it occurred to me that it would be possible
to bring out an English Bible which should contain, in
extracts from our poets, historians, lawyers, scientists and so
on, an expression of our national character and achievement
comparable with that contained in the Hebrew Bible. The
idea seemed excellent to various persons, who, however,
appeared to wish that it had emanated from a more august
source. So I substituted the idea embodied in the present
volume, which may be regarded as an introduction to my
original idea, and a stimulus to someone to put it into
execution.

After I had read the contributions which make up this
book, I pondered on the English genius as it shows itself in
the art of editing. In editing, as in every other English
achievement, there are two traditions, typified in *The Times*
on the one hand and in Dr. Johnson on the other. At the
present moment, when we compare ourselves with the
totalitarian states, we are inclined to over-estimate English
individualism. Really individual persons are more common
in England than elsewhere, but they are not numerous.
Ninety years ago Carlyle said that there were twenty-seven
million Englishmen, mostly fools. That was an unkind way
of expressing what is still true, except that the population is
now greater. The mass of mankind likes, and always has
liked, to have a few plain ideas at their disposal by means of
which they will be able to take up a simple attitude to any
problem of general interest. In the last hundred and fifty
years the Press has been the chief instrument for clarifying
and disseminating these ideas. Public opinion in England
is, of course, not completely uniform. One section of the
public favours one set of ideas, another another. Our
insular and relatively secure position allows us that much

latitude. But in any great crisis, such as a war or the events of December, 1936, the English become as cohesive as any dictator could wish. "Team spirit" is an English phrase, so is "playing the game" and "it's not cricket." Leading athletes in our public schools do not differ in any essential respect from foreign dictators, like them regarding the body to which they belong as the instrument of their own glorification. In England, as elsewhere, it requires the co-operation of a great many persons to make any particular person really pleased with himself.

Anyone who glances through the files of *The Times* during the last one hundred and fifty years will realise the powerful collective spirit which animates the English nation. The contributions to *The Times*, political, religious and literary, like the instruments in an orchestra conducted by Toscanini, blend with one another in a perfect harmony. Here is the genius of English editing in its most characteristic and, it must be admitted, most impressive manifestation. The other tradition, what I have called the Johnsonian, is very different. In the seventies of the eighteenth century someone had the idea that it would be a good thing to bring out an edition of the chief English poets. Someone else thought there ought to be an introduction to each volume, and suggested Johnson. In due course a number of booksellers (as publishers were then called), each with one or more poets whom he wanted written about, approached Johnson. Johnson fell in with the idea, wrote introductions to all the poets on the list, and added a few names, chosen less in the interests of poetry than of religion. The total effect was heterogeneous. *The Lives of the Poets*, as Johnson's introductions were called when published in book form, were in many instances not lives, owing to a lack of biographical material, and in many instances not poets, owing to a lack of inspiration in the persons under notice. Johnson was vaguely aware of these and other flaws, for he writes: "The poems of Dr. Watts were by my recommendation inserted in the late collection; the readers of which are to impute to me whatever pleasure or weariness they may find in the perusal of Blackmore, Watts, Pomfret, and Yalden." Nevertheless, the effect of *The Lives of the Poets*, quite apart from the genius with which they are written, is pleasing. In any other country an edition of its chief poets, with introductions by the greatest living writer, would have been a cut-and-dried affair, supervised by some responsible body. Poets of the standing of Chaucer, Spenser and Shakespeare would not have been omitted. Poets of the standing of Elijah Fenton and Thomas Sprat, not to mention Blackmore, Watts, Pomfret and Yalden, would not have been included. The total effect would have been homogeneous, but it would also have been lifeless. However attenuated it may be, there is in every Englishman a resistance to being regimented. Matthew Arnold used to complain of this, and spent much time trying to persuade the English to institute an Academy which should be, like the French Academy, "a sovereign organ of the highest literary opinion, a recognised authority in matters of intellectual tone and taste." His efforts were useless, for where the imagination is concerned there is no place for a collective authority, as the English, the most imaginative of races, instinctively realise.

In saying that the English are the most imaginative of races, it is not implied that many Englishmen have used their imaginative faculty to much advantage. Excellence of any kind is rare, and does not become more common by being detected where it does not exist. It is as absurd to praise a nation collectively as to indict it collectively. It may be pleasant to be told in speeches and books that the English are kindly and just, that they possess an ancient and inbred piety, that they are slow to anger but terrible when they are roused, that their affections are not given lightly, but once given, etc. All this, however, bears very little relation to the reality of harassed, narrow lives, seldom lit up by any impersonal emotion, and only at rare intervals revealing the divinity latent in every human being. Such differences as exist between the English and other peoples are not radical, and are far from being always in our favour, but such as they are they can for the most part be traced to our greater

imaginativeness, which has conditioned both our faults and
our merits. Our poetry, the greatest in European literature,
and our humour, the richest and most varied, are the finest
fruits of our superiority in imagination. At the close of the
Great War it was England that gave the world the two
symbols which commemorate its tragedy, the Unknown
Soldier and the Two Minutes Silence. On a lower level, the
English excel in ceremonial. The Prussian enjoys drill, the
Englishman prefers a beautiful uniform. The goose-step is
an assertion of power, Trooping the Colour is a kind of
ballet. Even our monarchy is a poetic conception as well as
a practical convenience, an image of the kind of existence
children think they would enjoy.

The weak side of our imaginativeness is that it quickly
becomes debased by false sentiment, which is more prevalent
in England than elsewhere, because we are more idealistic
than other nations and therefore more in need of a veil
between us and our everyday practice. We are romantic
about sex because we have an ideal of love which does not
square with the reality of lust. We are romantic about the
upper classes because we have an ideal picture of the aristocracy which we do not care to test by an unbiased survey of
those who constitute it. We are romantic about the poor
because we like to think they enjoy being exploited, and when
we possessed Ireland we were romantic about it for the same
reason. I remember going into the Coliseum a few days
after the Rebellion of Easter Week, and there was the
audience, fresh from seeing pictures of half Dublin in ruins,
tenderly joining in the chorus of "When Irish Eyes are
Smiling."

It might be possible to find another term than hypocrisy
for the English resolve not to admit the discrepancy between
their ideals and their practice, but few foreigners put themselves out to find one. A courteous Frenchman, however,
when I asked him whether he did not consider the English
hypocrites, replied: "Not hypocrites—amateurs of decorum."
He was not being ironical. The English had discovered a
new form of connoisseurship, and he wished them well.

A discrepancy between practice and theory always produces an internal discomfort, and I shall conclude this brief summary of our chief defects with a quotation from Johnson, bearing on the mistrustfulness and lack of geniality which characterise most Englishmen in the ordinary intercourse of life: "Two men of any other nation who are thrown into a room together, at a house where they are both visitors, will immediately find some conversation. But two Englishmen will probably go each to a different window, and remain in obstinate silence. Sir, we as yet do not enough understand the common rights of humanity."

In the contributions which follow, the qualities which have reconciled the rest of the world to our existence and at the present time attract the saner nations within our orbit are explained and illustrated.

H. K.

RELIGION

BY

W. R. INGE

RELIGION

THE Editor of this book is no doubt well aware how many snags there are in an attempted estimate of the English genius. Is there such a thing as national character? Does the real Englishman or American often resemble John Bull or Uncle Sam? How much, if any, of the continental prejudice against the Jews is justified? Is not our own society divided into sections or classes, each with its own traditions and ideals? It may make a great difference whether our public policy, which helps to create an impression of our ways of thinking and acting, is directed by our aristocracy, or our middle class, or by organised labour. Again, if there is a national character, has it remained unchanged? There may be alterations even in the predominant racial type of a mixed population. May there not even now be local characteristics, handed down from the times when the country was settled by immigrants from different lands? Is not the Northumbrian noticeably different in character from the native of Wessex? The very name of England raises difficulties, for we resemble the United States in having no proper name for our nation. America is the name of a continent or hemisphere, not of a nation; England is the name of a part only of the British Isles. The Scots will not allow us to include Scotland; and if we could, the Highlander is very unlike the Lowlander. Wales is not part of England; we cannot forget this when we are discussing religious movements and characteristics; Cornwall sometimes seems to be more Welsh than English in its reaction to revivals and its proneness to emotionalism.

We shall be wise not to pay very much attention to foreign judgments. There is hardly any quality, except meekness and loquacity, which has not been ascribed to us, for good or evil, by some of our neighbours. We have been accused

3

of "taking our pleasures sadly"; but another medieval critic writes of "Anglia plena iocis, gens libera, digna iocari." Napoleon called us a nation of shopkeepers, a business in which we are far inferior to the French; we have been accused of perfidy, though we are incapable, both from our institutions and our temperament, of long-sighted and crafty scheming. We are credited with indomitable will-power and with easy-going softness; with dogged industry and with slack indolence. Our national "spleen" was supposed to drive us to suicide, until statistics demonstrated that our suicide rate is one of the lowest in Europe. Such comments, even when they do not contradict one another, are not helpful.

And yet there are a few qualities which seem to persist as really characteristic of our people, though in every genera-tion there is a vast number who exhibit none of them. The typical Englishman is humane; cruelty excites him to violent indignation. He is a bad hater, and has a short memory for injuries. He is much more often proud than vain. He is a Stoic in repressing his feelings, and despises those who give way to emotion. He is, by intention at least, just, and will not take an unfair advantage. "Fair play," for him, is a duty which should govern his conduct in almost every relation of life.

Most of these principles are integral parts of the ideal of a gentleman, which is recognised everywhere as our chief contribution to ethics, and which is very far from being the standard of one class only. This ethical ideal has deeply coloured our religion. The standard which the Englishman sets before himself, he applies, *per eminentiam*, to the Deity. God must be the greatest of gentlemen. How much of traditional theology, which has been at various times pre-sented as Christian, is discredited by this canon, hardly needs to be set forth in detail. Some of it is still passively accepted, but not really believed.

Other characteristics of our people are intemperance, in eating more than in drinking, a habit common to all the nations of North-Western Europe, and much diminished in England in the last half-century; disinclination for hard and steady work, which has, on the contrary, become much more pronounced within living memory; a strange addiction to fads and crank-beliefs, a fault which we share with the Americans; and a peculiar sense of humour, which is often a saving grace in an Englishman's character, preserving him from fierce and cruel fanaticisms. "I hate the very sound of abstractions," said Burke, speaking on this occasion like an Englishman. "An Englishman hates an idea when he meets one," said Bishop Creighton. This is not mere stupidity or want of education. We think we have observed that the most irreparable mistakes are made by consistent doctrinaires, and we prefer to improvise a solution for each problem as it arises. But it must be admitted that we have too often addressed Britannia in the words of Charles Kingsley: "Be good, sweet maid, and let who will be clever."

Christianity is, I think, stronger in Great Britain than in any other European country. The presence of a Church party, called in Germany the Centre, in secular politics gives the hierarchy a bargaining power which it does not possess among us, except in the highly organised Roman Catholic body. But it is very questionable whether this political pull is favourable to religion as distinguished from ecclesiasticism, and the power of the Church in Catholic lands arouses an antagonism to Christianity which is rarely encountered in this country. The recent debate in Parliament on the revision of the Prayer Book was read with amazement on the Continent; we at home were surprised only by the unusual candour and eloquence of the speeches. Theology and dogma have decayed, and the superficial test of church-attendance has made many people think that Christianity is declining; but ethically we are still a Christian nation. The saying of the agnostic Mill that a man cannot do better than order his conduct so that Christ would approve of him would be accepted to-day by the vast majority of Englishmen. This is true even of the *déracinés* of our large towns, who have been uprooted from the soil, and from the wholesome pieties and wise traditions of country life.

It has often been said that the Englishman likes to find his own way to heaven. John Bunyan's "Christian," travelling alone or with one or two companions, is a very characteristic figure. And yet, when our countrymen wish to combine, for religious or for secular purposes, they are not undisciplined. They show a certain sanity even in their enthusiasms, and a decided wish to show their faith by their works. Among all our churches and sects none is more characteristic than the small Society of Friends. Alike in their individualism and in their mysticism, in their sacramental view of life which almost supersedes the need for particular sacraments, in their confidence that honest and productive industry may fulfil all the requisites of a godly life, in their humanitarianism and pacifism, and in their devotion to charitable and practical reforms, the Quakers are typical of English piety, though the large majority of our people would be unwilling to give up the traditions and practices which bind them to the greater Churches, whether Catholic or Protestant. What Troeltsch calls the sect type came into power for a short time after the Great Rebellion; but the Englishman is conservative in religion as in other matters, and the Puritans soon found that the popular love of the Church of England was far stronger than they had supposed.

The salient feature of English Christianity is not individualism, nor sectariarism, nor practicability, nor empiricism. It is that vein of idealism which has always been an integral part of our complex character. The notion that our nation is preoccupied with gross material interests is a libel. During the last century transitory circumstances made England the workshop of the world, and we had to adapt ourselves to that not very congenial part, in spite of the denunciations of our poets and moralists, who thought that we had forsaken our God for the golden calf. But in reality we are neither very covetous nor very industrious. Our national poetry, one of the finest in the world is, to a quite unusual extent, serious, moral, and spiritual, and inspired by a lofty imagination. A survey of English poetry, in any good anthology, will convey the impression that behind all the fluctuations of classicism and romanticism there is a vision,

a sense sublime
Of something far more deeply interfused,
Whose dwelling is the light of setting suns,
And the round ocean and the living air,
And the blue sky, and in the mind of man.

I know no other literature which is so strongly marked by
this noble idealism, and it is in the best secular poetry, rather
than in avowedly theological and devotional works, though
in these also our nation takes a front rank, that I find the
truest indications of the English genius on the religious side.

It is usually convenient to treat a subject of this kind
historically. I shall not attempt to find any national characteristics in the English Schoolmen, Duns Scotus and
William of Ockham, who appear in history as opponents of
Thomas Aquinas. But in the fourteenth century there was
a very remarkable group of cloistered mystics, whose works
have been rescued from oblivion, and who will always be
valued by students of devotional literature.

Besides the monasteries and convents, where the "religious"
lived a communal life, there were numerous anchorages,
often close to a church, where hermits of both sexes were
walled up. They never left their cells, which communicated
with the outside world by a window, covered by a heavy
curtain, which was drawn aside when the recluse wished to
give an interview. The very early *Ancren Riwle* is full of
wise and witty advice to three anchoresses at Tarrant Kaines,
Dorsetshire. They are not to be "staring" or "cackling
anchoresses" (*kakelinde ancren*); the true anchoresses are birds
of heaven that fly aloft and sit on the green boughs singing
merrily; that is, they meditate "on the blessedness of heaven
that never fadeth and is always green. A bird sometimes
alighteth on earth to seek food, but never feels safe there and
often turns herself about." A pretty comparison, made use
of by a French poet:

Soyons comme l'oiseau, posé pour un instant
Sur des rameaux trop frêles;
Qui sent ployer la branche, et qui chante pourtant,
Sachant qu'il a des ailes.

But the gem of our medieval sacred literature is the *Book of the Revelations of Julian of Norwich*, one of the most exquisite books of devotion ever written. It is entirely free from morbid erotic emotionalism, and with all its fervour breathes a spirit of cheerful and hopeful sanity. She was visited in her cell by that queer creature Margaret Kempe, and gave her, it seems, some shrewd advice.

Another admirable book of the fourteenth century is *The Scale(or Ladder) of Perfection*, by Walter Hylton, who died in 1396. This treatise is entirely on the lines of medieval mysticism; but in reading this literature we are often reminded of Maeterlinck's saying that a book grows old only by reason of its anti-mysticism. In the best mystical works there is very little to determine either date or place, or section of the Church. Christianity, in fact, has never been divided in the chambers where good men pray.

John Wycliffe, the most notable of the Reformers before the Reformation, illustrates the independent temper of English churchmanship. Long before the breach with Rome, the Anglican Church often showed itself intractable; but the Lollards made themselves unpopular by their strict Puritanical principles, and Wycliffe's movement had more influence among the followers of Hus in Bohemia than in our country.

The English Reformation had not much in common with the contemporary movements in Germany and France. It is a childish mistake to suppose that the private quarrel of Henry VIII with the Pope about his marriage did more than determine the form of the revolt. Lollardism had never died out, and in 1511 the Latin secretary of Henry VII wrote to Erasmus that wood was grown scarce because so much was needed to burn heretics, "and yet their numbers grow." The parliaments were anti-papal long before Henry broke off his allegiance to Rome, and the work of the English humanists, like Dean Colet, must not be forgotten. The possibility of making England an independent patriarchate under Canterbury was no new idea. The English people were determined to have the Scriptures in the vernacular—

the vernacular Bible had been banned in England, though
not on the Continent. The victory of the English Bible had
a long-lasting and important effect on the national religion,
which became to a large extent the religion of a book. The
uncritical and superstitious treatment of the text, and the
tendency to set the Old Testament on the same level as the
New, for a long time made English Christianity more Jewish
than the religion of the apostolic age and of the Fathers.
The Christianity which converted Europe was a Hellenistic
religion; the Catholic Church was the last creative achievement of the classical civilisation. This, however, was not
the view of the English Puritans or of the Evangelicals who
followed them. Bibliolatry and Sabbatarianism offended the
common sense of educated people at a time when education
was ceasing to be the privilege of the few. The newer
Evangelicalism is discarding these burdens, which unquestionably had become obstacles to the work of the
Churches. On the other side, the familiarity with the Bible,
which is no longer usual among the young and middle-aged,
had some great advantages. The Jacobean scholars who
made the Authorised Version were masters of a very fine
English style; the coincidence in time of this book and the
plays of Shakespeare did much to stabilise the language when
it was almost at its best. The records of an ancient Eastern
civilisation, and its poetry, always interesting and sometimes
sublime, had a considerable cultural value. And an intimate knowledge of the Gospels and Epistles, from which
many proverbs have passed into common speech, gave our
countrymen a far better idea of what Christianity was like
when it was fresh from the mint than is possible to the
majority of Roman Catholics, who learn what they know of
religion from other sources. The present neglect of Bible
reading must be deplored on many grounds.

The influence of Luther and Lutheranism in this country
has not been great. Luther was not a great theologian, and
his knowledge of Church history was slight. The early
Church was not so pure, nor the medieval Church so radically corrupt, as he supposed. The reverence for the "first

six centuries," which has played some part in Anglicanism,
is perhaps a legacy from Luther. By exalting faith and dis-
paraging works, he attached more importance to correct
belief than even the Catholics had done, and became the
founder of a new scholasticism, which did not take a firm
root in England.

Far more important in its influence upon British Christianity has been the teaching of John Calvin. His aim was to
make the invisible sovereignty of God as tangible a thing as
the medieval Church had been. We are soldiers in Christ's
army against the powers of evil; those who are predestined
to salvation are bound to a life of active combat in the war
of right against wrong. A strong and steady self-control,
extending over the whole of life, took the place of the mild
dietary rules and gentler discipline of Catholicism; a vigorous
political interest, not for the sake of the State; a steady
diligence, but not for the sake of riches; a meddlesome social
organisation, but not to increase human happiness; a zeal in
productive labour, without much interest in its objects—
these are the characteristics of a Calvinistic society. The
effect upon social life has been enormous. The modern man
of business, if he is not a child of the Ghetto, is usually a
grandchild of John Calvin. Calvinism has created a very
strong, austere, and virile type of character, and has brought
great material prosperity to the countries which have adopted
it. It is now in decay, corrupted in part by its own success; it
is to be found more often in Scotland and the United States
than in England. That a creed which denies free will should
have such results is one of the paradoxes of human nature.

Since the Reformation there have been periodical Catholic
revivals, which show that the rupture with the Latin Church
was not acceptable to all Englishmen. George Santayana,
in his beautiful book of *Soliloquies in England*, thinks that the
national character is Protestant through and through. "An
Englishman who becomes a Catholic ceases to be an Englishman." This is overstated, since there are natural Catholics
and Protestants in every nation. But we have, as I have said,
our own ideal of moral excellence, the perfect gentleman,

which differs in some respects from the Catholic ideal
of the saint; and the typical Englishman dislikes the idea of
making over his conscience, and still more that of his wife,
to the keeping of a priest. But there will always be many
who think it as reasonable to entrust a priest with the care
of their soul as a doctor with the care of their body and a
lawyer with the care of their affairs; and the Catholic system
of spiritual therapeutics, developed empirically through long
experience, is more scientific than can be easily obtained
elsewhere. Protestantism, however, can enter into closer relations with modern secular movements than Catholicism, and
is more free from the weight of the dead hand. It is most
unlikely that England will ever again choose to submit to
the yoke of the Western Catholic Church, which is more
decidedly Latin in its strength and weakness than it was four
hundred years ago.

It is a remarkable fact that the mind of our countrymen
has always found Greek thought more congenial than Latin.
John Scotus Erigena, in the dark ages, based his philosophy
on the system of the Christian Neoplatonist whom he knew
as Dionysius the Areopagite. The Renaissance reached
England in the time of Colet and Erasmus; Grocyn and
Linacre had studied at Florence in the famous Platonic
Academy there. Erasmus encouraged the study of Greek at
Cambridge, where as early as 1516 the young men were
reading Plato and Aristotle.

These men were primarily religious reformers. Colet
studied not only the pseudo-Dionysius, but the Greek
Fathers, especially Origen. After the breach with Rome
there was a group of Liberal churchmen—Falkland, Hales,
Chillingworth, Stillingfleet, and Jeremy Taylor, who wished
to make the Church of England as comprehensive as possible,
and so prepared the way for the famous school of Cambridge
Platonists, who must always be one of the chief glories of
Anglicanism. In the opinion of Bishop Burnet the corrup-
tions of the clergy at this time were so great that "if a new
set of men of another stamp had not appeared, the Church
had quite lost her esteem over the nation."

The Cambridge Platonists in the seventeenth century were glad to recognise in the Platonic philosophy "the old loving nurse" of their theology. "It is difficult," as Professor Muirhead says, "to exaggerate the essential unity of principle and spirit that pervades these two great systems." "Platonism might be called the intellectual side of Christianity." The abiding influence of this school upon English thought has not been sufficiently recognised. The Cambridge group was in conscious opposition to Hobbes, and before long discerned "a tang of the mechanic atheism hanging about" the Cartesians. Philosophy and religion were for them almost identical; faith and discipline lead to real enlightenment; in the apprehension of the absolute values, goodness, truth, and beauty, we have real knowledge of the nature of God. "God is not only the eternal reason, but He is also that unstained beauty and supreme good to which our wills are perpetually aspiring." "Nothing is more natural to man's soul than to receive truth." They fully accepted the act of faith on which Platonism rests, that "the fully real can be fully known," or that "that which is filled with the most real is most really filled." A few of their maxims, mainly from Benjamin Whichcote, whose "Aphorisms" are to be found in many old libraries, will show the general tenor of their teaching, and its very English character. "I will not make a religion for God, nor suffer any man to make a religion for me." "The mind of a good man is the best part of him, but the mind of a bad man is the worst part of him." "The state of religion lies in a good mind and a good life; all else is about religion." "That faith which is not a principle of life is a nullity in religion." "Heaven is first a temper and then a place." "Our Saviour accepts of no other separation of His Church from the other part of the world than what is made by truth, virtue, innocency, and holiness of life." "He that gives reason for what he saith has done what is fit to be done and the most that can be done. He that gives no reason speaks nothing, though he saith never so much." "The longest sword, the strongest lungs, the most voices, are false measures of truth." "If I have not a friend, God send me an enemy." "To seek divinity merely in books and writings is to seek the living among the dead; we do but in vain seek God many times in these, where His truth too often is not so much enshrined as entombed. No, seek for God within thine own soul." This last is from John Smith, a mystic of the type of Plotinus, whom he studied carefully. His also is the following: "Such as men themselves are, such will God Himself seem to be. There is a double head as well as a double heart." Like Plato, he aspires to a "naked intuition of eternal truth which is always the same, which never rises nor sets, but always stands still in its vertical, and fills the whole horizon of the soul with a mild and gentle light."

Half a century separates the Cambridge group from the next outstanding figure in English religion. William Law, non-juror, controversialist, moralist, and mystic, was born in 1686, and lived through a period when the fire of zeal burnt low, and the Church was too much conformed to this world. Law was not the man to adapt himself to the fashions of his time. His *Serious Call* is a tremendous indict-ment of lukewarmness in religion. Samuel Johnson called it the finest piece of hortatory theology in any language. "If he finds a spark of piety in the reader's mind," says Gibbon, "he will soon fan it into a flame, and a philosopher must allow that he expresses with equal severity and truth the strange contradiction between the faith and practice of the Christian world." About 1734 Law became acquainted with the writings of the German mystic, sometimes called the Teutonic philosopher, Jacob Böhme. The study of them coloured all the rest of his life, and inspired some of the most beautiful devotional treatises in our language. He acknow-ledges no obligations to Plato or the Platonists, but like all other philosophical mystics, he really belongs to them. He is as unique a figure in the cool, rationalistic, moralising eighteenth century, as Erigena in the barbarous age when he lived.

There is perhaps nothing specially characteristic of England about the two reactions against the eighteenth century, the Evangelical and the Catholic, except their insularity. Both arose when our island was intellectually more isolated from the Continent than at any time before or since. The Anglo-Catholic position is quite defensible, but foreign nations see in it only further evidence of the illogicality of the English mind. Liberal theology has never been a popular movement. It seemed to be forced upon all thoughtful Christians at a time when the sciences were confident and dogmatic. But the present wave of anti-intellectualism and pragmatism tends rather towards sceptical orthodoxy. Whatever suits souls is true, and truth has no other meaning except what suits souls. Catholic modernism can make terms with this disintegrating relativism; Liberal Protestantism raises its voice against it in vain.

I have already referred to the wonderful catena of religious poets in our language, from the Tudor Platonists through George Herbert, Vaughan, and Traherne to Crashaw and Quarles. Wordsworth is one of the great religious poets of all time; to understand "The Prelude" is to understand Plato. In the Victorian period Keble is the voice of those who lived "beneath the shadow of the steeple"; Tennyson and Browning interpret the lay convictions of their time, while Matthew Arnold and Clough give expression to its haunting doubts. There is a deep seriousness about them all, as there was in the period to which they belonged. We may say the same of more recent poets, such as Bridges and Masefield.

If I am to hazard any predictions about the future of religion in our country, I must protest to begin with that the future of institutionalism is not the same as the future of religion. The only true apostolical succession has been in the lives of the saints, who have been sometimes sheltered and sometimes attacked by the official hierarchy. The more loosely bound Church corporations are certainly losing ground; whether men and women are actually more irreligious than they were formerly may be doubted. Christ nowhere encouraged us to expect that the largest crowd will ever be gathered round the narrow gate; at all times many are called but few chosen. A popular religion, for this very reason, is not likely to be a true religion. Religion, as A. N. Whitehead has reminded us, may be and often is a very bad thing. Priest and prophet seldom agree except when "the prophets prophesy falsely, and the priests bear rule by their means." A Church may win what the world calls success by exploiting the superstitions of the vulgar, and by making unholy alliances. A degenerate people will have a degenerate religion, and will treat its true prophets as true prophets have usually been treated by their contemporaries. But in spite of all, the torch-bearers of the divine fire never fail. Christianity has lived through even the most corrupt ages.

Even those who do not believe in a revelation of God through Christ must recognise the extreme improbability that a religion which has lasted for nearly two thousand years, and has throughout that period satisfied, on the whole, the spiritual aspirations of the most civilised part of the world, will die out. Far too much importance is ascribed just now to the post-war revolutionary upheavals; they have stirred up the unsavoury dregs which every civilisation deposits; they have not changed human nature, nor its fundamental needs. Ecclesiastical institutions may be destroyed, their property confiscated, their buildings burnt, their priests murdered. But personal religion—the life of prayer, which is "the elevation of the mind to God," penitence and the craving for forgiveness, the ardent desire to rise above the fleeting shadows of this mortal life and to behold the land which is "very far off" and yet "closer to us than breathing and nearer than hands and feet," all that is summed up in the words devotion, contemplation, mysticism—varies very little from age to age and from east to west, and we may fairly assume that it is indestructible. The longing will never cease; our hearts, as Augustine says, are troubled until they rest in God.

Will these cravings and aspirations continue to be satisfied through Christianity? Why should they not? That religion has satisfied all legitimate claims made upon it hitherto, and we can no more invent a new religion than we can build a tree. Miracle may perhaps be relegated to the sphere of pious opinion; the function of myth in theology and even in philosophy may be more frankly recognised; but in official declarations the thinker will always have to defer to the opinions of the half-educated majority. This is no new thing, and does not threaten the permanence of the Church.

Should there be a national type of Christianity? I think there should. Every nation has its own contribution to make to the spiritual life of humanity. We may compare it if we will to an orchestra, in which many instruments blend their notes in a hymn to the glory of the Creator. The best English Christian will be an Englishman, and as such rather different from the best French Christian. There is so much that is good and noble in the secular character which we most admire that it only needs purifying and elevating by the principles of the Gospel to make it a very fine ideal. Already the idea of a gentleman has shed its adventitious associations with heraldry and property in land. It has no longer anything to do with class or occupation or absence of occupation. When we think of the best men and women whom we have known, do we not see a national as well as a Christian stamp upon them? Personally, I feel a little resentment when I read Newman's famous and brilliant sketch of the character of a gentleman. He so plainly dislikes the type that he misrepresents it as a matter of acting and seeking after effect, which at its best it certainly is not. Nor are the Englishman's self-respect and reserve justly called pride. Considering his upbringing, Newman ought to have understood his countrymen better. The Catholic nations themselves do not trust an "Italianised Englishman"—in fact, they used to say that he is "an incarnate fiend." We may become much better people than most of us are without ceasing to be ourselves, loyal citizens of the land of our birth, who "speak the tongue that Shakespeare spake, the faith and morals hold that Milton held."

ENGLISH VERSE
BY
HILAIRE BELLOC

ENGLISH VERSE

THE verse of a European nation takes its form from two things combined: the national temperament on its poetic side, including the political circumstance within which that temperament works, and the matter upon which that temperament is exercised—the national language.

The English temperament has become, after long moulding, an individual thing in Europe. The political condition within which that temperament works has also become an individual thing in Europe. The English language, the latest born of the great European vernacular languages, was moulded into its permanent form a little before the Reformation. It has been what it now is for four hundred years, and is, from the strange history of its comparatively sudden development, a thing equally individual with the national temperament (which is far older) and with the political circumstance (which is far younger) than itself.

To define a national temperament, even one as highly differentiated as is now the English temperament is not possible. The thing depends upon an inward spirit; it is manifested through a character and savour of its own to which obviously no formula can apply. You might as well try to formularise a scent or a colour. But its main characteristics are discoverable, and these are the spiritual forces which have built up the glorious body of English poetry—a thing the like of which, both for its possession of the reader's emotion and for its volume (wherein is included its variety) has, I believe, no rival or parallel in all the European mass of literature of which it is a part. For we must always remember that England is a part of Europe, a Province of Christendom, can only live as such and must decline or perish if it be too long cut off from the general

stem. We must not think of English verse as something
self-existent and indifferent to the general body of our
civilisation. Those who are already beginning to think thus
condemn themselves to fatuity, and if they were to become
the masters of our literary future they would condemn that
future to death.

We only live by the common life of Christendom, but
within that common life England has made things of her
own, distinct from all other European things. Of those
things that which perhaps a remote posterity will keep in
highest honour, that by which the name of England will be
most regarded is English letters: and of English letters not
English prose—which nearly achieved a norm yet failed to
do so—but English *verse* will stand supreme above the other
forms of English expression.

The national temperament of England is above all
emotional. It is constructively emotional, indeed its constructional power is at least as remarkable as its emotional
power, but its emotional power is, compared with that of
other European groups, more remarkable than its constructional.

That is why there has been no specific body of English
Architecture, at least no body of it comparable to that of the
Northern French Middle Ages, of the Italian Renaissance,
or of the great seventeenth-century classical period in France;
which we followed but wherein we did not originate.

The constructional genius of the English has shown itself
exceptionally in mechanics. It has shown itself also (though
this feature is usually exaggerated) in the region of Law. It
has shown itself somewhat (and this has been still more
exaggerated by a patriotic bias) in the region of political
arrangement. But it has shown itself strong beyond that
of any rival in the fabric of English verse. The English
temperament herein captured and dealt constructively with
an emotional power of unique intensity.

What were the characteristics of that emotional power?

In the first place a unique visual imagination. This
is, it would seem, the most permanent and the most vital

factor of the English mind. You see it in the fact that
English fiction has thrown up a whole gallery of individual
portraits, indeed of living imaginary individuals who crowd
and jostle each other throughout the whole story of English
dreaming and telling of tales. This vital current would seem
to run permanently through English literary effort, beginning
long before the formation of the English language and
continuing till yesterday; perhaps destined to continue into
the future uninterruptedly. Portraits stand out in the earliest
narratives appearing in this island. They stand out in the
Latin of the English medieval chronicles. They stand out in
Chaucer. They stand out in the private letters and dispatches—such few as remain to us—of the later Middle
Ages. They stand out to us in chance phrases of state
documents and brief biographies and epistolary work of the
sixteenth century. They crowd upon us in the descriptions
of the seventeenth and eighteenth but they come to a climax
and maximum in our own time. All Thackeray, all Meredith,
all Dickens, even Hardy, testify to that, and where you
may begin among the moderns with Sam Weller in *Pickwick*
you do not end a hundred years later with a triumph: the
character called Jeeves in the contemporary work of Mr.
P. G. Wodehouse.

Now in the matter of verse this violent driving power of
the English visual imagination is to be discovered principally
through the action upon the English mind of landscape. To
read the Fourth Book of *Paradise Lost* is like taking a great
journey through landscapes, splendidly imprinted, and
permanently, upon the reader. You may pick out at random
in an hour's turning over the leaves half a hundred pictures
of sea, sky and air; land and water; mist and evening and
morning; peculiar to this island and fixed for ever in a dozen
words, so that the man reading them possesses an experience
as exact and as acutely living as the experience of a short
unforgettable dream, or as one of those experiences equally
short, equally unforgettable, which come to us each in our
little passage through the daylight and remain a consolation
for living.

But there is another quality of the English mind which through the national temperament glorifies and stamps English verse: a combination of variety and active impact in the matter of rhythm.

Rhythm is common to all verse, English or Hottentot, but it would seem that English rhythm has about it something of that vigour which should proceed from the proximity of the ocean and from the power of the South-West Wind: which is an English power, if the South-West Wind will allow me to say so.

English rhythm, of course, has subtlety as well, but it does not live on subtlety as does French rhythm. It lives on something which is, if anything, an exaggeration of stress. Hence English verse is perpetually threatened with the vulgarity of exaggerated lilt. This temptation is increased by the age-long factor of alliteration upon which the remote ancestry of the Dark Ages, and for all we know, of Prehistoric Britain as well, too much depended. It has led to a thousand absurdities, and some of them of the most degraded rhymed stuff—especially in the patriotic vein—of modern time. This necessary appetite, which necessarily becomes a degraded passion for lilt, has done us all manner of harm, especially since the classics decayed among us. But being a passion—or at any rate a vital appetite—it has most assuredly invigorated our letters.

Of modern examples perhaps the best, as it is also the most varied as well as among the most emphatic, is Tennyson's incomparable "Ballad of the Revenge." That masterpiece reminds me of another truth closely allied to the power of the visual imagination: "Bad history makes good verse." But we are not here concerned with history but with verse. If the verse be good let the history go hang. Though upon a right reading of history depends the fate of nations, yet also upon verse depends the glory of nations when every other glory has passed away.

I have mentioned the presence of landscape in English verse and given as an illustration the Fourth Book of *Paradise Lost*. I must return to it again for a moment in its modern aspect. For modern English verse has achieved its highest emotional expression upon that theme. This again is directly in tune with the national temperament as it stood during the nineteenth century. Nowhere are men so moved by the aspect of Nature as are Englishmen. In the pictorial arts you find that continually, from Turner to the woodcuts of Whymper, which for my part I have always thought to be a high example of the national genius. The too often despised or forgotten mezzotints of Martin are an example in point and the striking coloured series on the harbours of the English coast. Well, English verse in all that modern period follows suit. In those rare passages of his total work where Wordsworth strikes deep he continually does so through landscape. The passages of "In Memoriam" which are most calculated to survive are not the confused sentimental theology which our fathers too much admired but rather the hints at landscape: "Ring out wild Bells"—and "Answer each other through the mist." Perhaps the summit of all single lines worthy of quotation from the Victorian poets is that in the "Morte d'Arthur": "Was a great water and the moon was full." It answers to and echoes the landscape motive in Byron's line: "The moon is up and yet it is not night." But instances perhaps equal or not much inferior crowd upon anyone who lets his memory wander over his reading of the English lyric from the beginning of the Romantic revolution for a hundred and twenty years. It is one of the worst symptoms of our present decline that this essentially national note of landscape is disappearing or has disappeared from contemporary verse of the younger generation to-day.

What we gained, however, in this department of landscape during the nineteenth century we lost in the gradual abandonment of rhetorical verse. The body of rhetorical verse appearing in the mass of the English lyric was not only considerable but of very high value. A man must have but a poor critical judgment who does not admire Macaulay's *Lays of Ancient Rome*. But rhetoric as a whole was oddly discredited towards the end of the nineteenth century among

English men of letters. I say "oddly" because that which Englishmen have most loved to praise in the way of letters and that in which they have been and still are (in quotation at least) most steeped, is essentially rhetoric and nothing else. I mean the more emotional passages of the Authorised Version. If ever there was the case of something following the Greek definition "neither prose nor verse but a mixture of both," it is the archaic English of the Jacobean Old Testament. Its texts are continually quoted as monuments of English prose. They are not that, and the word prose in their connexion is out of place. They are essentially masterpieces of rhetoric. In happy confirmation of the hope that English rhetòrical verse is not dead, or may perhaps revive, is that recent masterpiece, Mr. Chesterton's "Ballad of Lepanto," which for my part I find to be the best piece of *modern* verse in our language.

The national temper has a further special character, very strictly marked, which has affected English verse throughout its history: that character is *Creative Spontaneity*. The same quality in the English mind which produced modern machines and was parent to the Industrial Revolution has given its diversity to English verse.

The story of England as we know it begins with the creation of the new Protestant England and the Reformation. It was a process which did not mature until the later sixteenth century, and did not finally crystallise until the seventeenth. It is therefore during the later sixteenth century and the seventeenth that you have the formation of English verse as a body of European literature; nothing that came before was, properly speaking, the forerunner of what came after the Great Change.

Our Universities have attempted (unsuccessfully, I think) to claim an easy continuity between early Barbaric Saxon stuff and English verse as we now know it. They also, more naturally, with less violence, less necessitated gymnastics, attempted to claim continuity between *The Vision of Piers Plowman*, the work of Chaucer, and our present inheritance.

There is something in this latter claim, but, put as it

commonly is, that claim is misleading. The one thing we have in common throughout, dating from the earliest rough short lines of the local Teutonic dialects in the Dark Ages, is alliteration.

Most European verse uses alliteration, even the classics do so, but the constant use of it—I should call it an abuse of it—the *instinctive* and popular use of it is, I believe, peculiar to this island. It is a trick that gratifies men in the more civilised periods—and debauches them in the less civilised, because it is facile, a temptation to which the undisciplined mind easily succumbs. Anyhow, alliteration is always there in English verse, emphatic, and repeated from the beginning, it is the one link we have binding the medieval with the modern English poet.

For the rest, I repeat, English verse means verse since the middle of the sixteenth century. In that heaped treasure the mark of creative spontaneity is everywhere.

Foreign models of course existed. That was inevitable. But the English mind easily bent them to its own purpose. Even those great poets who are most steeped in classical and continental tradition gave to foreign models a new native accent. This was so even with the sonnet, the most rigid of models, while the purely native growths, of which I suppose the "Border Ballads" are the finest example, depended upon no influence external to our society. There has been noted by many a resemblance between the Spanish popular ballad forms and the English, for the various Spanish languages, and especially the Castilian, have in common with English a violent tonic accent: that same quality in English which continually puts us in peril of exaggerated lilt. But the similarity between the popular English and popular Spanish ballad is not derivative; the one did nothing to make the other.

Perhaps the chief proof and example of creative spontaneity in the English mind on its poetic side is the emergence of blank verse in the late sixteenth and seventeenth centuries.

Here was a form common to the stage, that is, matter which had to be written rapidly, written for popular acclamation, written for what was commonly regarded as ephemeral production. The national genius made of it a special language. Herein the spirit of Shakespeare was of course the main influence, but the thing was finally established by the astonishing faculties of John Milton.

Here was a man who deliberately decided upon a form still despised in his time, and who at one stroke (and advanced in life) raised that form to its highest level.

Let it be remarked that, of all forms, blank verse most easily degenerates. The classics were innocent of rhyme. The great monuments of antiquity, lyric, epic, didactic, are alive with rhythm but know nothing of rhyme or even assonance. It seems to have come in during that revolution of the mind which transformed pagan antiquity into Christendom. Those who are hostile to the Conversion of the Empire and who regret it as a prime disaster (a common academic attitude) deplore the advent of rhyme as something barbaric. They are fond of describing the Church and all its culture as a product of the lower classes swamping the upper: barbarians and common soldiers imposing disastrously their superstitions upon the fine order of the Greek and Roman World. There are those of course who come to an exactly contrary judgment and tell us that the Conversion of the Empire saved all that could be saved of pagan civilisation sinking in sterility to its death.

But both parties will agree that rhyme came in with the Great Change and, having come, it came to stay. Every one agrees that the body of verse in Christendom depends upon rhyme. The more remarkable is it that English poets should have produced the splendid anomaly of blank verse. The French did not do this, nor the Germans, nor the Italians. The English alone did it. A miracle, but a perilous one, for without a great and subtle diversity, without an avoidance of repetition most difficult to achieve, English blank verse becomes contemptible.

Whether more rubbish has been written in other languages than our own, by men under poetic impulse but lacking poetic talent to express themselves, I know not. I have no sufficient knowledge of other tongues. But of this I am sure:

that in the vast ocean of pseudo-poetic trash burdening our libraries, a good half or more of the worst is bad blank verse. Religious sympathies have made men praise Wordsworth, although for page on page he merely meanders, and on most other pages is scandalously bad. Now it was blank verse that led him astray.

It is commonly found that the supreme examples of any art appear at its origin. It is certainly so with the great sculptures of Assyria and Egypt. It is so with English blank verse. No one has ever touched the mark of Milton, and even the best of our modern poets, among whom I would certainly count Tennyson, fall continually into drivel when they touch this medium. Tennyson also did sublime things, but more things which might make one weep in pity for the frailty of man the singer.

If any man desires to possess and treasure a posy of bad verse, let him at once purchase a noble and invaluable book called *The Stuffed Owl*, an anthology of horrors due to the first-rate critical faculty of Mr. Wyndham Lewis.

I have hitherto forborne to quote in this essay, for quotation interrupts critical judgment and is I think an otiose habit when one is dealing with a general theme in letters, but I will make an exception here and quote from this sublime volume a rhymed extract. It is taken from the works of Crabbe.

> Something one day occurr'd about a bill
> That was not drawn with true mercantile skill,
> And I was ask'd and authorised to go
> To seek the firm of Clutterbuck and Co.;
> Their hour was past—but when I urg'd the case,
> There was a youth who named a second place,
> Where, on occasions of important kind,
> I might the man of occupation find,
> In his retirement, where he found repose
> From the vexations that in Business rose.
>
> The house was good, but not so pure and clean
> As I had houses of retirement seen;
> Yet 'men, I knew, of meditation deep,
> Love not their maidens should their studies sweep.

His room I saw, and must acknowledge, there
Were not the signs of cleanliness or care;
A female servant, void of female grace,
Loose in attire, proceeded to the place;
She stared intrusive on my slender frame,
And boldly ask'd my business and my name.

I gave them both; and, left to be amused,
Well as I might, the parlour I perused. . . .
There were strange sights and scents about the room,
Of food high-season'd, and of strong perfume; . . .
A large old mirror, with once-gilded frame,
Reflected prints that I forbear to name—
Such as a youth might purchase—but, in truth,
Not a sedate or sober-minded youth.
The chairs in haste seem'd whirl'd about the room,
As when the sons of riot hurry home
And leave the troubled place to solitude and gloom.

There you have really bad verse in its perfection. Such heights are rarely reached, but an approach to them is constantly made. Indeed I am here sorely tempted to begin again with some from Tupper, but to tell the truth Tupper's philosophy is not verse, it is inspired rather by the rhetoric of the Authorised Version: that most unequal book, responsible for great things and for many small, contemptible ones as well.

The effect of the political system upon the literature of a country is a matter too much neglected.

All that affects the body politic affects each particular activity of Society, and letters among the rest; thus the breakdown of central government in the West during the fifth century was the end of the old Latin literature, verse and prose, which during the sixth century grew degraded, and disappeared. The violence, the political chaos of the Revolution lowered the whole standard of French literary work, exalting, even absurdly, facile rhetoric and letting loose a mass of second-rate verse, which had only to be orthodox in its praise of social equality or patriotism, or arms, to be given a ridiculously exaggerated value. In all that welter André Chenier stands out, because there is no one else to be called a poet. The speeches, and still more, the political thought of Robespierre, are not negligible, but they are in no way great literature. Or again, in our own time, at the end of the nineteenth century, the complete security and the international supremacy of Great Britain fostered, in a mass of striking bad verse and prose, at the same time a sort of baseness in moral standards which degraded much of the verse by self-sufficiency and provincialism.

Instances might be multiplied indefinitely. The tone of a national literature in any phase of the nation's existence is not isolated from the political arrangements of that phase.

This is true of particular periods. It is equally true of a national literature as affected by the main political character of the nation.

Now the political mark of the English nation during the three centuries and more when it was rising in its modern form is Aristocracy: class government. England was distinguished from all her contemporary rivals between the first generation of the seventeenth century and the last generation of the nineteenth by taking its direction from the comparatively small wealthy class which began by destroying the monarchy; went on to make itself master of property and the soil; put an end to the peasantry, and through banking, foreign trade, and naval power, vastly increased the numbers and the wealth of the community.

The effect of this on English verse was marked.

For one thing, this vigorous new national organisation reacted strongly against foreign influence. The great foreign influence of the seventeenth and eighteenth centuries was French influence. Under that influence there was a general European tendency towards the classical spirit. This tendency England rejected.

There was a moment from the later seventeenth century to the middle of the eighteenth, when it looked as though English verse might take on a permanent classical form. With that strong bias towards the establishment of the classical spirit in English poetry we connect the names, especially, of Dryden and of Pope. Lucidity, intelligence, advance—and poignancy recedes. Accepted forms—the heroic rhymed couplet in iambic pentameters—are universally accepted as the general medium of verse.

I say it looked as though a classical spirit would conquer in this country. It did not do so, for this reason: national isolation, the product of aristocratic government, was too strong.

The classical phase disappeared. It did not disappear before the advance of great social changes during the Industrial Revolution, nor later through the new force of the French Revolution. It disappeared before the advance of something native and national, the resurrection of intense personal emotion, and that equally intense visual imagination which is the inheritance of the English people.

I may put it thus: before the last quarter of the eighteenth century had begun the epic and formal rhymed drama were no longer possible in England. The essential national lyrical form was again supreme.

England owes this rebirth of this specifically English poetical spirit to Aristocracy.

Yet Aristocracy had no effect on English verse, which is strange, for our verse was judged by an *élite*. A comparatively small number of men and women, the leaders of the English community on its intellectual and spiritual side, decided what should be accepted and what rejected. This was not true of prose. In prose, popular judgment had a greater effect; but in verse the gentry, their libraries, their drawing-rooms, their special scholarship, and their adherence. England was stamped by the patronage of the gentry over verse, just as France was stamped by the patronage over all literature of the monarchy, and of the intellectual members of the middle class.

In English prose the populace preserved Defoe, and took a large part (through *Gulliver's Travels*) in preserving Swift—the master of all English prose writers. It was general opinion, if not the populace, which founded the reputation of the

English novel—notably of Fielding, but it was class government which recognised, sanctioned, and advanced, the
national resurrection in poetry. Not that those who wrote
the more exceptional new verse were of the governing class.
Far from it. They were of all ranks, from the impoverished
gentleman like Byron, to one of the lower middle class, like
Keats. But it was a highly cultured, critical governing class
which discovered and promoted the new writing of verse.

In the nineteenth century this character became even
more marked. The lively, but second-rate, narrative verse of
Walter Scott was based upon a very general and uncritical
appreciation. But though this is in part true of Byron it is
not wholly true of him. Byron was understood by a superior
kind of critic, and later on, in the Victorian period, it was
the superior critic who made every reputation.

Two craftsmen as different as Tennyson and Browning
equally depended upon class recognition. It was not the
mass of readers who acclaimed Tennyson, though indeed
they did acclaim his worse work, even such shameful stuff
as "The Lord of Burleigh," but the high reputation (and how
well deserved!) of that great lyric poet was a reputation
framed by a special class in the midst of which he moved, and
by whom he was acclaimed. That he was just slightly connected with it in blood counts for nothing. The same class
recognised, and against greater opposition, the merits of the
obscure Browning. The same class awoke to, and acclaimed,
such part as is worthy (and very worthy it is) in the lyrical
flame of Swinburne.

Conversely, the decay of judgment by an *élite* best accounts
for the condition of English verse to-day.

There was a bad side to this dependence upon class judgment
for poetical recognition; and that bad side appeared, oddly
enough, in the department of humour, though it appeared
also, to a lesser degree, in another department—the academic.

In humorous verse, class government let loose during and
after the middle of the nineteenth century a mass of provincial folly based upon lack of reason. The general term
"nonsense verse" (the name of Lear is the most conspicuous

therein) describes only too well the character of this novelty. Unlike many unworthy things in letters it has no chance of survival, for it lived on the air at a particular time, lacking which it cannot breathe. It lived on the air of complete security, such as property then enjoyed through a national unity in which domestic conflict was unknown, and on an international supremacy which England came to take for granted until the turning point of the Boer War—whence we may date all our change of circumstance for the worse.

I have said that there was another bad side to the effect of class government on English verse, besides its effect on humour, and that this very bad effect was academic.

There rose in the complete class-security of Victorian, and especially of the later Victorian, period, an absurd over-rating of whatever verse attached to a particular wealthy centre: an over-rating of an Etonian clique, and a still worse and more general over-rating of an Oxford clique and of a Cambridge clique. This particularism stretched over no wide field. It did not create many false reputations, but such few as it created had a bad effect on the tradition of English letters. Matthew Arnold's work is an example; that of Mr. Bridges half a lifetime later is another. In verse nothing is worse than praise granted not for the excellence of the craft but for adventitious reasons of birth, wealth, acquaintance, and the rest.

To the evil of academic backwaters and self-praise by a clique has succeeded a far worse evil, the future of which none can see. It is no less than the loss of beauty. In criticism, still more in production, the would-be poet to-day thinks and speaks in terms of strength, shock, novelty, oddity, everything under the sun, but never in terms of beauty. Now of all human arts the one which lives by beauty, the one to which beauty is native, the one which without beauty must necessarily die, is the art of verse.

On that note I will end, proposing no remedy for there is none, save by such as can make the deaf to hear, the blind to see, and the incurably vulgar to hold communion with the gods.

HUMOUR

BY
HESKETH PEARSON

HUMOUR

F ALSTAFF is the father of English wit and humour. Although there was much humour and some wit in English literature before him, both qualities were suddenly crystallised and perfected in the knight, who remains England's greatest achievement in those fields, and the symbol of her greatest achievement in any field: her humour.

This quality, so common to the race that the peace of the civilised world has frequently depended upon it, so peculiar to England that she has been freer of religious and political strife than any country on earth, was first manifested in a literary form in the shepherds' plays of the old "miracle" cycles, and received its hall-mark in Chaucer's *Canterbury Tales*.

Our first great humorist, though no ascetic, was primarily a student of human nature. Humour did not bubble out of him as it did out of Shakespeare; he watched and recorded the humorous bubbles of others. His characters were seen from the outside; he did not enter into them; and so he has more affinity with Dickens than with Shakespeare. The *Canterbury Tales* were written by a man, to quote his own description, "Dumb as a stone, studying and reading alway, till his head ached and his look became dazed, so that his neighbours, living at his very door, looked on him as a hermit."

Between Chaucer and Shakespeare the humour of the people expressed itself in many forms. The father of English doggerel, laureate in the time of Henry VIII, was John Skelton, whose verses were ironic, Hogarthian, indecent and thoroughly English; pulpit-humour is traceable to Bishop Latimer, whose caustic comments on the supposed miraculous images of the Virgin Mary got him into trouble with the Catholics and brought him to the stake; while Sir Thomas

More's *Utopia* has passages of a playful fun which appears to have been habitual with him, for not even his wife knew when he was being serious, and he met death with a quip.

With the Elizabethan, John Lyly, whose *Euphues* was the first novel in the language to deal with contemporary life, we come to the parent of a long line of dramatists whose love of epigram and verbal fence has been greater than their interest in human nature. The plays of Lyly are entirely lacking in characterisation. They are full of quips and quirks and puns and conceits and innuendoes. He was what would now be called a highbrow playwright. Nothing gross, nothing common or popular interfered with the play of words and rattle of repartees. This type of entertainment was transformed into the comedy of manners by Congreve and Sheridan, was transformed again into the comedy of merriment by Oscar Wilde in *The Importance of being Earnest*, and has reappeared in our own day, with a much closer resemblance to the original, in the comedies of Noel Coward. It should be added that Ben Jonson was the first dramatist to satirise types, to ridicule folly, affectation, cant and pretension. *Every Man in his Humor* was a new thing in native comedy, and in that respect Jonson was the progenitor of Congreve and Sheridan; but their glittering dialogue, with its rapier-like thrust and parry, has more in common with Lyly's than with the straightforward, hardhitting manner of "Rare Ben."

Throughout the sixteenth century the playwrights for the most part modelled their comedies and farces on those of Plautus and Terence, and the first specimen of purely native work, coarse, broad, jocular, was *Gammer Gurton's Needle*. But Shakespeare's chief predecessor in stage humour was John Heywood, who wrote farces and interludes in the reign of Henry VIII and who created several recognisably human comic characters, though it is clear that the court of Bluff King Hal could only be moved to uproarious laughter when the theme was cuckoldry.

The wit of Lyly and Skelton and the humour of Heywood

and even of Chaucer were, however, but the faint streaks of
light that heralded the dawn of Shakespeare, whose prentice
work, *A Midsummer Night's Dream*, made his predecessors
seem amateurish, and whose master-work, *Henry IV*, makes
his successors look dwarfish. Falstaff was the first great
comic creation to be seen on the stage and will probably be
the last. Wit and humour are rooted in his nature; they
grow out of him; they are not grafted on to him. He differs
from every other humorous character in literature in that he
is the comic spirit incarnate. We look at life through his
eyes, and therefore do not laugh at a comic man but at a
comic universe. With his imagination he creates a world as
he goes along, making mountains out of mole-hills. Bardolph's red face and bulbous nose were to his other friends
just a red face and bulbous nose. To Falstaff they were
something more:

Bar.: Why, you are so fat, Sir John, that you must needs
be out of all compass; out of all reasonable compass, Sir
John.

Fal.: Do thou amend thy face, and I'll amend my life:
thou art our admiral, thou bearest the lantern in the
poop, but 'tis in the nose of thee; thou art the Knight
of the Burning Lamp.

Bar.: Why, Sir John, my face does you no harm.

Fal.: No, I'll be sworn, I make as good use of it as many
a man doth of a Death's-head or a *memento mori*. I
never see thy face but I think upon hell-fire, and Dives
that lived in purple: for there he is in his robes, burning,
burning. If thou wert any way given to virtue, I would
swear by thy face; my oath should be, "By this fire,
that's God's angel." But thou art altogether given over;
and wert indeed, but for the light in thy face, the son of
utter darkness. When thou ran'st up Gadshill in the
night to catch my horse, if I did not think thou hadst
been an *ignis fatuus*, or a ball of wildfire, there's no
purchase in money. O, thou art a perpetual triumph,
an everlasting bonfire-light, thou hast saved me a

thousand marks in links and torches, walking with thee in the night betwixt tavern and tavern; but the sack that thou hast drunk me, would have bought me lights as good cheap, at the dearest chandler's in Europe. I have maintained that salamander of yours with fire any time this two and thirty years, God reward me for it!

Such flights of humorous fancy were not made again for two centuries, when Falstaff appeared on earth in the flesh, disguised as a parson named Sydney Smith, who, upon being told that a young Scot was going to marry an Irish lady of imposing girth, burst forth:

"Going to marry her! Impossible! You mean a part of her; he could not marry her all himself. It would be a case, not of bigamy, but trigamy; the neighbourhood or the magistrates should interfere. There is enough of her to furnish wives for a whole parish. One man marry her! —it is monstrous! You might people a colony with her; or give an assembly with her; or perhaps take your morning's walk round her, always provided there were frequent resting-places, and you were in rude health. I once was rash enough to try walking round her before breakfast, but only got half-way and gave it up exhausted. Or you might read the Riot Act and disperse her; in short, you might do anything with her but marry her."

Shakespeare's immediate successor in comedy was Philip Massinger, whose play *A New Way to Pay Old Debts* contained two such showy characters, Sir Giles Overreach and Justice Greedy, that it held the stage for above two centuries. Massinger foreshadowed Dickens; his characters are melodramatic and his humour is theatrical. He was followed by James Shirley, the last of the fun-makers before Puritanism set in. Shirley cribbed Shakespeare, Jonson and Massinger, and is only noteworthy as the man who emitted the last laugh of the Elizabethans. But the laugh that was gargantuan in Shakespeare had become a giggle in Shirley.

It is perhaps worthy of remark that Robert Burton, whose *Anatomy of Melancholy* was so thoroughly pilfered without acknowledgment by Laurence Sterne, was the connecting link of humour between the Elizabethans and the Puritans, and that his particular brand was the humour of pessimism.

The spirit of Falstaff, like his body at the battle of Shrewsbury, had to sham death on the stage during the Puritan regime, but it went marching on in (one feels sure) the rear of the cavalier army, and two of the most typically English works of humour were produced under Cromwell's very nose.

Thomas Fuller was a clergyman with a passion for anecdotes. He was also one of the first authors to make writing pay. Sauntering along in the tail of a marching column, he spent his time in picking up stories of English "worthies," and when not on duty he sat patiently for hours on end listening to the prattle of old women in order to obtain snatches of local history and tradition. He wrote as he talked, racily, and he made the interesting discovery that character could best be revealed by anecdote. *The Worthies of England* is still one of the most entertaining books in the language. As might be expected, such an author was very well able to look after himself; he made the best of both worlds, being helped to a living by Cromwell's chaplain and becoming chaplain extraordinary to Charles II. Falstaff could have done no better.

Sir Thomas Urquhart was a Scot, but as he was responsible for what is, after *Henry IV* and almost any English version of *Don Quixote*, the richest mine of humour we possess, he must here be considered as an Englishman. He came tramping down from Scotland with the Royalist army and made the very un-Falstaffian error of under-estimating Cromwell; for instead of shamming death at the battle of Worcester he was captured. But his first action as a prisoner made up for this. Having sized up Cromwell, he tried to impress him by tracing the genealogy of the Urquharts back to Adam, inserting a brief sentence in the pedigree to account for an unavoidable hiatus: "Here is the Flood." He was released

on parole, but remained in London, and his translation of
the first two books of Rabelais appeared in 1653. We do
not know whether this displaced the Bible as Cromwell's
bedside-book, but he left the translator alone. Urquhart
was abroad in 1660 when he heard of the Restoration. The
news threw him into an uncontrollable fit of laughter, from
which he died.

A direct result of the Commonwealth was *Hudibras* by
Samuel Butler, who like his Victorian namesake was also a
painter, but his pictures were chiefly used to keep out the
rain from a windowless house. *Hudibras* expressed the
average man's hatred of Puritanism; in it Butler "naturalised"
burlesque, its formlessness being typically English, thus
earning the dislike of French critics reared in the classical
tradition.

With the Restoration the national genius reasserted itself
and found expression in new forms of wit and humour. John
Dryden wrote the first and best English political satire,
Absalom and Achitophel, which has a detached and therefore
more tremendous effect than the malicious digs of Alexander
Pope. The geniality of Dryden enlarges his objects; the
malignancy of Pope diminishes his. Dryden had something
of Shakespeare's humanity in him. Pope had nothing but
Pope, the wittiest of all versifiers.

Although Cromwell, different from his fellow-puritans,
had connived at a certain amount of furtive activity on the
part of the old players, the drama had been dead for nearly
twenty years when the famous group of Restoration playwrights—Wycherley, Farquhar, Vanbrugh and Congreve—
began to try French comedy on the English stage. It never
took root here, though the genius of Congreve would have
nourished it if the fun had been cleaner. Shakespeare apart,
Love for Love is the wittiest and most entertaining comedy in
the language until we come to *The Importance of being Earnest*.
One brief scene, typical of the whole, must be given. A half-
witted beau named Tattle, "vain of his amours, yet valuing
himself for secrecy," is talking to Valentine and his friend
Scandal:

Tat.: Valentine, I supped last night with your mistress, and her uncle old Foresight; I think your father lies at Foresight's.

Val. Yes.

Tat.: Upon my soul, Angelica's a fine woman. And so is Mrs. Foresight, and her sister Mrs. Frail.

Scan.: Yes, Mrs. Frail is a very fine woman; we all know her.

Tat.: O, that is not fair!

Scan.: What?

Tat.: To tell.

Scan. To tell what? Why, what do you know of Mrs. Frail?

Tat.: Who, I? Upon honour I don't know whether she be man or woman, but by the smoothness of her chin, and roundness of her hips.

Scan.: No?

Tat.: No.

Scan.: She says otherwise.

Tat.: Impossible!

Scan.: Yes, faith. Ask Valentine else.

Tat.: Why then, as I hope to be saved, I believe a woman only obliges a man to secrecy, that she may have the pleasure of telling herself.

Scan.: No doubt on't. Well, but has she done you wrong, or no? You have had her? Ha?

Tat.: Though I have more honour than to tell first, I have more manners than to contradict what a lady has declared.

Scan.: Well, you own it?

Tat.: I am strangely surprised!—Yes, yes, I can't deny it, if she taxes me with it.

Scan.: She'll be here by-and-by; she sees Valentine every morning.

Tat.: How?

Val.: She does me the favour, I mean, of a visit sometimes. I did not think she had granted more to anybody.

Scan.: Nor I, faith; but Tattle does not use to belie a lady;

it is contrary to his character.—How one may be de-
ceived in a woman, Valentine!

Tat.: Nay, what do you mean, gentlemen?

Scan.: I'm resolved I'll ask her.

Tat.: O barbarous! Why, did you not tell me——

Scan.: No, you told us.

Tat.: And bid me ask Valentine?

Val.: What did I say? I hope you won't bring me to
confess an answer, when you never asked me the
question?

Tat.: But, gentlemen, this is the most inhuman pro-
ceeding——

Val.: Nay, if you have known Scandal thus long, and
cannot avoid such a palpable decoy as this was, the
ladies have a fine time whose reputations are in your
keeping.

The strangest addition to the field of English humour in
the years that followed the Protectorate is to be seen in the
work of Samuel Pepys and John Aubrey. It is the unconscious humour of curiosity and revelation, the humour of the
significantly insignificant. The curiosity of Pepys about
himself, the curiosity of Aubrey about other people, resulted
in two works that have no parallel outside those of Boswell,
who was equally curious about himself and other people.
The *Diary* of Pepys owes its chief charm to the unconscious,
or at most half-conscious, humour of self-revelation. The
Brief Lives of Aubrey delight us because of the seemingly
trivial details recorded about important people; for example,
that the famous philosopher Hobbes was much afflicted
when bald by flies and that his favourite diet was whitings.
Because he was the first to realise that a man's private habits
are more interesting and revealing than his public behaviour,
Aubrey was the parent of modern biography.

Close on the heels of these naïve and life-loving men came
the frightening figure of Jonathan Swift, who despised human
beings, whose main effort in life was directed to an exhibition
of their stupidity, barbarity and utter futility, and who

imparted the most ferocious irony to the most lucid prose
ever written. Swift was one of the three greatest English
conversational wits. In that sphere he was only equalled
by Dr. Johnson and only beaten by Sydney Smith. Like
the first he could use the bludgeon effectively. "I would
have you know, sir, that I set up for a wit," said a dignified
young man. "Do you, indeed? Then take my advice and
sit down again," retorted Swift. On hearing that William
III had told a mob, shortly after landing in England, that
"We are come for your good—for all your goods," Swift
remarked, "A universal principle of all governments; but,
like most truths, only half told—he should have said goods
and chattels." When the wife of a Lord Lieutenant observed
that "the air of Ireland is very good," Swift fell on his knees
and begged "For God's sake, madam, don't say so in England,
for if you do they will certainly tax it." A man who had been
savagely lampooned by Swift çalled upon him to disavow
the writing or take the consequences. "Sir," said Swift,
"when l was a young man I had the honour of being intimate
with some great legal characters, particularly Lord Somers,
who, knowing my propensity to satire, advised me when I
lampooned a knave or a fool never to own it. Conformably
to that advice, I tell you I am not the author."

It is the cant of many critics that the French are a much
wittier race than the English. There is a certain logicality
about Gallic wit that sometimes gives it sharper point; but
the best English wit is more imaginative because it is usually
based on humour. In Swift's *Directions to Servants* humour
and wit are so exquisitely blended that it is difficult to
distinguish the one from the other. Here are a few samples:

"*Directions to the Butler*

"If you are curious to taste some of your Master's
choicest Ale, empty as many of the Bottles just below the
Neck as will make the Quantity you want; but then take
care to fill them up again with clean Water, that you may
not lessen your Master's Liquor.

"When you clean your Plate, leave the Whiting plainly to be seen in all the Chinks, for fear your Lady should not believe you had cleaned it.

"When a Gentleman is going away after dining with your Master, be sure to stand full in View, and follow him to the Door, and as you have Opportunity look full in his Face, perhaps it may bring you a Shilling; but, if the Gentleman hath lain there a Night, get the Cook, the House-maid, the Stablemen, the Scullion, and the Gardiner, to accompany you, and to stand in his Way to the Hall in a Line on each Side him: If the Gentleman performs handsomely, it will do him Honour, and cost your Master nothing.

"*Directions to the Cook*

"If a lump of Soot falls into the Soup, and you cannot conveniently get it out, stir it well in, and it will give the Soup a high *French* Taste.

"You are to look upon your Kitchen as your Dressing-room; but, you are not to wash your Hands till you have gone to the Necessary-house, and spitted your Meat, trussed your Fowl, picked your Sallad; nor indeed till after you have sent up your second Course; for your Hands will be ten times fouler with the many things you are forced to handle; but when your Work is over, one Washing will serve for all.

"There is but one Part of your Dressing that I would admit while the Victuals are boiling, toasting, or stewing, I mean the combing your Head, which loseth no Time, because you can stand over your Cookery, and watch it with one Hand, while you are using your Comb in the other.

"Lump three or four Pounds of Butter together with your Hands, then dash it against the Wall just over the Dresser, so as to have it ready to pull by Pieces as you have occasion for it.

"Directions to the Waiting-Maid

"If you are in a great Family, and my Lady's Woman, my Lord may probably like you, although you are not half so handsome as his own Lady. In this Case, take Care to get as much out of him as you can; and never allow him the smallest Liberty, not the squeezing of your Hand, unless he puts a Guinea into it; so, by degrees, make him pay accordingly for every new Attempt, doubling upon him in proportion to the Concessions you allow, and always struggling, and threatening to cry out or tell your Lady, although you receive his Money: Five Guineas for handling your Breast is a cheap Pennyworth, although you seem to resist with all your Might; but never allow him the last Favour under a hundred Guineas, or a Settlement of twenty Pounds a Year for Life.

"I must caution you particularly against my Lord's eldest Son: If you are dextrous enough, it is odds that you may draw him in to marry you, and make you a Lady: If he be a common Rake, (and he must be one or t'other) avoid him like *Satan*; for he stands less in awe of a Mother, than my Lord doth of a Wife; and, after ten thousand Promises, you will get nothing from him, but a big Belly or a Clap, and probably both together."

Swift, by the way, was partly responsible for the first popular success of the modern stage, for it was out of his remark to Gay, "A Newgate pastoral might make an odd, pretty sort of thing," that *The Beggar's Opera* was born. And we must not quit the age of Swift without observing that the short humorous essay, to be perfected by Charles Lamb, was popularised by Addison and Steele.

In the eighteenth century the English novel became the chief vehicle for the expression of native wit and humour, and the giant figure of Fielding reduced his French and English contemporaries to the size of pygmies. It was as if the genius of Shakespeare had forsaken dialogue for description, losing some richness but gaining some calmness in transit. The gentle but all-seeing irony of Fielding was a new thing in our literature. He was also a master of meiosis, one of the distinctive features of the best English humour, and all that is good in fiction since his day is directly traceable to his influence. The masculinity of his writing is in strong contrast with the style of another famous eighteenth-century novelist, Laurence Sterne, who was the originator of the "tear-behind-the-smile" form of humour, which has had such a lowering effect on English literature ever since.

The two extremes of both wit and humour are contained in the writing of Fielding and in the character of Dr. Johnson, in the freedom of the first and the restriction of the second, in the artist's detachment and in the moralist's concern. Tranquillity is the keynote to Fielding's wit, which expresses the ease of a man who is sure of himself and whose philosophy of life mirrors his nature. Discord is the cause of Johnson's wit, which too often expresses the uneasy acceptance of a belief out of harmony with his nature. In his youth he rebelled against the authority of his parents, just as in later years he subconsciously rebelled against the authority of religion, and when his mother called him a puppy he asked her if she knew what they called a puppy's mother.

The discomfort of his faith sat heavily upon him, making him so wretched that he could not bear the thought of happiness outside it. When Boswell championed Lady Diana Beauclerk, who had very wisely left her brute of a husband for another man, Johnson brought the discussion to an end with: "My dear sir, never accustom your mind to mingle virtue and vice. The woman's a whore, and there's an end on't." Another time Boswell was arguing in favour of suicide as a happy release for a swindler who had been found out, but Johnson delivered this broadside: "Let him go abroad to a distant country; let him go to some place where he is *not* known. Don't let him go to the Devil, where he *is* known." The strongest example of his refusal to believe that anyone could be happy was his retort to a man who declared that his wife's sister was entirely so: "If your sister-in-law is really the contented being she professes herself, sir, her life gives the lie to every research of humanity; for she is happy without health, without beauty, without money, and without understanding." As the lady in question was present when this remark was made, Mrs. Thrale thought it in the worst of taste; but Johnson told her not to worry: "The same stupidity which prompted her to extol felicity she never felt," he explained, "hindered her from feeling what shocks you on repetition. I tell you the woman is ugly, and sickly, and foolish, and poor; and would it not make a man hang himself to hear such a creature say it was happy?"

One cannot help regretting that Johnson and John Wilkes were so polite to one another. A battle of wits between these two would have given Boswell the best pages in his biography, for they had nothing in common except the ability to express their differences. "Wilkes," said the Earl of Sandwich to the dissolute democrat, "you'll die either on the gallows or of the pox." Wilkes replied: "That depends, my lord, on whether I embrace your lordship's principles or your mistress." But Wilkes, though he attended to Johnson's table-wants with the utmost assiduity, did not carry servility too far and was spared the fate of the man who laughed immoderately at everything the Doctor said and who was suddenly stunned by Johnson with: "Pray, sir, what is the matter? I hope I have not said anything which you can comprehend."

Samuel Foote would have been another antagonist more worthy of Johnson's wit than any member of the Literary Club. Foote once agreed with a second-rate dramatist who declared his future intention of laughing at his critics: "Do so, for in this way you will not only disappoint them, but lead the merriest life of any man in England." But Johnson feared Foote's ridicule and Foote feared Johnson's retaliation, because when Foote proposed to "take off" the Doctor on the stage, the latter bought a large stick with which to lay the mimic out; so their acquaintanceship did not ripen.

Sometimes Johnson's wit took a gentle turn, as when Mrs. Siddons called on him and his servant spent some time in fetching a chair: "You see, madam, wherever you go, there are no seats to be had." But the salt of his best sayings is in their bite. "Here's such a stir about a fellow who has written one book, and I have written many!" exclaimed Goldsmith when Beattie's *Essay on Truth* was being universally praised. "Ah!" replied Johnson, "there go two and forty sixpences to one guinea, you know." When Boswell complained one day that the volume of conversation on the previous evening had given him a headache, Johnson said: "No, sir; it was not the noise that made your head ache; it was the sense we put into it." Boswell weakly asked: "Has sense that effect on the head?" Johnson answered: "Yes, sir, on heads not used to it." Boswell never shrank from playing the magnanimous butt. Once he asked if Johnson did not consider that a good cook was more necessary to the community than a good poet. "I don't suppose there's a *dog* in the town but thinks so," returned Johnson. After their visit to Scotland Boswell was anxious to obtain the favourable testimony of the great man on as many points as possible. For instance: "You have now been in Scotland, sir, and say if you did not see meat and drink ,enough there." He was unprepared for this: "Why, yes, sir, meat and drink enough to give the inhabitants sufficient strength to run away."

David Garrick was always desirous to conciliate Johnson, whose butt was perhaps the only part in the world he never wished to play. Johnson, however, frequently enjoyed "benefit" nights at the expense of the great actor. "Why did you not make me a Tory when we lived so much together? You love to make Tories," said David. Johnson pulled a number of halfpennies from his pocket and asked: "Why did not the King make these guineas?" One more remark of Johnson's must be quoted. A friend who loved discussing his health and dwelling upon the symptoms of his maladies was admonished by the Doctor: "Do not be like the spider, man, and spin conversation thus incessantly out of your bowels."

Though few people read him nowadays, Johnson wrote some of the greatest pages in English biography. As an example of restrained humour there could be nothing finer than his account of the death of Edmund Smith:

"Having formed his plan and collected materials, (for a drama on Lady Jane Grey) he declared that a few months would complete his design; and, that he might pursue his work with less frequent avocations, he was, in June 1710, invited by Mr. George Ducket to his house at Hartham, in Wiltshire. Here he found such opportunities of indulgence as did not much forward his studies, and particularly some strong ale, too delicious to be resisted. He eat and drank till he found himself plethoric; and then, resolving to ease himself by evacuation, he wrote to an apothecary in the neighbourhood a prescription of a purge so forcible, that the apothecary thought it his duty to delay it till he had given notice of its danger. Smith, not pleased with the contradiction of a shopman, and boastful of his own knowledge, treated the notice with rude contempt, and swallowed his own medicine, which, in July 1710, brought him to the grave. He was buried at Hartham."

By the beginning of the nineteenth century the wit and humour of the race had found expression in nearly every form and had permeated every branch of literature. Henceforth, although the wit might be sharpened or the humour enriched by the genius of individual writers, they would remain essentially derivative. The greatest writers of the nineteenth century owe most to their predecessors, such novelty as there was coming chiefly from the lesser figures.

Among the former we may note Jane Austen, whose lambent satire played upon the country gentry with a delicacy Fielding would have liked; Frederick Marryat, whose eccentric portraiture owed much to the Scottish novelist Smollett; Dickens, who created a fantastic world of his own, in some respects richer than that of Fielding and Smollett but in no respect so true to life; Thackeray, whose brighter fancy and keener sensibility enabled him to paint more vivid scenes than any other English novelist, but who, like Dickens, deserted reality on the smallest provocation and indulged the maudlin sentiment and mawkish morality of his epoch; Meredith, who brought the comedy of manners into the novel; and H. G. Wells, whose Mr. Polly sits among the immortals.

Of the lesser figures in the last century we may note Thomas Hood, whose genius as a punster could produce

> Like the sweet blossoms of the may
> Whose fragrance ends in must;

Thomas Love Peacock, who specialised in the humour of humours, his cranks, epicures and drunkards being gifted with a neatness and brilliance of speech that recall Congreve; Edward Lear and Lewis Carroll, both of whom practised the art of Nonsense, which has achieved its apotheosis in the works of P. G. Wodehouse; Samuel Butler, whose peculiar contribution to literature may be described as the humour of the unexpected; and W. S. Gilbert, who made the curious experiment of looking at the world through his legs and basing his humour on the view enjoyed from that position.

We began with the comic spirit embodied in Falstaff and we must end with the comic spirit embodied in Falstaff's only legitimate heir, Sydney Smith. In his preface to the present writer's *Life of Sydney Smith*, G. K. Chesterton described the famous clergyman as "the real originator of Nonsense." But the first great creator of Nonsense in our literature was the first great creator of Humour, and if G.K.C. had remembered Falstaff on Bardolph's nose, or Falstaff playing the part of Henry IV, or Falstaff's chat with the Lord Chief Justice, he might have reconsidered his description. It would be much truer to say that Sydney Smith was the real originator of Sense, his air-free spirit enabling him to talk more sound common sense than the earth-bound Johnson and the earth-clogged Swift put together. His spiritual freedom gave him a sanity to which they were strangers. Johnson's horror of death and Swift's hatred of life were equally alien to Sydney's laughter-loving temperament. Like Shakespeare, he saw through life and saw that it was good; and so, like Falstaff, he was the poet of reason and absurdity, of sense and nonsense, of wit and humour.

On the whole, it must be admitted, a large proportion of English wit has been produced by Irishmen, but no one was ever so persistently and spontaneously witty as Sydney Smith, whose writings have influenced such brilliant Irish improvisators as Oscar Wilde and Archbishop Magee. To take a single instance, Magee had been mobbed and insulted by a crowd of rioters while he was consecrating a cemetery, but when the matter was raised in the House of Lords he dealt with it in the very accents of Sydney Smith: "I inflicted on them the ignominy of an episcopal benediction, and dismissed them from my mind."

The only wit who can be compared with Sydney is Voltaire; but French wit, as already remarked, has not the poetic quality of the best English wit; moreover Voltaire lacked the rich and racy humour, the soil in which the wit of Sydney flowered. Two examples of this humour must suffice, the first written, the second spoken:

(1) In order to undermine the power of Napoleon on the continent, the English Chancellor of the Exchequer, Spencer Perceval, prohibited the exportation from this country of certain medicines, e.g. rhubarb and quinine (known as Jesuit's Bark). Sydney doubted whether such a measure would make the French see reason:

"What a sublime thought, that no purge can now be taken between the Weser and the Garonne; that the bustling pestle is still, the canorous mortar mute, and the bowels of mankind locked up for fourteen degrees of latitude! When, I should be curious to know, were all the powers of crudity and flatulence fully explained to his Majesty's ministers? At what period was this great plan of conquest and constipation fully developed? In whose mind was the idea of destroying the pride and the

plasters of France first engendered? Without castor oil
they might for some months, to be sure, have carried on a
lingering war; but can they do without bark? Will the
people live under a government where antimonial powders
cannot be procured? Will they bear the loss of mercury?
'There's the rub.' Depend upon it, the absence of the
materia medica will soon bring them to their senses, and the
cry of *Bourbon and Bolus* burst forth from the Baltic to the
Mediterranean."

(2) In the summer of 1831 Macaulay went to a large party
in order to meet Ramohun Roy, a Brahmin who had become
an Unitarian and was being lionised by Society. The Indian
failed to turn up but Sydney Smith was there and Macaulay
said that meeting him was some compensation for missing
Ramohun Roy. The cleric was shocked:

"Compensation! Do you mean to insult me? A bene-
ficed clergyman, an orthodox clergyman, a nobleman's
chaplain, to be no more than compensation for a Brahmin;
and a heretic Brahmin, too; a fellow who has lost his own
religion and can't find another; a vile heterodox dog, who,
as I am credibly informed, eats beefsteaks in private! A
man who has lost his caste! who ought to have melted
lead poured down his nostrils, if the good old Vedas were
in force as they ought to be."

And now, having pursued wit and humour through the
centuries, with several pauses for sustenance on the way, we
may finally refresh ourselves with a few jets from what G. K.
Chesterton called "a bubbling and boiling fountain of fancies
and fun."

Extracts from Sydney Smith's Letters

(The subject of the first extract, a well-known economist,
held the view that the size of the population ought to be
restricted.)

"Philosopher Malthus came here last week. I got an
agreeable party for him of unmarried people. There was
only one lady who had a child; but he is a good-natured
man, and, if there are no appearances of approaching
fertility, is civil to every lady.

"She is, for a woman, well-informed and very liberal:
neither is she at all disagreeable; but the information of
very plain women is so inconsiderable that I agree with
you in setting no very great store by it. . . . Where I
have seen fine eyes, a beautiful complexion, grace and
symmetry, in women, I have generally thought them
amazingly well-informed and extremely philosophical.
In contrary instances, seldom or ever. Is there any
accounting for this?

"Agar Ellis looks very ill; he has naturally a bad constitution, is ennuied and blasé, and vexed that he cannot
procure any progeny. I did not say so, but I thought
how absurd to discontinue the use of domestic chaplains
in cases where landed property is concerned.

"Lord Tankerville has sent me a whole buck; this
necessarily takes up a good deal of my time.

"You have met, I hear, with an agreeable clergyman:
the existence of such a being has been hitherto denied by
the naturalists; measure him, and put down on paper
what he eats.

"My house is full of country cousins. I wish they were
once removed.

"Luttrell was very agreeable, but spoke too lightly, I
thought, of veal soup. I took him aside, and reasoned the
matter with him, but in vain. To speak the truth,
Luttrell is not steady in his judgments on dishes."

Some Sayings of Sydney Smith

"If I had a son who was an idiot, by Jove, I'd make him a
parson!" said a country squire. "I see that your father was
of a different mind," said Sydney Smith.

"We shall be on our knees to you if you come," said

someone, anxious for his presence at a party. "I'm glad to hear it," he replied: "I like to see you in that attitude, as it brings me in several hundreds a year."

To his wealthy brother: "Bobus, you and I are exceptions to the laws of nature. You have risen by your gravity, and I have sunk by my levity."

Speaking in favour of the proposition that St. Paul's Cathedral should be surrounded by a wooden pavement, he said: "Let the Dean and Canons lay their heads together and the thing will be done."

His comment on Milman's *History of Christianity*: "No man should write on such subjects unless he is prepared to go the whole *lamb*."

On reviewing books: "I never read a book before reviewing it—it prejudices a man so."

On doctors: "The Sixth Commandment is suspended by one medical diploma from the North of England to the South."

On a contemporary bishop: "I must believe in the Apostolic Succession, there being no other way of accounting for the descent of the Bishop of Exeter from Judas Iscariot."

During his last days he suffered much from languor and was forced to confess: "I feel so weak both in body and mind that I verily believe, if the knife were put into my hand, I should not have strength or energy enough to slide it into a Dissenter."

This last remark, which could only have been made by an Englishman, illustrates the fact that unlike any other people in the world humour is in our blood. We laugh at everything about ourselves, at our serious beliefs no less than at our silly prejudices, at our heroism and patriotism and at our cowardice and selfishness. Our true Patron Saint is not St. George but Sir John. Humour is the current coin, or perhaps we should say the Treasury note, of our everyday dealings. It is so much a part of us that we frequently fail to notice it; and the foreigner, taking us at our face value, thinks us a dull people. A rapid survey of modern politics will convince anyone except a Fascist or a Communist that we are the most civilised people in the world, the reason being that we are the most humorous people in the world; and if it is urged that we, too, once had a dictator, we can reply that it took a long and bloody civil war to establish a dictatorship here, and that in any case it was soon laughed out of existence.

Humour, then, is our natural element, but what of our wit? Broadly speaking it may be said that wit is a product of the mind, humour of the heart. Thus we usually exercise wit at the expense of others, humour at our own expense. Wit is a sign of superiority, humour of equality; wit is the aristocrat, humour the democrat. But again we must differentiate between French and English wit. The best French wit is cynical, the best English wit is genial. The first pierces, the second only bruises. The Frenchman leaves his antagonist dead on the ground, the Englishman delivers a temporary knock-out blow. The explanation of this is that our wit, being fertilised by our humour, is a much richer product than French wit and carries its own antidote in the picturesqueness of its imagery. We sometimes speak of our mother-wit; but a truer phrase would be our mother-humour, which is the fruitful parent of our wit.

CLIMATE AND CHARACTER
BY
WILLIAM GERHARDI

CLIMATE AND CHARACTER

THERE are two ways of writing on controversial subjects. One may write of them with assurance, as if one *knew*. But his confident stride merely serves to show how profoundly unconscious he is of all the contrary truths he does not know.

For my own part, I shall not base my assertions on any carefully assembled body of facts, nor sustain an argument in any special direction. I propose to be as arbitrary as a professor who has sorted out his facts to suit his own theory, but without pretending to be authoritative. As I thread my way in and out of the labyrinth of what may be called the English character I must not be considered as either praising or denouncing it. It is altogether too easy to praise or blame by suppressing the opposite view. I can merely suggest by allusions, citations, contrasts and comparisons. An essay on national character cannot claim to be either definite or exhaustive. All it can hope to be is stimulating and gently suggestive of new aspects, new vistas, new facets, and a more and more deeply furrowed conviction of the relative nature of national values.

Perhaps the simplest, if the most presumptuous, way of illustrating my conception of that which is English in Englishmen is by comparing the English character to the Deity. If you consider the Deity as the sum total of all individuals, and the number of possible individuals as corresponding to the number of possible combinations of individuality contained in the Deity, and at the same time remember that each individual, fashioned in the image of God, is the undivided reflection of the *whole* of the Deity, you get a glimpse into the microcosm of the English individual who contains in different degrees the characteristics common to the English race, while differing from every brother Englishman.

While the basic elements producing the complex of phenomena called the Englishman are probably very few, the variety of combination is very great. Each character element consists of an almost endless number of sub-elements, each of which represents the main element in a more or less varied way. On the one hand, all Englishmen can be said to be essentially alike; on the other hand, there is no Englishman exactly like another. It all depends on the standpoint one assumes and on the standard one applies. An illustration: inspected closely there is no one leaf of a tree exactly like another. Yet these variations, taken as a mere phenomenon, are only accidental and represent different forms of expression of a common basic law. The scientist, knowing that all leaves are different, is concerned with the basic law to which all leaves are subject; but to the layman who knows nothing of these laws they seem, prima facie, alike. The same applies to the judging of national character. According to your standpoint, you are able to discern the more accidental or the more fundamental features, or both, and what you do not notice does not, in fact, exist for you.

Let me, before I entrench myself in the national characteristics of the English race, suggest to you the eminently practical consequences of the theory set out above. The more you are conscious of the difficulties of the problem of defining the national character, the less likely you are to embark on national panaceas. This, from every point of view, is an advantage. Everything that is most tiresome and crippling to-day proceeds from men who, unable to think themselves into a state of tranquillising coma, translate their imperfectly digested thoughts into political action. It should be clear to the meanest intelligence that to achieve the peace of the world nothing more radical is required than the abolition of centralised government in countries which have already achieved an inter-urban habit of amity. Supposing the Government of Great Britain were rescinded, it would be unlikely that the City of Manchester would march on the City of Sheffield. Such passions for rivalry as may exist have already found their expression in organised competition in the sporting fields. But consider the inestimable advantage of such a step in international relations. The Mayor of Birmingham pays a courtesy visit to the Mayor of Lyons, which visit is in due course returned without anything of international significance having taken place to acerbate an unexisting problem. Some British sailors on leave have misbehaved themselves in a beer garden in Hamburg. In the existing situation of centralised national governments with diplomatic representation, a *casus belli* might arise which would require the concerted efforts of all the chanceries of Europe to avert a major war. But in my suggested plan there is no German Chancellor, no English Prime Minister, no Foreign Secretary and no government in either or in any country. The Mayor of Deal remembers having paid a courtesy visit to the Mayor of Nuremberg, but he is not acquainted with the Mayor of Hamburg, and the incident instead of ending in a total of twenty-seven million casualties fizzles out with half a dozen black eyes.

It is in the English character to appreciate the common sense of non-partisan relationships and to hand on the torch. Is this so far-fetched?

Is the opposite system of bilateral international agreements really rooted in human nature? Consider. Human beings of the same nation so hate and suspect each other that it is a wonder why certain householders in London should not have formed bilateral agreements with other householders in order to ensure a defensive arrangement against the concerted attacks of other groups of householders. But the fact is that no such groupings and alliances are contemplated because the thought of doing so has very reasonably failed to occur to anyone. If we could induce the same forgetfulness and negligence in regard to the larger groupings of units by lulling ourselves, through the hypnotic effect of profound thought, into a benignant inactivity, we should reap the same fruits of subtle, vivifying peace.

Naturally such a state of mind is not one in which

"ideologies" will grow to fruition. But we shall all be the happier for that. "Heil Hitler!" I can hear wise old Goethe saying to Eckermann were he alive to-day: "Freilich, damit ist nicht viel gesagt." And yet it is a sign for working yourself into a frenzy of denunciation as though the people who said "Heil Hitler" and the people who said "The Party" were in fact two opposite sets of men. The truth that they are not two opposite sets of men is already proved by the wholehearted conviction with which they call each other unutterable blackguards while regarding themselves as commendable fellows. In political sense England has always been in advance of other countries. William the Conqueror united England in 1066. Now the real trend is in the opposite direction—that is, of a nation so closely united as to be able to afford to dispense with a central government in order to avoid a focus of international friction. Because Hitler has done in 1938 what William the First achieved in 1066, is that a reason why we should introduce a totalitarian system we have outgrown by eight hundred and seventy-two years?

Why am I starting a train of thought which does not seem to have any direct bearing on the English character? Because it eminently has. It is the most consistent, deep-rooted and cherished conviction of the Englishman that denunciation is a synonym for untruth and that he who is angry is unjust, and he who is unjust and unfair is not to be admired by English standards.

Here, indeed, we place our finger on the motor-centre of the English nervous system. In suggesting a political path which the world may follow in the distant future I am, while I seem to be digressing from my subject, really bearing witness to the English political genius. That political genius which is rooted in an instinctive understanding of individual freedom of conscience, coupled with a mellowed, time-honoured tradition of quiet, anger-shunning expression.

There is another reason for introducing the German analogy. The Englishman, indeed, cannot be explained without the German. The Englishman is a more intelligent

German. The English language is a twig of the Primitive Germanic branch of the Aryan mother tongue. It is indeed apparent to anyone knowing German that the English language is a more intelligent German language. English, a lucid and therefore threadbare tongue, is perhaps not quite so rich and leafy in its lyricism as German; and the Germans are certainly not inferior to the English in feeling and the expression of feeling. But when it comes to the prose of life, is it not evident that only a befuddled race could have put up so long with the tortuous, involved atrocities of German expression? Neither Luther, nor Wieland, nor Goethe, who had, in turn, tried to give their dear Germany a prose style, have advanced matters appreciably. Journalists and laymen alike still express themselves in a prose propelled not so much by meaning as the unduly strong flavour exuded by German words.

Here, indeed, is the real intellectual frontier of England and Germany. The English is the stronger mentality. Whether owing his intellectual advantage to the vigour of a bracing climate, or the infusion of some Celtic and Latin blood, the Anglo-Saxon has mastered his language: the German has succumbed to the incoherence of his tongue. In no other language do innocent words carry so strong and bogus a suggestion of erudition and profundity. It is almost impossible in German to say a simple thing simply. If, with luck, you avoid inflated compounds like "Weltver-besserungswahn," "Weltpolitik," "Weltanschauung," "Welt-schmerz," "Weltall" (and all the other words suggesting the inveterate provincial's veiled nostalgia for a world empire) you still cannot avoid nouns all absurdly magnified with a capital. The German language is a confession that prestige values loom large in the Teutonic consciousness. The German is notoriously thorough, and he leaves nothing unexplained. But the Englishman is a carefree German. He carries his education and his citizenship of the world lightly, like his clothes. He does not know, and he does not care, what effect he creates. The German, that backward Englishman, cares terribly. The reason for it is not far to seek.

The German is not sure of himself. This essay does not purport to be a glorification of the Englishman at the expense of the German, though at first sight it may seem to be so. I am merely getting at the nucleus of the English character by abstracting him from that hinterland, Germania, of which he is essentially a product. Far from praising him indiscriminately, I must confess that he is a queerer bird than that blind owl of Central Europe who is his real ancestor. I think that the Teuton is in many ways a more solid piece of work than the Englishman, who in comparison is a will-o'-the-wisp.

The English in relation to the German are more or less what the Japanese are in relation to the Chinese. We are in fact the Japanese of the western hemisphere. We have, and with good cause, been disliked in the past for meddling in the affairs of Europe, as the Japanese are now being disliked for meddling in the Far East. Here we have been, as they have, packed on a tight little island with the waves lashing around us, our gaze fixed on the far horizon. Japan, too, had its native "Celts" and diverse invaders; but whatever they may say to the contrary, it is clear enough that they are mainly Chinese as we are German.

Here, then, are the English: a stream of Germans bottled up on a small island, with a few ingredients of native Celt, Roman and Norman French, a few currants and some yeast to make the cork pop: and the fine mixture not unnaturally spurts to the other end of the world, and in time overflows one-fourth of the habitable globe. The resemblance of the English to the Japanese can be further extended to cover other points. The Japanese, for example, are likewise insouciant. They are as proudly indifferent to the effect they produce on people who are not Japanese as the English on all the doubtful world which isn't English. I daresay the Japanese don't care what the Chinese think of them. The old English caste system had its parallel in Japan. The Samurai, with their rigid discipline imposed on themselves in the interests of making Japan a land fit for the Samurai to live in, is not unlike its English counterpart. *The Forsyte*

Saga contains the record of a caste which, while willing to impose a certain discipline of behaviour and obligation upon their own members, so that the England they have loved may remain just as they loved it, with their own hegemony unimpaired, yet consider the rest of the population as almost a race apart.

To love your own country is something distinct from praising only colonels, bishops and viceroys. He who revels in national glory is usually a person who, lacking personal distinction, develops an appetite for praise and merit as a member of his nation. Smith, a man of notorious insignificance, recalls with satisfaction that Cromwell and he are both Englishmen. In appraising national character one must bear in mind that the virtues of a nation cannot be absolute, since a nation is composed firstly of classes, and secondly of individuals, who have little good to say of each other. The moral reason why a nation (Spain, for example) should not bother to resist foreign invasion is because Spaniards do not apparently love other Spaniards well enough to spare their Spanish lives. Well may we ask: what is this famous love of Spain? It cannot be merely houses and scenery. I am not sure whether the Englishman to-day, should the occasion arise, would show himself capable of depriving other Englishmen of their English lives on the ground that they do not see eye to eye with him as to what is best for England, when, where, why and for whom. And what is this unreasonable fear of invasion (moreover, quite improbable), seeing that England has always absorbed every invader? If Hitler invades England to-day, somebody will boast two hundred years hence: "We Goerings are a very ancient English family; our ancestor came over with Hitler." And some invading fighting cock, Sir Somebody Mackenzie, will, at another date, prove to be the first of a proud line of patriotic Prussians calling themselves von Mackenzen. I am of opinion that the Englishman at his worst is the class-opinionate Englishman. It matters little who he is, whether a clergyman patronising the working-man, instilling into him his own notion why the social *status quo* is best in this best of all possible worlds and the British Empire under Providence the greatest agency for good; or whether it is the working-man in strident tones demanding the abolition of everything mellow in life: the effect is equally painful.

The love of one's country usually takes the form of hating two-thirds of the people who live in it. Like virtue which is merely the salt in the dish of life and should be taken for granted, love of one's country and what is called patriotism should be seen but not heard. Only cads beat the big national drum. Patriotism is indeed the last refuge of a scoundrel. But so is any "ism." A love of communism, of fascism, of internationalism, of pacifism, militarism, even deism is in reality always the same disgusting habit of over-salting the soup. It is always the same bankrupt confession: "As Smith, Schulz, Laporte, Popoff, I am nothing—nobody. But as an Englishman, a German, a Frenchman, a Russian, a Conservative, a Nazi, a member of the front populaire, a communist, internationalist, left-and-right deviationist, I am the pride of creation!"

Where, then, is the Englishman we all love? You expect me to produce Shakespeare or Samuel Johnson, Charles Lamb or some rustic of sterling qualities. Not at all. I will show you.

Mr. Percy Lubbock draws a delightful picture in a book of his published fifteen years ago, called *Roman Pictures*, of a typically English family spending a winter in Rome. Mr. and Mrs. Clarkson, Miss Agnes Clarkson, respectable, gentle-mannered Britons, had been spending the winter in the south because Mr. Clarkson has a delicate chest. Here is the real England. Here, indeed, mixed with the gentleness, kindness, even a certain superficial and pathetic helplessness, is the insidious, the incurable and unconquerable bulldog race. "No need for them to create their colony with laborious arts; Mr. Clarkson spreads his game of patience on the table, his wife winds her wool over a chair-back, his daughter goes out to buy a cake for tea—and the thing is achieved. True they are not as comfortable as they were at Torquay, and they miss the Marshams; but you can't have everything, and the English chemist is very obliging, and what with the English banker and the English news-agent Mr. Clarkson can always find an object for a walk."

Were you to ask them why they had risked the treacherous climate of Rome when our nice mild "English Riviera" conforms so much better to their needs and habits, they would not know how to answer this question. One goes to Rome for the winter because it is what one *does*. And next winter, when they are happily restored to Torquay, they will be able to tell the Marshams about the intensely interesting time they passed in Rome.

Even better than the Clarksons is Mr. Bashford who, calling on the Clarksons in Rome, has made them forget the long chill of the Roman winter, as he tells Mr. Clarkson that he has found it advisable to use an iron upon the fourth tee at Ilfracombe.

Mr. Bashford, moreover, knows the Marshams.

"Do you hear that, Agnes?" cries Mrs. Clarkson.

Agnes had seen a great deal of the Marshams at Torquay, and it was worth while having come to Rome for the unexpected chance of talking to Mr. Bashford about the Marshams.

"Have you heard from them lately?" she asks.

Mr. Bashford had received a letter quite recently from the Marshams, and he was now telling Miss Agnes that they had this year selected Bournemouth for their winter retreat, and had there been enjoying the best of weather.

"Do you hear that, Mother?" exclaims Miss Agnes. "The Marshams have been at Bournemouth."

The Clarksons, very remarkably, had themselves been at Bournemouth the year before last, and Mr. Bashford had cause to envy them the experience.

But no understanding of the English character, with its insidious penetration into foreign climes, would be complete without Mr. Bashford. I allow myself the freedom of using as far as possible Mr. Lubbock's own words in presenting

the case of Mr. Bashford because Mr. Bashford is a complete
refutal of the theory freely credited by scholars of all kinds,
that it is the climate and the climate alone which has made
of all the rich inheritance of Celts, Romans, Danes, Saxons,
Normans, Dutch, French, and other races that phenomenon,
the Englishman. Here is the story of Mr. Bashford to refute
the facile but, as it will be clear, unfounded theory that
climate makes the man.

"Mr. Bashford was not noticeable in appearance, at
least upon the golf-course at Torquay; though for the
streets of Rome he was perhaps too weather-bronzed, too
tawny-haired, too baggy in his homespun clothing. One
may well wonder how it happens that Mr. Bashford, who
certainly hasn't a delicate chest, can have strayed so far
from the first green at Bournemouth in this fine spring
weather. He and Mr. Clarkson are there again, it seems,
as they fall into an absorbing discussion of the merits of
the course—Mr. Bashford knows it well, having played
many a round there a few years ago. 'Now they're off!'
says Mrs. Clarkson, smiling over her book; and she too,
good soul, might be seated in her corner of the ladies'
drawing-room at the Sea View Hotel, while she tran-
quilly enquires of another English guest whether she isn't
badly 'wanting her tea.' "

Mr. Bashford has transplanted the Clarksons to their
native soil; they breathed again the kindly and temperate
air of the Marine Parade. Mr. Bashford therefore, you may
assume, is just another native Englishman, like the Clarksons. But if you assume this you are mistaken.
Mr. Lubbock tells us that later on he learnt the story of
Mr. Bashford and found to his surprise that this golfing,
gossiping, puffing Englishman, with the red face and the
yellow moustache, was actually *romano di Roma* in all the
conditions of his life. "He had been born in Rome, he had
lived all his years in Rome; he possessed by inheritance a
tenement in the Piazza Navona and a farm in a valley of the

Volscian hills; English weather had counted for nothing in
his complexion, and to the English golf-club he had only
been admitted as a holiday-making stranger from foreign
parts." He was the son, the author discovered, of a certain
mid-Victorian amateur of the arts, an independent gentleman of some quality, who had been an early and earnest
disciple of the eloquence of Ruskin "—Ruskin whom one
pictures, a grave and blue-eyed young man, stepping out
into the early summer morning of a little Tuscan town to
set up his easel in a deserted sacristy, an echoing cloister—
where he will work through the long hours with piety and
concentration, glorifying the beauty that a simple industrious God-fearing peasantry (if only they would bear
it in mind) may always possess and impart to a man of
feeling, trained among the refining influences of Gothic
architecture at Oxford." This was the devotee who settled
in Italy—"whether" (as he puts it in his diary) "for health's
sake or for love of St. Ursula I know not"—settled in Italy
with a wife ("my entirely precious and meek-eyed Dora,"
says the same document), "and there became responsible
for this weather-bronzed, tawny-haired baggy Englishman
in his homespun clothing. Ruskin and St. Ursula—Italy,
my Italy—the ineffable meekness of dear old Brother
Angelico: by names, by phrases of this kind I suggest the
atmosphere that was about the cradle of Mr. Bashford the
son. But human children, we know, have long ago brought
to the highest pitch the art of self-protection; and little
Bashford, I dare say, was not yet weaned when he cautiously
shut the doorways of his head against the assault of his
parents' enthusiasm. It was firmly done, it was final; little
Bashford proceeded to grow as he pleased into the big, red,
middle-aged Bashford who is now before our eyes. In other
circumstances he might have allowed his nature to remain
more plastic, at least in the cradle; but his was a special case,
an English babe exposed to culture in foreign parts. There
was nothing for it but to guard himself utterly and absolutely; and I think we may say that only an English babe
could have carried the affair so successfully through to the

end. For forty years and more an insidious culture, reinforced by the unwholesome excitement of foreign ways, had
been beating upon the skull of Mr. Bashford, and all without
creating the faintest disturbance within it; secure behind its
powerful sutures he had lived the life of which the accidents
of his birth had conspired to deprive him. He was in no
position to trifle with the danger. He, poor lamb, thrown
from the beginning upon the dubious world of all that isn't
English, must take his own deliberate precautions; and he
doesn't hesitate, he begins in time—and at forty he will meet
you in the Via Sistina with the certainty that his clothes and
his speech and his colour belong unmistakably to the land in
which he wasn't born."

Mr. Bashford, of course, is the real English gentleman.
No inquiry into the English character would be complete
without some investigation into that essentially English
term which has overrun the world and which in fact nobody
is quite clear about, since it may mean so many different
and opposing things—the word "gentleman."

The word gentleman springs from the word gentle. The
gentleman is a propertied man, and he is gentle compared
with the roughs and tramps who lack the gentleness which
springs from a sense of security and well-being enjoyed by
the propertied man who relies for protection from the
roughs, the homeless and lawless, on the loyal ruffians who
are dependent on his wealth. So he is strong, but relying
on his rough-necks to protect him, can afford to remain
gentle. The gentleness of a gentleman is to be found in his
faculty to delegate the necessary churlishness incumbent on
his privileges to others and for the rest expressing himself in
genial and endearing amiability. The head of an attacking
force, the judge who can destroy a fellow-man, need have no
strength at all, and they are invariably gentle men. A general
need never fire a shot at the enemy, and so long as he does
not shoot his own troops he will be looked upon as a gentle
man. No need for a judge to use even violent language to
the man in the dock, knowing as he does that the violence
about to be done to the prisoner will lose nothing of its force,

when, by a process of delegation, the prisoner in the dock is presently hoisted on a rope.

Sometimes you meet the most kindly and courteous men who would not willingly pain another human being by a wrong word, as a certain English doctor, now dead, I met some years ago, who, however, after he had recounted to me his love of bird life, made me question whether one could in truth apply to him the beloved English word of gentleman.

"Always was a lover of birds," the doctor said. "When I was a lad of fourteen I used to climb over the wall into the vicarage and listen to the nightingale. Loved listening, I did. You know, thrilled me, it did, through and through. I always was one for birds. In the dentist's garden which gave on to the heath I knocked down a cock pheasant one morning and sold it to the landlord of the Red Lion. In the woods on the edge of the moors I have seen partridges, goldfinches, bullfinches, and most of the English birds you can mention. I caught two brown owls by baiting a live rat in St. Herbert Jason's park, and sold them to a Mr. Worrel, who kept a grocer's shop on the common." The doctor smiled with pleasant reminiscence of his boyhood. "I secretly set a brick trap one day in a garden beyond the old mill, just under the wall, and caught a bullfinch and a robin. I released the robin because I was always told it was unlucky, and sold the bullfinch for twopence to a butcher's roundsman at Dr. Martin Fraser's back door. Now I am a grandfather, but I can still enjoy the bird life of Coventry." Perhaps we can scarcely call him a gentleman, after all. He may best be designated as a sportsman.

Then there is the kind of man—clean-limbed and upright, called a "good sport" by similar good sports—who appears to a sensitive and imaginative person as peculiarly cruel, who delights in the testing of an animal's powers of endurance (which he naïvely calls "sport"): in reality, he is amiable and clean-limbed, and would knock down a man in the street for beating a horse. He is inclined to call other men cads who do not conform to his standards. But it does not occur to him that, judged by a more intelligent standard of ethics than his own, he would appear a greater cad than the men he so facilely despises. He ignores all the realism of a situation; he is temperamentally blind to it. What might have made him a less disappointing individual? The answer is: if he had had less faith in his own standards and more shame in his heart. An example from war—he is essentially the army type. The sight of a human being having his entrails interfered with by a bayonet would, you might think, convince any unsophisticated observer that there was something radically wrong in such an operation. Not so to him. He will be satisfied with the knowledge that the man was serving his flag. In former days it would have been "his church"; in days to come "his class." His type does not change. He is, however, complete. If he is a fool, he will be a complete fool; and that, too, is not without a certain weight in the natural balance of things. Whatever the cause, heredity or upbringing, he is sure of himself where a wiser man might tread with caution and circumspection. His very lack of insight operates to his advantage. It is as if Nature herself had transformed his lack of perception, commonly a weakness, into self-confidence—a strength.

But the sporting Englishman does not always conform to type. There are many variations. He may even possess intellectual tentacles with which he gropes after other resting-places. He may have an intellectual side. He may have a cosmopolitan side. Far from being shy and retiring, like Mr. Clarkson, he may pride himself on being a veritable vessel of continental information. He lets it be known that in days of yore he had been very worldly, a native of the great world, or, if the occasion called for it, equally at home in Bohemia—when Bohemia really *was* Bohemia, before Soho restaurants were so altered. He is a cosmopolitan, but also a thoroughly countrified Englishman, at once a product of Sandhurst, and a bearded intellectual, and, if the occasion calls for it, a hunting-squire: ever an authority because he had been each of these things at the most propitious time, when these things really were at their best and he at the height of his powers, and he notes the changes with the insight of a man who, unlike yourself, knew Vienna when it *was* Vienna—in other words, knows more than you.

Now we come to the pioneer. I do not mean the bearer of the white man's burden. I mean the man of grit and dreams, generally a North-country product. Of him a great deal may be written. He must be explained with a certain amount of circumlocution.

Goethe confessed to Eckermann that palatial surroundings did not suit his nature. He would avoid rather than seek an opulent interior, which he considered to be detrimental to poetical expression. His own working-room was bare, stark, simple. Whenever in his writing he was called upon to describe magnificence he would sit facing a blank wall to allow his imagination free rein. From this confession it may be deduced, by reversing the process, that to describe a blank wall, Goethe would achieve the happiest expression by staring at furniture of the period Petit-Trianon. The imagination is in effect assisted by contrasts. The reason, if we delve into our common experience, is not far to seek. Physical bodies stand in their own shadow. It is as if the dead clay blotted out the living spirit, as two equal figures, superimposed, obliterate each other's outlines. Which explains why fulfilment in this life falls short of the promise of desire. Complete fulfilment would have necessitated the perception of the outline of desire at the very moment of the two figures merging into one.

All contrast is an expression of the same half-realised yearning when the soul perceives in clear outlines whole continents of promise. Vivid dreams swim into view in circumstances of exceptional gloom and sordidness such as the industrial north alone can provide. Natives of ugly, squalid, ever-drizzling Lancashire must dream. O what dreams! Extreme force of character is developed from extreme bleakness and bleariness of surroundings. And what do we see? A dreary, drizzling, intermediate climate, not quite inclement enough to force the North-countryman to entrench himself against Nature in wind-proof shelters, yet steeling him by constant exposure to the moodiness of the

weather, is responsible for the paradox of a people which, by
sheer grit developed through an infinite capacity to support
all the abominations of soot, fog, sleet and rain, has become
the custodian and trustee of most of the fair places of the
earth.   The sunny acres of palm and orange groves and magic
casements opening on the foam of perilous seas in fairy lands
forlorn are controlled, not unnaturally, by a people walking
nine months out of twelve under umbrellas and mackintoshes.
I am reminded of a most fascinating experience of mine when
travelling on Christmas Eve by the night train to Bolton,
and reflecting that the corner of England where the first
railway was run in 1830 should be among the last to continue
to suffer the indignities of smoke and soot; but also reflecting that here in this carriage with me were the very people,
the natives, who had with their milk imbibed and resisted
the germs of this abomination.   Simple folk with their
extraordinary love of home, roughing it to spend twelve
hours of Christmas at home in Bolton.   Here, then, was the
real native genius, in its native genius-breeding surroundings.   Having steeled their souls with the endurance of so
much gloom, ugliness and dreariness, they have, on the other
hand, taken the world in their stride.   Euston looked as if
I had entered purgatory.   The yellow fog hung over everything.   Every platform was chock-full of Lancashire natives
intent on spending Christmas at home.   The sound of hissing
steam under the glass roof augured the vicinity of hell.   The
platform was crowded from end to end.   An empty train
steamed backwards into the platform.   We all put down our
arm-rests, giving the impression of chocolates nicely spaced
out in a symmetry which no sensitive person could wish to
disturb.   We were settling down to a satisfied contemplation
of our good fortune when sounds of commotion reached us
from the far end of the carriage.   A last crowd of passengers
rushed past us on the platform and then a stream with bags
and suit-cases pushed along the corridor.   A woman with
a babe in arms, a grave old man, a youth with a bandaged
jaw and eyes which said he was in the throes of neuralgia,
shuffled down the corridor, and from behind them came the

irritable and peremptory voice of the guard, shouting:
"I can't help that. Room's got to be found. Two more in
here. Three more in there." Our door was rudely opened
and a draught of cold air blew upon us. "Two more in
here," said the guard. And with a look of stricken social
conscience we lifted our arm-rests.

Then the train moved. I noticed all the men in my compartment wore dark-blue serge suits, new and neatly pressed.
And their shoes were well polished, their hair freshly cut, and
there was an air about them not so much of well-being
perhaps as of well-doing. I discovered the reason for this a
little later. The man next to me from the moment he had
planked himself down had closed his eyes and gone to sleep.
He just sat rigid where he had planted himself and did not
wake till we had reached Crewe. Then he opened his eyes,
and another man called out: "Merry Christmas!"

"Merry Christmas to you all!" said the man, rubbing his
eyes. Till that moment they had all been silent. From that
moment on they never stopped talking till they reached
Bolton. Every one in the compartment both came from and
hailed for Bolton. They talked slightingly of London people.
One could never really get friendly with London people, they
said. London folk kept their real thoughts at the back of
their minds and you never felt they really liked you. They
didn't like Lancashire people getting jobs in London and
asked them why they didn't go back to Lancashire. Two
men in the compartment discovered that their people in
Bolton lived almost opposite each other; and when they had
expressed their surprise how small the world was they
discovered that in London too they both lived off Ladbroke
Grove, practically round the corner of each other. "Why,"
said the wife of the man next to me, "*we* live at th' corner of
Ladbroke Grove, that'd be nearly touching your back door."

"Are ye reely? Bah goom! World's small it is an' all!"

The wife of one man asked the other man whether he
knew a girl called Maggie who lived in the same street in
Bolton, and he said, "Why, Maggie's me sister!" "Why,"
said the wife of the other man, "me and Maggie was as pally

as could be at school and then we worked at Simson's together!" "Why," he said, "she works there still!"

They heaped more and more surprises on each other; and then the brother told them a story of Maggie. "Maggie was a grand girl, she was, as sharp as needles, Maggie was, and with a tongue to match. She could twist any feller round her little finger, Maggie could. Once when no more than a lass she and a girl friend she had in those days missed the train at Blackpool and they went out on Chorley New Road and waved their arms as they see car coomin' along, 'oping as they might get a lift like. And aye, sure enough, car stops and inside was coople o' fellers. Sure enough, 'op in, and off they go. But fellers got fresh, so Maggie says hi! stop car, I don't want none of that, and out they get, her and 'er pal, the fellers arguing like, in the middle of Chorley New Road all alone at night like, when up cooms 'nother car, flash lights an' all, and they wave their arms and scream like mad an' all, and sure enough car pulls up and in car there's two more fellers like. In they get and off they go and, aye, sure enough lads get fresh again like, and what could lasses do on dark night on Chorley New Road all alone like with two chaps getting fresh an' all? But Mag she's got 'er 'ead screwed, that lass. Fellers thinking time's coom now for a bit o' foon like by side of road, they slow down, but Mag, she says drive on, she says, I know nice quiet spot where we can have foon an' all and no one interferin' like, drive on, says Maggie, she says, and 'e says you show the way, and, aye, sure enough she shows 'im, first right, second left, and first right again and round corner like till they pull up at 'er own front door, and out they jump, Maggie and 'er pal. 'Good night' and slam th' door on 'em. That's Mag for you. Only when fellers 'ad driven off, they remembered like."

"Aye, and there was pair o' boots in car."

"Aye, I was cooming to that. 'Ow ye know?"

"Why, I was lass in car wot bought them boots in Blackpool."

"Bah goom! World's small it is an' all!"

The train, running uninterruptedly since we had left

Crewe, began to pull up abruptly, the brakes screamed and we came to a stop at an obscure station, something knocking underneath the carriages. We all hazarded what the station could be. A man as obscure as the station passed by—clink-clink-clink, testing each wheel; and as if the tired train enjoyed the sensation there followed the sound of brakes letting off steam. Somebody pulled open the door and a cold whiff of the sooty night air rushed into the overheated compartment, and we caught fragments of conversation from the adjoining compartment—an argument why this could not be Stockport. One of them yawned, and then the yawn was caught and repeated by all in turn. It felt cold, and somebody pulled the door to. Then the train puffed on gently.

Maggie's brother was telling the married couple that from the moment he set foot in Bolton to the moment he took the midnight train on Boxing Day and arrived at Euston at 5.20 in the morning in time for a wash and brush-up before he went back to work, he would spend the two days and the intervening night solidly in visiting old friends from house to house, everywhere partaking of a nice cuppertea and not taking off his best new suit till going back to work on Tuesday morning. The married couple said they had a different plan. They would be taking to-night the 11.50 back to London, spending the whole of Boxing Day in sleep to make up for two uninterrupted sleepless nights in the train; they had sent the old folks a postcard informing them of the time at their disposal, and the old folks, as they had done the last twelve years, would have sent word round to all their pals in Bolton, who would all be cooming over this afternoon for a cuppertea and a chat till it was time to board the tram to get back to the station.

Presently I dozed off. Every time I woke I caught fragments of Maggie's brother's narrative. I gathered that he was talking now of his younger brother called Eddie, the apple of his father's eye. "Eddie 'ad been courting young Bolton lady when all of a sudden like she goes to Loondon. Well, Eddie 'ad got 'is 'cart set on lass, so off 'e goes to

Loondon to look for work like. It nearly killed 'is old dad—
'e was that fond of th' lad. 'Well, Ed,' 'e says, 'if you can't
find work in Loondon, you come straight back 'ome to
Bolton.' Eddie was 'airdresser's apprentice like, and the
girl too was in the 'airdressin' business, permanent waves
and all—that's where 'e met her. Well, Eddie goes to find
'er, and, aye, sure enough 'e gets a job in the same shop—
'e's that likeable our Ed is, that anyone'd give him a job
even if there wasn't noon to be 'ad."

I dozed off again, and when I woke I gathered that the
girl, for reasons missed by me, had got the sack and gone
back to Bolton and that Eddie at once chucked his job and
followed her. "She set up an 'airdressin' place on 'er own
at corner of Beek 'ill and when Eddie 'e goes round to see 'er
she wants 'im to join 'er in business as partner like—take
on the gents. But Eddie didn't want to—thought site wasn't
right for trade, and when she 'ears 'e won't join 'er in
business, she gives 'im the bird—which fairly broke his
'eart. 'E went back to Loondon, but poor Eddie 'e couldn't
get lass off 'is mind. Can't sleep—not a wink. Keeps gas
on and reads an' all to take 'is mind off like. Two months
of that and he went clean off his choomp. Doctor said it
was nervous breakdown or soomthin' like. Can't live without 'er. In 'ospital two months, and when 'e cooms back to
Bolton to get well again like and looks for lass she's oop and
gone. Business gone smash—not right position for shop.
Eddie was quite right. And lass gone some place, nobody
knows. Well, Eddie goes to Blackpool to get 'is 'ealth back
like and there first day he boomps into 'nother lass in
tobacconist shop an' all. And next week they were wed.
Eddie took 'er down to Loondon. Dad went down for the
weddin', didn't like it, thought lass wasn't up to mooch—
not good enough for 'is Ed—not 'is class like. Didn't seem
right like, weddin' 'er without a-courting. Dad's strict like
that. Now Eddie's down in Loondon. Not cooming up
this Christmas. Not done so well this past year."

At Manchester the train seemed to have got stuck in the
station for an interminable time, and the weariest of early

dawns looked in, bleary-eyed, through the rain-stained
window, and there was the sound of shifting cans—a mourn-
ful clang of echoing activity this yellow hour of 4 a.m. on
Christmas morning at Manchester (Victoria).

We were already nearing Bolton when the conversation
drifted to keeping a fish-and-chip shop. The train whistled
hopefully over the still dark and sleepy fields, over which a
faint yellow light was just breaking, and the faces of my
fellow passengers had an oily shine and their hands looked
grimy. Fish-and-chip shops were the thing for making
money. No doubt about it. Sure thing, said one. Aye,
but mooky work, said the other, going up to fish-market
early each morning and cleaning and cutting up fish all
day—smelly. Chimneys showed black in the dim slate sky,
and the whirling fields had patches of snow on them. The
train gave another whistle, full-lunged and yearning, and
by the sign that seven genuine Boltonians were getting up
and putting on their coats and hats and taking down their
parcels and cases it was evident that we were within a few
minutes of running into the station.

There were no porters, and I carried my suit-case up the
iron-shod stairs. Then I stood on the wet pavement outside
the station. It was five o'clock on a Christmas morning.
The pavements had been covered with ice which was just
thawing and they were very slippery. No sign of a taxi
anywhere. The tramlines looked innocent of conveyance.
But the air, after the bad smell of the overheated compartment, was good for the lungs. I lifted my suit-case and went
down the slope of the station, crossed the empty street and,
not being too sure of my direction, followed the empty tramlines. The flag-stoned streets were slushy, but less slippery
than the uneven pavements to which the ice still clung with
some pertinacity, remembering it was Christmas and winter.
It was still dark. I scanned the endless ugly road stretching
interminably under a milky sky. The empty tramlines proclaimed the dawn of Christmas Day, and it was touching;
I almost felt the trams had gone to church. At first, to
right and left of me, there were torn posters displaying in

the dim light Lord Nelson in a cocked hat advertising some commodity which assured you the Nelson touch and stamina if you partook of it for breakfast. There began to the left a low row of houses; to the right stretched a wooden fence with more posters. Eat Toby's Lancashire Hot-Pot and Digest In One Hour, they urged. Then, crossing an inconspicuous bridge, houses appeared on both sides, the road rose a little and sank again and turned imperceptibly, first to the right, then to the left. The houses grew bigger, then smaller, and there began a long row of stark workers' dwellings with stark fronts and stark doors opening straight on to the pavement. These dreary rows of doors and windows stretched for miles till Bolton ceased to be Bolton and became another town. I put down my suit-case and took a breath of air. Rain fell from an invisible sky. The road stretched before me for ever. Bolton looked like the bottom of a pond with the water drained off. Sleet on the roofs, on the street—everything shining. In the bleary-eyed dawn the street lifted its shiny back like a hippopotamus which at any moment might disappear again under water.

Here was the cradle of a conquering race; here was the wealth and the glory of industrial England which was supplying sun-scorched India with light summer materials; here was that pearl set in a silver sea; here were the people who, if they could endure this, could endure anything.

LAW
BY
E. S. P. HAYNES

LAW

IN 1912 there appeared a volume of lectures given in America by Sir Frederick Pollock which was entitled *The Genius of the Common Law*. Sir Frederick mentioned that the word "genius," according to the Roman idea, was a "symbolic personage. He combines all elements of fortune and is rather an unseen comrade on a higher plane, *natale comes qui temperat astrum*, than a master or a mentor. We may call him a clarified image of the earthly self, a self represented as bringing forth the fruit of its best possible efficiency but always of its own."

In accepting this definition I should perhaps explain that English Law is more than the Common Law. It is as various a blend as the English people are by descent. It has tributaries from the old Roman Civil Law and the ecclesiastical Canon Law as well as from national custom. Then we have Equity, founded on the King's Conscience, which remained independent of the Common Law until 1873 and which is now administered by the Chancery Division of the Supreme Court. It was originally conceived as supplying a moral element which could not be found in law, though in the result the Chancery precedents became as rigid as any other Case Law. It is from Equity that the whole system of trusts is derived, both as regards real and personal property, and from it again grew up an armoury of protection for women and children against cruel or unscrupulous husbands or relations.

The law of our constitution has a marked affinity with the law of the subject. We have, for instance, no written constitution and the working of it is dominated by traditions and conventions. This is in harmony with the English legal doctrine that outside the region of statutes everything shall be decided by the precedents of Case Law as opposed to any codification or abstract declaration of legal principle.

83

This system has both advantages and disadvantages. It has the advantage of giving more flexibility to legal decisions; but it is dull and uninspiring for a philosopher interested in law. It may be partly responsible for a remark of Mr. Belloc to the effect that "Protestants think in paving stones."

Side by side with this dislike of abstract doctrine there appears a very strong instinct for personal liberty which was no doubt derived from our Germanic ancestors as described by Tacitus. It runs all through Anglo-Saxon history and has a very marked effect on Criminal Law. The Continental criminal system, which involves the secret examination before a magistrate, has a Roman and ecclesiastical sentiment to justify it; but in England the criminal has always had the advantage of publicity, and of a rough "natural justice," although until recent times he has not usually had the advantage of counsel to appear for him, and there was no Court of Criminal Appeal until 1907.[1]

The criminal fared badly before the Star Chamber when it existed, and in treason trials; but, generally speaking, he has never been punished without due process of law, and he has also been defended against unlawful imprisonment. Sir Frederick Pollock points out, however, that "the development of auxiliary criminal jurisdiction in the Star Chamber was exactly parallel with Equity (as Bacon told us) and did quite honest service for a century or more. It was ruined not by inherent vice but by abuse; the Star Chamber was doomed when Charles I made it an engine of political and ecclesiastical persecution."[2]

Anyone who wishes to understand the spirit of English Criminal Law will enjoy reading Mr. Anthony Berkeley's recent novel *Trial and Error*, which illustrates in a very pointed and amusing manner the legal obstacles encountered by a man who wishes to confess to murder in order to release another man who has already been convicted by a jury. Such a case actually occurred in the 'seventies.

These elements of Criminal, as of the Common, Law are

[1] He was, however, much handicapped as to calling witnesses in defence.
[2] *The Genius of the Common Law*, by Sir Frederick Pollock, p. 66.

due to the establishment of a central justice in England
under the early Norman kings, and to the fact that the people
were turbulent and anti-clerical islanders. Owing to anti-
clerical sentiment there was, for instance, no legitimation
by subsequent marriage until 1926 and, with certain local
exceptions up to the eighteenth century, no *legitima portio*, as
in Continental countries and in Scotland. The judges, as
from the time of Henry II, were mostly laymen and disliked
ecclesiastical rules and procedure, although they were unable
to prevent the Canon Law ousting the Civil Law as regards
marriage and wills. These judges had more regard for local
custom and less regard for foreign notions of law than
ecclesiastics had. Moreover, the Norman element of the
population contributed a stability and order not achieved
by the Anglo-Saxons and only made possible by a central
system of justice reposing on an insular security.

The English Criminal Law has flourished better than might
have been expected. As Sir Frederick Pollock remarks, it
has "achieved success, for it would be hard to name a British
possession where it does not prevail in one form or another.
It has almost every possible fault, especially in the matter
of definitions, and criminal offences have been created by
statutory offences without any continuous plan and with
much inefficiency." Yet "the Genius of the Common Law
has somehow contrived to extract from all the theoretical confusion a body of law which is quite well understood by those
who handle it, and quite sufficient for everyday needs, and has
the reputation of being, on the whole, just and merciful."[1]

The Indian Penal Code has not only been in force in
British India more than half a century, but has been largely
copied in other countries under British rule or influence from
Hong Kong to the Sudan and among them Ceylon, where
we found Roman–Dutch law in possession. In the same way
the old French laws and usages of Lower Canada in Criminal
Law have been ousted by the English Criminal Law, and in
the Crown Colony of Mauritius the Criminal Law is English,
though the Civil Law is French.

[1] Op. cit., p. 86.

English lawyers have always shown great powers of acquisition and assimilation, and perhaps the best example of this is the Law Merchant. Up to the seventeenth century the Law Merchant stood outside the ordinary law of England; but in the seventeenth century it could be said that the Law Merchant was part of the Common Law because the parties appeared before an English Court on the understanding that they agreed to be bound by the custom of Merchants. In the eighteenth century Lord Mansfield presumed to take judicial notice of any item under the Law Merchant which had come to the knowledge of the Court without requiring it to be proved in evidence. "Thus general Mercantile custom, provided it were really general, became in the fullest sense a matter of law," and Sir Frederick points out that we owe certain reforms, such as the summary Order XIV to the Law Merchant. The victory of the Common Law in this matter is certainly due to Lord Mansfield, who, "being a Scotsman by birth, followed the Scottish tradition of cosmopolitan jurisprudence rather than the insular learning of the Inns of Court."[1] On the other hand only one law of the English Common Law has ever gone forth into the world beyond the narrow seas under or in company with the British flag: and wherever the British flag has gone much of the spirit of the Common Law has gone with it if not of the letter also.[2]

Just as the Law Merchant was assimilated to Common Law so by a similar instance of judicial dexterity the Commercial Court was created by a simple exercise of administrative discretion on the part of the High Court judges. This was made possible by the late Lord Gorell when sitting as Admiralty judge announcing in 1893 that he was ready to put causes of a commercial kind in a special list, expedite all interlocutory stages, and abridge or wholly dispense with pleadings, if the parties would only undertake not to raise merely technical points and to admit all substantially un-contested facts.

Yet whereas in France and other countries there is a line

[1] Op. cit., p. 84.   [2] Op. cit., p. 85.

drawn between, e.g. the *droit ancien* ending in 1789 and the *droit actuel* being modern law since 1789, there is no such distinction in English Law. "As recently as 1922 the question arising whether a wife could be guilty when the husband was found guilty, on presumption of marital compulsion, the judge had occasion to trace this doctrine to the laws of Ine of the seventh century, which declared that a wife cannot be punished for receiving goods stolen by her husband."[1] There are many other instances such as the decision in 1818 that a defendant could challenge a plaintiff to Ordeal by Battle. The old manors with their medieval customs were often responsible for legal complications largely due to dearth of records and historical information, and the same is true of our peerage law, in which success has often been obtained by men like Sir Harris Nicolas, who was perhaps more of an antiquary than a lawyer.

There is also another strong link with the past in the British doctrine that personal status is determined by domicil and not by nationality. The old Roman test of domicil continued in Continental Europe till the ardour of modern nationality obliterated it there; but the domicil test still survives in Great Britain, throughout the British Empire, and in the U.S.A. Under the Roman peace the citizen's rights were determined by the jurisdiction which prevailed in his permanent home, and the same still applies to the British Empire. The personal status of a British subject cannot be determined except by reference to his domicil, and an "English citizen" (to use an ignorant phrase of Italian lawyers) is merely a *chimaera bombinans in vacuo*. This doctrine certainly has an atmosphere of peace in so far as it ignores the enmities of nationality.

English lawyers are perhaps too fond of glorifying their own system, and English Law has the serious disadvantage that under it no question comes to be decided unless and until litigation takes place. There is a further disadvantage that at least one litigant on any new point has to pay for the interpretation of the law (statutory or not) out of his own

[1] *The Law*, by Sir Henry Slesser, London, 1938, p. 21.

pocket. On the other hand codification does not abolish litigation, although no doubt an admirable statute like the Partnership Act 1890 makes it much easier for partners and others to settle their disputes without litigation. Much good has also been done by the Committee for Law Reform which started work under the late Lord Hanworth and which has clarified the law by a process analogous to the culinary operation known as stewing.

Sir Henry Slesser defends the English system with some ingenuity. He writes:—"It may be said that the whole temperament of Englishmen towards their law, and, indeed, their politics, has been based upon the empirical method of dealing with problems as and when they arise; there has always been a desire to refrain from over-definition and proleptic law. It would be a very grave and revolutionary step to break with a habit of life which has become second nature not only to lawyers but to nearly all the inhabitants of this country and those other parts of the world which they have peopled."[1] Secondly, he argues that the English system "is far more elastic and organic in its nature than is the occasional and necessarily infrequent promulgation of law didactically by a legislation which leaves no room for change between one issue of a code and the next." Thirdly, he points out that "a system of case law is far less liable to abuse by despotic persons than is a decision under a system of codes or acts or edicts, alterable at will."[2] He adds, "It is not mere accident that the Judiciary in the Common Law stands upon so much higher a plane than do the judges in the Continental system; for the one are called upon to enforce the law of which they themselves, as spokesmen of the common will, participate in the making, while the other have merely to interpret the will of their masters. In most countries where the Roman Law obtains, not only is the judge subject to such dictation, but he is himself avowedly the servant of the Executive."[3]

There are of course unkind laymen who suggest that English lawyers praise English Law because they are very

[1] Op. cit., p. 16.   [2] Op. cit., p. 17.   [3] Op. cit., p. 17.

highly paid. The suggestion is that litigation is only the
privilege of the rich on the principle of the often quoted,
but seldom printed, lines:—

> Adultery and fornication
> Are for those of higher station—
> Pastimes of the Great.

Even if this were so, freedom from litigation might be counted
as one of the blessings of poverty. I have already pointed
out that judge-made law is made largely at the expense of
litigants; but lawyers are scarcely responsible for the am-
biguities of Parliamentary draftsmen and the exuberance of
modern bureaucracy. Then again the litigant may often
be bled by the possibility of two appeals against the Court of
first instance. Nevertheless the public have only themselves
to blame in regard to the enormous fees paid to eminent
counsel who have achieved newspaper publicity, but who
are often not much better than colleagues who have not
received so much advertisement.

Even so, I doubt if in medicine the ordinary general
practitioner earns so much less than the ordinary solicitor,
and a fashionable surgeon certainly earns as much as a
fashionable King's Counsel. Some years ago it might have
been reasonably argued that the poor were better provided
for in medicine than in law; but to-day the poor man gets
far more work from lawyers than he ever did before and
men in what may be called the class of *genteel poverty* are
quite as badly squeezed in the matter of health as they are
in the matter of justice, especially since hospitals have
started charging for their charitable activities.

Law costs are certainly higher in the United States of
America than they are here. They are lower in Scotland and
in most European countries; but in those countries the lawyer
has lower expenses in the matter of rent and labour. The
main defect in English Law is in the deficiency of local justice.
It is, for instance, absurd that divorce cases are not dealt with
in local courts, and I expect that some such reform will
become absolutely necessary in order to make the new

Matrimonial Causes Act work at all for the poor man. Meanwhile it may be as well for the reader to remember that a lawyer's fee of 6s. 8d. for an attendance was fixed in the reign of James I where it was equivalent to about thirty shillings of our money!

English Law may possibly at times have been over-praised; but there has never been anything sacrosanct about it either among lawyers or laymen except perhaps in certain sentences of Hooker and Blackstone or in the talk of Dr. Johnson. In other countries one often finds copious ridicule of lawyers in plays and novels but rarely any satire of the law as such, while in England there is a perpetual stream of satire directed against the law itself not only by lawyers but also by poets, playwrights, and the Year Books and Chaucer to the present day.

Selden particularly embodies the humorous spirit of the English Law as when he writes:—"A man may plead Not Guilty and yet tell no lie, for by the Law no man is bound to accuse himself, so when I say 'Not Guilty' the meaning is as if I should say by way of paraphrase, 'I am not so guilty as to tell you if you will bring me to trial and have me punished for this you lay to my charge; prove it against me.' " This is a refreshing contrast to the confessions which were habitually obtained by torture up to the end of the eighteenth century in Continental Europe and which are so frequent in the trials of the modern totalitarian state. In the same passage Selden proceeds to excuse an apparently tyrannical maxim. "Ignorance of the law excuses no man," he writes. "Not that all men know the Law but it is an excuse that every man will plead and no man can tell you how to confute him."

Examples of humour can also be found in Archdeacon Hale's *Precedents in Criminal Causes* (1847). This book most vividly records the ecclesiastical equivalent of police court proceedings up to 1640. Even there the same tradition of free speech often prevails and women in particular are often unrestrained in their language and behaviour in spite of the ducking-stool, pillory, and whipping-post, which in those days were not confined to men. An amusing example is recorded on May 6, 1614, in regard to a parish clerk "who will not kneel on his knees in time of divine service . . . and for that he singeth the psalms in the church with such a jesticulous tone and altitonant voice viz squeaking like a gelded pigge."

Not more than fifty years ago there was a scene at Assizes which reminded me of Hale's book. A well-known judge of sensitive intelligence but not very imposing appearance was trying an important case at Assizes. (Some kind person once remarked that he was rather like a monkey on a barrel-organ!) The day before the scene he had very properly sentenced a baby-farmer to a period of penal servitude. Not expecting a conviction, she fainted with astonishment when sentenced. For the rest of that day, however, and through all the following night she made such a noise that no one could keep her in order. Her excuse for this was that she had forgotten to say something important to the judge about the sentence. The Governor at last prevailed on the judge to hear what she had to say and she was duly shown into the dock. The judge rather curtly told her that if she had anything to say, she had better say it as quickly as possible, whereupon the virago violently shouted, "My Lord, you are a b—— b——."[1] The judge did no more than reply rather querulously, "But I'm not a b—— b—— at all," whereupon the woman began shouting, "Yes, My Lord, you know you are," more than once before being removed. I presume that in a totalitarian state the woman would have had her head cut off; but in a modern English Court episodes like this crop up just as they did in the merry England of the past.

Mr. Bumble's remark, "The law is a hass," has become classical and continues to be repeated. In fact, it now carries more weight than it ever did owing to the mass of ill-drafted and ill-digested legislation which seems to become worse every year. Nevertheless even the Year Books testify, as Bacon subsequently did, to the English attachment to law

[1] I use the police court euphemism.

as representing an authority superior to any other power in the state.

Sir Maurice Amos refers to the number of laws which have fallen into desuetude and points out how many medieval and modern enactments have been systematically ignored.[1] He rather ingeniously, however, reconciles English individualism with English respect for law as follows:—"It is not abstract law as such which has commanded allegiance in England but law regarded as the expression of reason and common consent. Laws which are neither congenial to popular views of policy nor designed to create or protect private rights, have often been overruled by the jurisdiction of the man in the street, a jurisdiction which is only another expression of the national aptitude for self-regulation. You cannot, it seems, have a confirmed national habit of continually creating law by custom and convention, without having at the same time the converse habit of correcting by neglect the less successful experiments of the legislature."[2]

It is no doubt this characteristic which makes it possible in England to dispense with a written constitution. It must have astonished any foreigner to read that the Parliament Act of 1911 was carried in the first instance by a bare majority in the House of Commons and that this majority was ultimately confirmed by an Irish vote due to the reduction of the Irish whisky tax. Nevertheless I doubt whether so far as public opinion goes the House of Lords is not in a stronger position to-day than it ever was and I suspect that any attempt to abolish its limited right of veto would meet with strong opposition.

National equanimity may also explain the success of a constitutional monarchy in this country, especially after the strain imposed on that institution by the events which led up to the abdication of King Edward VIII. National amiability has, of course, the defects of its qualities, for it undoubtedly leads to toleration of gross abuses in public finance on which the Treasury nowadays exercises very little

[1] *The English Constitution*, London, December 1934, p. 49.   [2] Ibid, p. 49.

control either in the case of politicians or bureaucrats. This is bound up with a certain sense of decorum in public life which foreigners call hypocrisy and which certainly screens a number of scoundrels who know how to defeat the law and square the Press; but on balance it may be argued that this is better than the French system under which financial scandals constantly destroy the continuity of administration. Indeed it may be argued (as Bagehot did) that a certain amount of owlish lethargy is essential to political harmony so long as it is not combined with any scandalous defiance of the law. It is in fact a homage paid to virtue so long as the law remains virtuous.

The House of Commons has fostered various kinds of corruption such as the enclosures of the eighteenth century, the neglect of canals in the nineteenth century, and (quite recently) abolishing the right of appeal to the County Court from the often discreditable activities of local councils in the matter of destroying old buildings and erecting luxury flats.[1] Nevertheless, even political if not municipal corruption is still subject to exposure in the Law Courts, and judicial independence still remains our principal security for public integrity. Whatever tyranny may threaten us, the old maxim is still valid. "The King ought not to be under any man but under God and under the Law, because the Law makes him King. . . . Let the King render to the Law what the Law renders to him, that is, dominion and power, for he is nothing, if his will rules and not the Law." It is significant that King Charles I and his supporters made their appeal to law as against the illegal violence of the Parliamentary Party.

It is perhaps inevitable for any English lawyer writing about English Law to be constantly reminded of Sir Frederick Pollock's wise comments on it. He was a brilliant philosopher and historian of thought; but he also had a practical sagacity which enabled him to appreciate the more prosaic and cautious elements of our law. "Sometimes," he

---

[1] The decisions of the County Court, while its power lasted, are worth studying.

writes, "it is a gift rather than a defect not to see too far
or too wide at once; it may save us from fighting against the
gods,"[1] and again, "With us it is not 'What memorable
thing can we achieve? But How shall we get this business
through?' "[2]

Chinese observers have often remarked on the success
achieved by English merchants and business men in places
like Shanghai, where the business of the day comes first and
is harmonised by a consistently international spirit which
is not easily found among other European nations. It is
this spirit which has made the foundation of the British
Empire at all possible, combined with the desire to confer
autonomous freedom. I venture to think that both these
characteristics are intimately associated with the laws which
regulate an Englishman's life and career from boyhood and
which are not marred in administration by the pompous
and overbearing manners which may be observed in other
countries and their colonies. "I suppose that this is the
only country in Europe where quite a large proportion of
important affairs from the Constitution downwards are
worked by just doing the thing you want and saying as little
as possible about it even to yourself."[3] These words were
written in 1898 before the days of modern bureaucracy; but
I hope that they may still hold good in regard to the in-
articulate sentiment which moulds public opinion.

Perhaps, however, we can find one clue which unites
English Law both in space and in time. That clue is a revolt
against the tyranny of any one individual or corporation in
the state. We can see this spirit at work throughout the
British Empire and even in the United States of America.
Looking back to 1100 when English Law begins to assume
its distinctive form, we find that the law is the means of
moderating the tyranny of feudal magnates and it emanates
from the King. This process occurs much later in Continental countries, and even in the sixteenth century is
not so complete in France or Germany as it was earlier in

---

[1] *The Expansion of the Common Law*, London, 1904, p. 58.
[2] Ibid., p. 59.   [3] *The Etchingham Letters*, by Sir Frederick Pollock, p. 99.

England, while in sixteenth-century Italy we see a growing tyranny of the city state despots and oligarchies.

In England under the Tudors there was a distinct danger of something approaching to the totalitarian state. Parliaments become subservient and bodies like the Star Chamber begin to flourish at the expense of liberty. But for the misfortunes of the Stuarts English history might have taken a very different turn; but the Stuarts, with the exception of Charles II, were singularly obtuse to public opinion and never so careful as the Tudors were to preserve legal decorum. Their misfortunes were also largely due to the changes of currency which compelled them to go to the House of Commons for money. It is noteworthy that although on the whole the law was on the side of the King and his prerogative, yet it was Coke and other exponents of the Common Law who became the strongest supporters of the Parliamentary Party against the King. The power of the lawyers survived that of Parliament under Cromwell, and they were able to save Lincolns Inn Fields from the builders of the day in spite of Cromwell supporting the builders.

The balance of power among the classes remains fairly equal during the eighteenth century except for the cruel treatment of the lower orders in respect of the Criminal Law and the oppressive enclosure of common land carried out by the big landowners. At the close of the eighteenth century the whole balance is rudely disturbed by the industrial revolution, which results not only in a financial tyranny stronger than that of the landowners, but also in the inhuman condition of mines and factories which took so long to reform. From 1840 onwards the balance is perhaps better maintained except that successive extensions of the franchise eventually led to the formation of a Labour Party which ultimately eclipses the Liberal Party. Yet throughout this period, as always, one observes the value of the Law Courts as a bulwark against tyranny and especially in our day against the bureaucratic tyranny which is the principal danger of democracy.

This was particularly conspicuous just after the Great War

in such cases as the *Wilts United Dairies* (1921) where the Food Controller was prevented by the Court of Appeal from levying money from the Wilts United Dairies Company for a licence of twopence on every gallon of milk purchased. The same principle prevailed in the case of *De Keyser's Hotel* (1920), which severely limited the right of the Crown to take premises under the prerogative so as to avoid paying the compensation which was due if the Crown acted under statutory powers. We may properly compare this tendency of the English Law with the old principle of our foreign policy, which was to control the power of any Continental tyrant, and this is perhaps one of many reasons why Great Britain is never likely to become a totalitarian state.

To judge from the manifestations of public opinion in the newspapers and particularly in the cinema, the modern dictator like Stalin or Hitler or Mussolini is as much hated by our generation as Napoleon was by our ancestors, and so long as this spirit prevails in England we are not likely to suffer from any violent revolution. The crucial test came in 1926 with the National Strike, when the whole population revolted against the tyrannical movement initiated by the activities of a Communist Minority in the Labour Party and found protection under the law as expounded by Sir John Simon.

I do not want to suggest, in the fashion of Blackstone, that English Law is at any given moment perfect, especially in our day when it embodies a number of clumsy and verbose statutes for the most part enabling bureaucrats to become public despots instead of public servants. What I do suggest is that the intellectual atmosphere of the law keeps in being a spirit of fair play and a habit of precise thinking which is a valuable aseptic in public affairs. One cannot take up any English newspaper to-day without perceiving a continuous decline in any sort of dialectic or grasp of principles. Theology in any exact sense has disappeared and the modern substitute of what is vaguely called "science" is seldom illuminated by close reasoning, for it is saturated with question-begging conjecture.

Modern youth is distracted by scraps of undigested information and is *not taught how to think*. Modern sermons, debates in the House of Commons, newspaper leading articles and correspondence have a certain note of pompous futility which points all too clearly to a growing lack of intellectual discipline and a sad ignorance of pass logic. The Law Courts at least preserve a sort of intellectual gymnasium, the efficiency of which is perhaps best advertised by the objurgations of those who wish to solve every political problem by the short cut of violence.

PUBLIC LIFE
BY
DOUGLAS WOODRUFF

PUBLIC LIFE

THE British Empire will rank in history as the greatest of the commercial or trading empires. Its inhabitants have a genius, an inborn aptitude and zest for making and selling things. Its thinkers have led the world in discovering and formulating the conditions under which the greatest number of things can be made and sold; and the outstanding characteristic of its public life as it has developed through the centuries of commercial expansion, is the modest view which those who govern in Britain take of the function of rule. Men who live under governments do not easily consider that rulers ever take a modest view, the dignity of state requiring pre-eminence and ceremony; but by comparison with most rulers through history, who have approached their vocation with a high theological view of their rights or of their moral responsibilities, or as military chiefs, thinking it their essential business to consolidate and to extend, British Government in the last two centuries, has thought of itself quietly, as ancillary to the creation of wealth.

Just over a hundred years ago Disraeli, in "the Spirit of Whiggism," asked in what lay the genius of the English nation, what was the prime characteristic of the English mind, and without hesitation · answered, "Industry." A thousand circumstances, said he, convinced him that the salient point in our national psychology is the passion for accumulating wealth of which industry is the instrument. Disraeli lived to see, nearly half a century on, the replacement of the old whiggism against which he had fought by the new liberalism of Mr. Gladstone's final phase. From out of the heart of the old toryism came, in Disraeli and Gladstone, the two great streams of imperialism and radicalism, and the characteristic and symbolic man of the age was Joseph Chamberlain, the Birmingham Radical, who

was also the incarnation of the new sense of Empire. The
Tariff Reform Campaign of 1903 was of profound significance. It failed at the time; a quarter of a century was to
pass before Chamberlain's son was to enthrone the Tariff
in the English system, not as a temporary war expedient but
as part of a conscious effort to take control of the national
economy. In 1931 the tariff was made law without much
excitement; but the issue had settled an election in 1923 and
had been only second to Ireland as a political irritant before
1914, because in that controversy was involved the contrast
between two opposed ideas of Government. The Liberals
imagined that they embodied and championed eternal principles: but in championing economical freedom they were the
creatures of yesterday, the embodiment of an epoch which
came in with the younger Pitt and Huskisson and lasted, in
its full flower, less than a hundred years.

The twentieth century is rejoining the eighteenth, and,
indeed, the whole of previous human history in regarding
economic matters as things which rulers must regulate.
We live in the age of the new mercantilism, but the framework of our institutions and our public life presupposes the
Liberal Economic Era. It presupposes, that is, a common
philosophy, and agreement about the end of government.
Disraeli charged the Whigs with stealing two periods of
power, in the eighteenth century for fifty years, in the nineteenth for ten, by lending their support, to bring into the
circle of privilege first the merchants and then the manufacturers. The Whigs, he said, adopted the commercial
interest in the eighteenth century, and the secret of Walpole
was in that adoption. Lord Grey and his friends of the
Reform Act of 1832 had adopted the manufacturers. What
both the trading and financing City of London and the
northern manufacturers wanted from the state was to see
enthroned, in law and public opinion, a profound respect for
the canons and dogmas by which their callings could flourish.
They wanted the state to withdraw from fields it had from
time immemorial occupied. Queen Elizabeth and James I
might have legislated about the size of London: let the

Georges keep their ignorant hands off the suburbs. Elizabeth and James I might have enjoyed telling their subjects
not to meddle in matters too high for them. The tables
were turned now, when the whole lesson of the new science
of political economy was that Kings, and Parliaments, must
not meddle in matters too high for them. What triumphed
from Pitt to Cobden was the spirit of

> And while our statesmen do not itch
> To try their hands in matters which
> They do not understand,
> So bright will be old England's rays
> As in Victoria's golden days.

Nineteenth-century statesmen agreed that the less they
did the better, and it was money more than anything else
which induced this humility. The younger Pitt, with his
clear head, understood finance better than any statesman
since Walpole, perhaps since John de Witt, but he died in
1806 and the war with France and the Continental blockade
made it only too plain that the movements of money and the
decisions of monetary policy were as important as they were
difficult. Noble statesmen had not been prepared for those
questions—they had studied the classics and expression at
Eton and Oxford when they had studied anything, and it is
not surprising if, in the person of their chosen workman, the
laborious Robert Peel, they judged it best to hand those
matters over to the professionals. The whole of the nineteenth century that was to be is contained in the decision,
in the first of Peel's Bank Acts, in 1819, that the key matter
of regulating the amount of money should rest not with
ministers of the Crown but with the Bank of England.

The year 1816, which established the gold standard, the
year 1819, when Parliament made the directors of the Bank
of England responsible for determining the volume of money,
the most important decision to be taken in the country, and
the Governors protested against having such a responsibility
thrust upon them, but accepted it; these years stamped the
character of government in Victorian England. Statesmen
did not consider the whole field of life as their province;

they sought to obey economic science, which now enjoyed the authority of an accepted theology. Parliamentary struggles, in consequence, were not about fundamentals; the credit system was accepted by all sides; the supreme issue of the nineteenth century became the government of Ireland, which was quite plainly a secondary matter. In the final stages of the Home Rule controversy, the German fleet had come into existence, and Unionists could argue that an autonomous Ireland would be a menace. In the nineteenth century, with the British fleet incomparably stronger than the French, that argument had no plausibility.

The paradox is plain that the Houses of Parliament enjoyed an enormous prestige during the decades when their business was least important. To be a Member of Parliament in Victorian England was a high distinction, while the respect which accompanied membership of the Cabinet remains embalmed in the novels of Anthony Trollope, and then of Mrs. Humphrey Ward. It was a respect which went to men who already enjoyed sufficient deference, because very few commoners sat in Victorian Cabinets. The House of Lords, in its richer members, kept most of the chief positions, at a time when Cabinets consisted of twelve or thirteen members. The work was not exhausting, unless a man of prodigious industry, like Peel or Gladstone, made it so; the House did not sit for long or inconvenient stretches, unless the Irish were bent on making things uncomfortable. But for the accident of the Home Rule Party, with its love of forcing all night sittings, Parliament would have been what the governing aristocracy meant it to be, something that was not allowed to interfere unduly with their splendid private lives. In the biographies of Lord Salisbury and Earl Balfour, the survival of this tradition into the early twentieth century can be observed.

When Mr. Belloc, in 1911, published his attack on the Party System, saying outright what he had already said plainly enough in a succession of political novels, he failed to bring conviction because he made collusion between the

Front Benches a conscious matter; and all those who took part in public life and who knew their own excited and keen antipathies, particularly in the years before 1914, were slow to perceive the great truth of the thesis that both parties were agreed on all the large fundamentals, and in particular on maintaining and working the system. The things which divided them were altogether trivial by comparison with the things upon which they were so firmly agreed that they never even thought it necessary to discuss them or bring them into the light of day. Englishmen only came to realise, often with a shock, the superficial nature of their party warfare when they saw what happened to parliamentary institutions in foreign countries which had adopted the English model because of the prestige of England, but lacked the English unity and brought into their chambers real and passionate differences about the nature of the state.

Most of the battles of the nineteenth century were for political and not for economic or social privilege. The characteristic creation of nineteenth-century England was the Liberal Party, whose *raison d'être* was to put the Non-conformist tradesman and artisan on a complete official equality with the Church of England gentleman. The perorations about Liberty issued in legislation in the extension of votes or the abolition of tests, and it was fitting that the final stage of universal suffrage for both sexes was reached just after the close of the Great War, coinciding with the disappearance of the old Liberal Party. What was not realised, although it was fundamental to the whole business, was that the character of the electorate was transformed, as the qualifications were reduced. Disraeli, in 1836, wrote of England as a country devoted to industry, as a place where all men might seek their fortunes according to their qualities. He was writing at the moment of the Poor Law Reform, with its tremendous insistence upon the distinction between deserving and undeserving poor. The great change which set in about 1870, the beginning of what Professor Dicey named the collectivist trend, came through the realisation that the great mass of the population, a population which had doubled itself in half a century, was certainly not going to rise by its own endeavours, and had to be looked after. Robert Lowe's dictum, "We must educate our masters," expressed the philosophy behind the Education Act of 1870, which followed immediately on the extension of the vote to working-men in 1867, to rural labourers in 1885. What we may call the Joseph Chamberlain period, with its creation of new ministries and increasing range of government activity, culminating in compulsory insurance and state pensions for poor men, was not the consequence of competitive political programmes. Indeed, most of the time Conservative administrations won the elections. These things were the consequence of the existence of a proletariat.

The new electorate, the children taught in the new state schools, lacked altogether the fire of the old. It was an electorate which looked to the state as its forefathers had looked to the King, for protection. It could not at the same time think of Parliament as its servant, or view it as could free men owning property and paying small taxes to make Parliament possible. The point is of capital importance to-day. A statistical habit of mind, that quantitative approach which a preoccupation with economics and natural science fosters in the mind, makes men attach importance to-day to political gatherings according to their size, and not according to the enduring intensity of emotion or tenacity of will they represent. In essence, Albert Hall and Queen's Hall rallies on which the Labour Party in particular spends so much energy, are only Hyde Park meetings, and Hyde Park is part of the English tradition as an irresponsible safety-valve. These minority meetings can never have the significance of meetings of real minorities, of permanent minority interests, as the Irish were, and they do not embody real determination or fixity of purpose.

Indeed, the chief characteristic of Labour Party rallies on foreign affairs is their eclectic fickleness, the readiness of the same people to start agitations and then to become interested in something else, to turn from Abyssinia to Spain, from Spain to China, and from China to Central Europe. This is not the spirit of the Anti-Corn Law League, or the Women's Social and Political Union. Only the League of Nations Union keeps alive the spirit of political persistence. It is true, of course, that all this political activity has an unchanging end, to increase the strength of the Labour Movement, and that to that extent there is an abiding will and sustained purpose.

The Labour Party is the characteristic political development of the twentieth century. The Liberal Party in the nineteenth embodied the principle of the subordination of government to classical economics. The Labour Party embodies, more consciously than its opponents, the reaction, the aspiration to control. It is true that the Labour chiefs, from their preoccupation with economics, tend to be peculiarly at the mercy of academic experts and so of the old established dogmas of the schools. But that is accidental, and may pass. What is fundamental is the new type of public man which the Labour Party is producing, in the ranks of its opponents hardly less than in its own.

The Victorians never thought of Parliament as a paid or a full-time occupation. It sat in the afternoon and evening, for the convenience of those of its members who had active professional lives to lead. It took care not to interfere with the long week-end; constituencies were small, and made no great claims on their members. The M.P.s of to-day get salaries and free railway passes, but they excite less awe than their forerunners, and they work vastly harder. They are more closely disciplined, they sit on more committees compelling morning attendance, they have far more political work to do at the week-ends in their own or other peoples' constituencies. It is now proposed to give pensions to ex-M.P.s because so many cases have occurred in which conscientious members have by consequence lost all other means of livelihood. The professional politician, in the full sense of the word, is something new: a portent.

He is an immense departure from the English aristocratic tradition by which government was seized by the landed interest, not at all because its members wanted to devote themselves heart and soul to the work. They resolved to govern primarily in order not to be governed, and their great virtue was not that they governed particularly well but that they prevented anybody else from governing either well or badly, and above all from governing too much. The central government at Westminster was an extension, in a country whose social basis was agricultural, of life in the innumerable villages and small towns which made up England. No one can look at the Statute Book in the eighteenth century without noting the hard core of class selfishness which secured the domination of the landed interest. Innumerable private acts of enclosure were passed through an assembly in this respect quite unrepresentative of the country. *Pari passu*, the criminal code was increasingly stiffened to achieve that security which trade pre-eminently requires, yet the reign of the squire in the village was, comparatively viewed, humanised all the time, because his sports and tastes were those of his poorer neighbour. His house needed no fortification against armed enemies. The country had seen no foreign invaders for centuries. There was not, there did not need to be, any military tradition, and while it is doubtful how far the preparations against an invasion by Napoleon would have proved militarily adequate, they disclosed a deep unity of national outlook in the very years in which the rich were taking the most complete advantage of the poor.

The glorious constitution to which Burke and the Duke of Wellington loved to refer was viewed by its eulogists as a balance between estates and interests, between property and popular feeling. As late as 1866 the word democratic, which no statesman dare omit from his vocabulary of praise to-day, had primarily a bad significance, derived from antiquity, as meaning the capricious rule of the lowest elements in the nation. Mr. Gladstone had, in that year, in defending his suffrage proposals, said to a Liverpool audience, "You will tell me this is democracy. I reply it is nothing of the kind." A democracy, when it came, proved very unterrifying. Even the town crowds came, like all Englishmen, from the country, two or three generations back at the most, and in their blood was the whole political approach. The school teacher in England, surprised to find how readily her pupils look to her to tell them which is the greater, Tennyson or Browning, is the residuary legatee and heir of the choleric, dogmatic eighteenth-century squire, who laid down the law on very different subjects from the school curriculum, but who laid it down with such authority and expectation of obedience that the acceptance of authority has remained in the English blood.

The hungry sheep look up. The new claimant to the Duke of Omnium's seat is the teacher or the official, not the popular Press, which does not speak with authority, but very much as a scribe, which seeks to please and finds its historical pedigree in the cheapjack at the village fair. The penny daily paper delivers its patter, hoping to interest and amuse and hold the attention and keep the crowd round its particular booth. Only secondarily can it seek vehemently to establish that such and such a proposition is true.

Those who now seek the seats of authority, for the quiet pleasure of saying what shall be done and seeing that it is done, are to be found, in the main part, in the new permanent civil service, the vast incorruptible leviathan that wallows in paper by the side of the Thames at Westminster. The most cursory glance at the public life of our country must include these quiet important people to-day.

We all have faces not our own which we will carry with us for ever, and there dwells with me the red and angry face of a man in a bowler hat, who accosted me in a railway carriage some little while since. I was listening to an acquaintance, fresh from Nigeria and full of its difficulties, and after a time Bowler Hat could stand it no longer. "And what about this country?" he said. "Doesn't this country want thinking about and talking about? What's happening to it? It's being given over to pen-and-inkers. Look at Whitehall there, building after building filled with pen-and-inkers. And take it from me, pen and ink never made anything useful."

He had a good deal more to say in rebuke of the ever-growing bureaucracy, and he foresaw the day when Government offices would reach, he thought, from London to Land's End (for he was a West Country man), eating up the good earth for temples for inkpots and pens.

Let the reader come then on a brief tour of inspection of Whitehall, the seat of government, the centre of imperial rule, and consider the great departments which have grown rather than been consciously created or desired. They live, for the most part, in heavy Renaissance buildings. The Houses of Parliament, on which we will later on cast benevolent but discerning eyes, are Gothic in the best Victorian spirit. But the need for Government Departments adequate to the growing volume of minutes to be filed and letters to be kept and answered, was only tackled in the middle of the last century, and as it happened, Lord Palmerston had the final voice, and Gothic and all it stood for he refused to stomach. His patrician taste was for something classical with statues, but most of the statues—for there are a few— the Treasury knocked off the design for economy, and the result is the heavy square buildings in which His Majesty's Civil Service lives out its busy days.

There are some three hundred thousand of these Civil Servants, but this alarming figure includes postmen, whose harmless activities are known to all of us. Alone of the Civil Service, postmen are not supported out of the taxes, but by those who make willing use of them, and the G.P.O. is a huge business showing a profit every year. But the ordinary departments spend the taxes, and so there lives in their midst, to watch the spending of every penny, the Senior department, His Majesty's Treasury. It is many years now since Disraeli described Treasury officials as combining the manners of the Publican with the morals of the Pharisee. They are not popular, nor do they expect to be. Their reward is not affection but power, a power so extensive that a large part of the energies of every other department is taken up in tugs of war with the Treasury. If there were no Treasury control, how enormously larger all the great departments of state would be. They may look large to us, walking down Whitehall, but they do not feel large, but starved and overdriven.

The departments to-day bear little resemblance to the secretaries' offices out of which they have grown. In the earlier stage of the growth of our institutions, the great state offices were posts in the king's household. The Norman kings governed their realm as men administering an estate, employing various kinds of agent. But the offices took on characters and traditions of their own, and finally became things for which kings and their nobility fought political battles, because whoever held the office, although he might be in theory completely subject to the king, in fact enjoyed very real and wide authority of his own.

In similar fashion, the modern departments with their permanent heads, began as secretariats to assist the different Secretaries of State. The theory of the last century saw a great gulf between the Minister and his anonymous confidential advisers, secretaries and clerks. It was assumed that he would be a man of substance and position, whether or no he held any political office. It was not expected that the work of his department would require much specialised knowledge or a long apprenticeship. Colonies and war, for example, were combined in one political office until after the Napoleonic Wars. The theory is still maintained; the political head of the office affixes his name to everything and carries the responsibilities, defending his department and, on rare occasions, resigning when its conduct incurs blame. But in real fact, the departments to-day are organisms living busy lives of their own, directed by permanent heads, who expect their political chiefs, not, indeed, to be transient and embarrassed phantoms or purely constitutional monarchs, but who do expect them to stay on an average some two or three years and not to frame fresh policies but to observe the continuity of administration.

So there has been produced in a century a new type in English public life, the permanent Civil Servant. Institutions are animated by men; the most venerable of them, even the Bank of England or *The Times* are pantomime animals, deriving their life from the men who are content to live anonymously, and to let their strength and cunning be manifested in the activity of the institution. For the best part of a century, year by year, young men have appeared, the products of Oxford and Cambridge, men knowing themselves to be good at examinations, and hoping to win through that gift places in the Civil Service. There is a certain amount of moving from one department to another, but in general, a Civil Servant has all his eggs in one basket, and if he is ambitious, becomes absorbed in the work of one office. Each year that passes is a fresh hostage given to official fortune.

The fruits of this absorption are reflected in the whole structure of public policy. The governing principle has always been self-sufficiency. The defence Ministries, the Ministry of Health, the Colonial Office, even the Ministry of Agriculture, could each of them easily spend on their special interests most of the national revenue. The Civil Servants in these departments have to devise policies which will help, e.g. British farming or the Colonies, without making avoidable fresh charges on the Exchequer.

The Treasury control is the great pruner of planning mentalities. Civil Servants sometimes complain of the high proportion of their daily energies which they expend, when they have reached the top walks of their departments, in fighting with equally costly public servants in other departments and at the Treasury, yet this friction and partial mutual stultification is of the essence of the English system. No one individual must have too much power, not even when he is an anonymous Civil Servant.

The division of powers which eighteenth-century theorists so much applauded has been in practice magnificently achieved to-day, as power has drifted into the hands of great departments of state which are fiercely and perhaps providentially jealous one of another. The weakness is that modern England in its public life presents the picture of a great deal of separate first-class work rather hazily co-related.

What is strikingly absent in our polity in 1938 is anything central and authoritative, giving direction to the whole. The Cabinet, and in the Cabinet the Prime Minister, do this for the business of the day, but it is a work of supererogation to expect Cabinets to add to their immediate troubles by looking very far ahead. Sufficient unto the day is their instinctive motto.

The monarchy tends of itself to make accretions of strength, given time. Yet it is plain to-day that, with all her firm virtues, Queen Victoria left the Crown vastly weaker at the end of her reign than it had been at the beginning. The frontier line marking what a constitutional sovereign could or could not do was drawn ever tighter, till the twentieth century has seen the theory stated that there is no constitutional limit to the advice of ministers, nothing with which, as the representatives of Parliament and the nation, they may not claim to be concerned. This constitutional theory would have staggered and alarmed all English sovereigns before Edward VII. There are strong arguments for it and against it, but what is indisputable is that the monarchy is not to-day an independent source of initiative or leadership but a medium through which the Government of the day acts.

There is no order of powers making an estate of the realm and able to claim the position of national leadership, and, in the widespread absence of belief, the Bishops of the Established Church have to pick their topics and their words with care. In so far as anybody can claim to speak with a generally accepted authority in modern England it is the heads and spokesmen of the two great professions of medicine and law, and they are the most fruitful source of *obiter dicta* from above at the present time. Certain scientists, if they master the technique of apparent modesty, can include themselves among the elders, but in general no great empire in the past has ever been so denuded of accepted councils of wise men, chief priests, and leaders of the people. There is, in consequence, little responsible attempt to avoid waiting upon events. Politicians treat the trend of the times as something they must observe and allow for and to which their measures must be accommodated. They do not think of it as something they can tackle or deflect. In 1931, when a National Government asked for a doctors' mandate and won a huge majority, the country was intellectually prepared to hear the most far-reaching things, to be told that the drift of decades must be forcibly and perhaps painfully changed, that the national economy must be recast and made a more even balance between agriculture and industry, even that there plainly had to be a great redistribution of the population of the Empire. Merely to name these things is to show how they were beyond the scope of practical politics, which had to move in a world of immediate compromise between entrenched interests, of ten per cent tariffs, of Agricultural Marketing Boards and small changes in the rate of interest. No one, in short, is in charge, although there is a large, comforting, belief among the mass of the people that wiser heads are directing and are able to see comfortably far ahead.

Yet it is among the defects of the new professional pressure of public life, as it determines the day to day preoccupations both of members of Parliament and the higher and busier Civil Servants, that they get less and less time for long views, for retrospective and prospective meditation. Indeed, they are in great danger of lessening their immediate effectiveness if they indulge in such things.

The English public man, said Walter Bagehot, should have first-rate capacities and second-rate ideas. He must not get out of touch with his followers, who are not given to original thought or sustained study. He must not run the risk of being thought impracticable or a dreamer of dreams. The predominance of the Commons, the effective destruction of the other parts of the constitution, nowhere carries a greater threat for the future than in this: that it requires and selects certain qualities and aptitudes in its members, and it destroys others, highly necessary but not at present adequately represented in the framework of our public life. Short views are often, it is true, the highest wisdom, and even if they are not they are the easiest to take.

By a profound instinct the mass of the population refrains from taking public business too much to heart. The newspapers reflect very accurately how much people really want to know or really care, and by the tests applied in the interests of their own revenues by acute commercially minded men, the conclusion is exceedingly plain that most people care very little. If a paper costs twopence, however high the quality of its public writing, its circulation becomes one-tenth or less of a paper costing a penny, with no such claims to serious attention. So a penny makes all the difference, which is a sobering reflection for those who are fond of talking boastfully about our democracy, that it should be so, that so many people for whom the extra penny is an inconsiderable fragment of their expenditure, should not have sufficient curiosity or interest to want to pass beyond the easy and sensational penny paper, which, with all its great merits, as an entertainment, has few claims as a serious guide.

"Clear your mind of cant," said Dr. Johnson, "public affairs vex no man." It is well for human happiness that it should be so, and there is no more melancholy figure in our midst than the type of earnest idealist. His extravagant belief in the rapid improvement of his fellow men by exhortation and political measures soon leads him to despair at the cussedness of human kind and his own powerlessness to change them. There is too much needless unhappiness and disappointment produced by over-ambitious idealist movements for us to be quick to condemn the cheerful apathy with which the mass of the people regard public life, and their bland, unfounded, but comfortable assumption that legislators and officials have a clear connected picture in their minds of what they are trying to do. But all the aims of practical men are severely limited, and the larger issues are in fact left to take care of themselves. To-day that sounds alarming because we are so accustomed to think in terms of dynamic movement and change which must either be left to chance or consciously directed, but the older, and perhaps the more normal, conception does not think of society as a great body out on an adventure, with government in the van. It takes, rather, a static view and sees the Government, like the village constable, who only intervenes to make adjustments from time to time, in order that the village, the disturbance over, may once again resume its quiet agreeable round; and it is that modest, preventive or remedial, view of public affairs which best expresses what most Englishmen have felt and still feel about affairs of state.

MONARCHY
BY
CHARLES PETRIE

MONARCHY

IT has become such a platitude to say that the throne has its roots deep in the national traditions of England that the truth of the observation is liable to be ignored. The fact is the more remarkable when one considers that the crown has so often been worn by foreigners, for Danes and Frenchmen, Germans and Dutchmen have been among our rulers, as well as two dynasties, the Tudors and the Stuarts, which hailed from other parts of the British Isles. In spite of this hereditary kingship has endured, while the monarchies in other countries, such as France, Prussia, and Austria, which on the surface appeared more national, have been swept away. Perhaps the principal reason for this paradox is the adaptability which the wearers of the English crown have generally displayed down the ages, combined with the fact that in this country the monarchical principle has for several centuries meant more than the sovereign of the day. Never was this latter attitude more openly displayed than during the crisis which resulted in the abdication of King Edward VIII. English monarchs have shown a surprising aptitude for interpreting the wishes of their subjects, as a glance at the national history clearly proves. When strong government was the order of the day, as in Plantagenet and Tudor times, the throne supplied it, and when it was necessary to ride with a looser rein, the kings usually did that too. The flexibility of the monarchy has always been one of its most prominent characteristics.

Before the Norman Conquest the King had, for a variety of reasons, of which decentralisation was by no means the least, little effective power. The Normans and early Plantagenets were generally capable rulers, if not always very estimable in their private lives, and they were determined that the Crown should be supreme over both the Church and the nobility. It represented the interest of the nation as a whole, and the monarchs looked to the people for a support which was rarely refused. As Rudyard Kipling so well expressed it:

> When King and People understand each other past a doubt,
> It takes a foe and more than a foe to knock that country out;
> For the one will do what the other one asks as soon as the need is known,
> And hand in hand they can make a stand which neither could make alone!

Our medieval ancestors fully appreciated this reasoning, and from William I to Edward III they did not object to the autocratic methods of rulers who kept order at home, and made the country respected abroad. If they had any doubts as to the need for strong rule, they were set at rest by the anarchy that marked the reigns of Stephen and Edward II.

The fifteenth century saw that curious anticipation of Parliamentary government known as the Lancastrian Experiment, but it proved a complete failure. Parliament appeared to exercise control, while it was in reality itself subject to the pressure of the great nobles, and the result of their strife was the Wars of the Roses. For many a long day the memory of this catastrophe closed men's ears to all arguments for weakening the power of the Crown, and it was one of the main supports of the Tudors. It takes a long time to unsettle a nation, but once that has been done the recollection of what has happened remains for generations, and there is a universal demand for strong government to prevent a recurrence of the trouble.

Arbitrary, and often tyrannical, Henry VII and his successors may have been, but there can be no question of their popularity. There was no standing army and no police in those days, and if the Tudors had gone against the wishes of their subjects they would not long have been protected by the few halberdiers who lounged at the gates of their palaces at Richmond and Greenwich. They all knew how to appeal to the people, as Mary showed when she called the City apprentices to arms when Wyatt's rebels were already at

Southwark, and Elizabeth in her famous speech at Tilbury
at the time of the Armada. For whatever injustices were
committed during this period the whole nation was responsible, for it supported its rulers, and it must not be forgotten
that the Tudors acted with a careful regard for the letter of
the law.

It was not until four generations had passed away that the
power and the existence of the throne began to be called
in question. Even so, the agitation was at least as much
economic (due to the fall in the value of money) as political
in its origin. "None more fond of a King," as a contemporary observed, "than the English, yet they departed from
him to ease their purses and their consciences."

In due course the issue came to the arbitrament of the
sword, and in place of the old traditional monarchy the
English found themselves with, first a regicidal republic, and
then with a dictatorship. Cromwell was not, as the historians of the nineteenth century would have us believe, the
first great Liberal in British history: on the contrary, he was
the precursor of Lenin, Mussolini, and Hitler, and, like them,
he achieved power by the use of his private army in the
name of an idea. What the Red Army, the Blackshirts, and
the Brownshirts are in our own time the New Model was in
that of our ancestors. Cromwell's dictatorship was characterised by arbitrary arrests, crushing taxation, and an
economic crisis, and these were hardly atoned for by a few
successes in the field of international politics. It was little
wonder that after a short experience of "the rule of the
Saints by the sword" the vast mass of Englishmen were
praying for "a speedy deliverance out of the power of the
Major-Generals, and restore us to the protection of the
Common Law." This experience has never been forgotten,
and to the present day it subconsciously influences the attitude of innumerable people who know nothing of Cromwell
save his name. The death of Charles I and the tyranny
which succeeded that event established for ever the principle
of hereditary kingship in England. The arguments in
favour of another republic were strong, and they were ably

put forward by important statesmen, at the beginning of the
following century, but they passed unheeded. Even those
who were most bitter against the Stuarts preferred a "wee
wee German lairdie" to a second essay in republicanism.

This sound instinct that in some mysterious way the small
man was better off when there was a King to co-ordinate
conflicting interests received confirmation in the eighteenth
century, for with the first two Georges but the puppets of
the Whig oligarchy the rights of the common people were
most flagrantly violated. As soon as it became obvious that
George III was prepared to make a stand against the
governing clique, the country rallied to him, and for the
rest of his active life it supported him in spite of the appalling
mistakes he sometimes made. The loyalty thus re-kindled
was even strong enough to survive the regency and reign of
the First Gentleman of Europe.

A new chapter in the history of the monarchy began with
the accession of Queen Victoria. This is the more extraordinary in view of the fact that in fashionable circles in
London a hundred years ago it was generally believed that
kingship in England was doomed. The superior people at
Holland House and elsewhere who took this view ignored
the deep-rooted convictions of their fellow-countrymen, and
they little realised the character of the sovereign who had
just mounted the throne. They saw only that the Reform
Bill had conferred political power on the middle classes, and
there seemed no reason why these should support an institution which could have little meaning for them. Those who
argued along these lines forgot that Queen Victoria was the
grand-daughter of George III, and that he had received the
steady support of his people in spite of the sneers of the
West End. It was to be the same with the new Queen.

The Victorian era represented an important, though
essentially temporary, phase in the national history. It was
the period of middle-class predominance, and it reflected
the strength and weakness of that section of the community.
By some dispensation of Providence the Hanoverian Queen,
who came of bad stock and had not had an English ancestor

for seven generations, shared to the full the prejudices of the
dominant class of her subjects. The carousals of Carlton
House and the Pavilion at Brighton gave place to the
domesticity of Osborne and Balmoral, until every respectable citizen looked on the Court as the very model of
propriety. There was undoubtedly a stiffness there which
had not been known in Stuart times, but this did not matter,
for it was a prim and proper age. For a brief space in the
middle of the reign there was a republican agitation, but it
had no roots, and it only served to show the firmness of the
foundations upon which the monarchy stood. The Queen,
as she grew to be an old woman, came to personify for the
great majority of her subjects the country herself, and the
new Imperialism, of which Disraeli and Chamberlain were
the prophets, intensified this tendency. The Diamond
Jubilee was an event unparalleled in the history of kingship,
and it was a tribute to the adaptability of the Queen during
a particularly difficult era of transition.

The fact that Queen Victoria did so much to raise the
prestige of the throne cannot disguise the decline in its direct
political power during her reign. George III had insisted
upon dissolutions of Parliament, and William IV had dismissed a ministry with a majority in the House of Commons,
but their successor never dared to act in such a manner,
though on at least one occasion she seriously contemplated
similar heroic remedies. Not that there was any legislative
diminution of the power of the Crown, but rather, as Sir
Sidney Lee put it, "Many times did she write to a minister
that 'Never would she consent' to this or that proposal; yet
her formal signature of approval was always at his service
at the needful moment." If she was a great Queen, she was
also a very human woman. When she died the great pre-
rogatives of the Crown were that of mercy, the dissolution
and convocation of Parliament, the dismissal and selection
of ministers, the declaration of war and peace, the making of
treaties, the cession of territory, the creation of peers, and
the nomination to official appointments. In addition the
monarch might refuse assent to a Bill, but this right had not

been exercised since the reign of Anne. One of the proofs of the Queen's adaptability was her realisation that times had changed.

On the other hand Queen Victoria, owing to the accumulated experience of so many years, was able to exercise very considerable influence over her ministers. In the latter part of her life she could quote from personal experience precedents relating to events that had occurred before some of them were even born, and this gave her an enormous advantage in her dealings with them. This role of impartial adviser was a new one, and in adopting it the Queen set an example which her son and grandson were not slow to follow.

By the end of the nineteenth century the basis of political power was shifting from the middle to the working classes, and it was the supreme merit of King Edward VII and his son that they fully realised the fact. They made the masses as enthusiastic for the Crown as Queen Victoria had rendered the *bourgeoisie*, and they did this without any lowering of the prestige of the throne. It would have been so easy to play to the gallery like a Louis Philippe, but they knew their people well enough to realise that it is the appeal to the higher, not to the lower instincts, of the English which pays in the long run. Indeed, it was what may be described as the July Monarchy atmosphere which sometimes attached to the behaviour of King Edward VIII that weakened his position among those who were, by tradition and conviction, most loyal to the throne. The result of the policy of King George V and his father was seen in 1918, when the fall of so many thrones was entirely without repercussion in the British Isles.

Ten years later it was announced that the King was seriously ill, and for some weeks he actually hovered between life and death. The effect upon the country came as a surprise even to those who were most convinced of the monarchical instincts of the British people. In a moment it was clear that the best-loved and most respected man in the Empire was its sovereign, and every class among his subjects shared the anxiety of the Royal Family as the bulletins raised or lowered its hope. There had been nothing like it since the illness of the Prince of Wales over fifty years before, and for anything in the nature of an exact parallel one must go back to 1744 when Louis XV lay at death's door at Metz. Since the Armistice many an eminent Parliamentarian had sickened and died without the nation giving him more than a passing thought, but the whole Empire was in spirit by the bedside of King George V. While only too many of the politicians had been endeavouring to rivet the attention of the public by posturing in the limelight the King had won the nation's confidence by his unostentatious devotion to duty and its interests.

The value of the monarchy, and the influence of the monarch, were seen when the crisis broke in 1931. When it occurred the King was at Balmoral, and as soon as the announcement was made that he was coming to London a sigh of relief went up from the whole country. He alone inspired universal confidence as standing above the parties, the representative of the interests of the nation and Empire as a whole. Those who are inclined to question the value of hereditary kingship would do well to reflect upon what would have happened had Great Britain been a republic in August, 1931. The President would have been either a colourless nonentity or a violent partisan. If the former, he would never have dared to adopt a definite policy of his own, and at a time when every hour was of importance if catastrophe was to be avoided, days, and probably weeks, would have been wasted in consultations with the various party leaders before a new administration could have been formed. Had the President been a partisan he would not have possessed the confidence of the nation to a sufficient extent to have rendered his intervention decisive.

If it be admitted, and few will deny the fact, that the prestige of the monarchy has never been higher than it was at the death of King George V, has that prestige been seriously dimmed by the events of the succeeding twelve months? It is useless to deny that the abdication, and the circumstances which produced it, gave the Empire a severe shock. It seemed to many people that King Edward was preferring his personal inclinations to his duty, and they thought of the tens of thousands of men who had without question sacrificed all that was dearest to them for the sake of their country in the war. To the whole Empire it appeared incredible that anything or anyone could be preferred to the proudest throne on earth. Yet it was at this moment that the good work of King Edward's three predecessors was most obvious. The principle was more than the man, and after a week of conflicting hopes and fears, the British people at home and overseas settled down under King George VI. It would be idle to say that no resentment is felt on account of what then occurred, but this resentment is in no way directed against monarchy as an institution.

The difficult circumstances in which King George VI and Queen Elizabeth ascended the throne have won them widespread sympathy, and this has been strengthened by their behaviour. His Majesty appears to have the happy knack of combining the "popular touch" with the dignity of his position, and one has only to travel up and down the country to realise how successfully he has overcome the initial obstacles. There will be rocks ahead, but he has made an admirable start. Perhaps the position can best be summed up in the phrase used by an old cricketer to the present writer, "He went in to bat on a very sticky wicket, but he has played himself in magnificently." Furthermore, Queen Victoria taught the British public to look to Buckingham Palace for the pattern of family life, and this tradition has been revived. In the Royal circle the man-in-the-street sees the reflection of his own household, and to a home-loving people like the English this means a great deal. As the Prince Consort put it at a public dinner so long ago as 1853: "In the progress of the Royal Family through life is reflected, as it were, the progress of the generation to which they belong, and out of the common sympathy felt for them arises an additional bond of union amongst the people themselves." "I am a very ordinary person when I am allowed to be," the present King once observed, and in saying so he put his finger upon the secret of his success.

The basis of the monarchy is that it is popular in the etymological sense of the term. The English like to see their sovereigns, and the most popular have always been those who took obvious pleasure in showing themselves to their subjects. Charles II walking in St. James's Park and feeding the ducks, where every Londoner who wished could see him, is the model which the wise King of England will always keep before him, though, of course, changed circumstances impose different standards of behaviour. King Edward VII owed a great deal of his popularity to the delight which he clearly took in appearing in public, and King George V would not have been able to render such enormous services to the state had he not early won the affection of the people by appearing among them on the occasion of the national sporting festivals. It was not pure chance that the withdrawal of Queen Victoria from public life for so many years after the death of the Prince Consort should have been followed by the growth of a definite, if short-lived, republican movement. There must not be, either in theory or in practice, anything exclusive about Royalty in England, and the attempt of the earlier Hanoverians to bring this about was not the least of the many causes of their unpopularity.

Gradually the Court has once more come to reflect these sentiments, and the fact is generally appreciated. It is in no small measure due to the tact of King Edward VII, for in abandoning some of the exclusiveness which had characterised his mother's relations with the outside world he greatly broadened, as has been shown, the basis upon which the monarchy itself rested. In this the Crown has set an example to the whole country. Society in the Victorian era despised what it called trade, and the pages of such writers as Trollope contain innumerable examples of this prejudice. It was, incidentally, a somewhat illogical attitude, in view of the fact that what was termed society was largely composed of the children and grandchildren of "nabobs" and profiteers of the Revolutionary and Napoleonic wars. Readers of Disraeli will remember his reference to "Mr. Canning, long kept down by the plebeian aristocracy of Mr. Pitt as an adventurer." King Edward VII and his son set their faces against such folly. In their reigns the King once more delighted to honour any who showed themselves worthy, whatever might have been their origin. They made the Crown national again on its social side. Had their example been followed abroad, there would be more thrones in Europe to-day.

This tradition of accessibility is enshrined in the Constitution in the Petition of Right. The doctrine that the King can do no wrong, and the fiction that the law courts are his own, have the effect of making it impossible for a subject to sue the Crown in the ordinary way if he has sustained injury, so the procedure of Petition of Right came into existence. This, it may be observed, is employed only where the relief claimed is for money due under a contract, or for restitution of property of which the Crown has obtained possession. Where a tort has been committed by any servant of the monarch, the appropriate remedy is by action against the servant personally. "I am above the law," James II told the Duke of Somerset, whom he had asked to attend him to Mass. "But I am not," replied the Duke, and remained outside.

The price of kingship in England is an infinite attention to detail. The King is probably the only man in the country who never gets a real holiday free from the daily cares of his work. If one has occasion, for example, in August or September to communicate with a Government Department or an industrial concern, it is highly probable that no definite answer will be forthcoming until the return of this or that individual from his holidays: if the approach has been to Buckingham Palace, the King's pleasure will be taken in a day or two, and the necessary decision given. Pictures of the King shooting in Scotland or yachting at Cowes should not be allowed to obscure the fact that after breakfast and before dinner there is official business to be transacted.

Nor is this all, for the King must keep in touch with every aspect of his subjects' activity, so that it may be truly said of him *nihil humani alienum*. During the course of a single day he may be expected to display at any rate a nodding acquaintance with a score of widely different problems, and to make intelligent conversation with men and women each of whom is an expert upon his or her special subject. Many of these people have never spoken to him before, and are unlikely ever to do so again; thus a momentary impression may last a lifetime, so that it is of the utmost importance that it should not be disappointing. At the same time it is essential that the King should on every possible occasion extract the maximum amount of information from those with whom he is brought in contact; and the task of doing this, without appearing rude, is indeed formidable.

In addition, there is an amount of ceremonial which would in itself appal one not born to it. The English people are rightly very partial to the pageantry which is traditionally attached to Royalty, but this imposes a severe strain upon the wearer of the Crown. An actor on screen or stage is free for a time when he has played his part, but a King has to pass on at once to something else, possibly just as arduous. The opening of Parliament is a gorgeous spectacle, but one sometimes wonders whether the cheering thousands along the route realise that the central figure in it is a man as well as a monarch; a man who did not choose his position, but has accepted it as his duty towards God and his fellow men.

To-day a fiercer light beats upon the throne than ever before, and the events of the last two years have done nothing to lessen it. Napoleon told Caulaincourt: "*La royauté est un rôle. Les souverains doivent toujours être en scène.*" One of the many drawbacks of a republican regime is that the whole tone of society is lowered by the absence of a Court, and from the capital this demoralisation spreads to all parts of the country. But if the reverse is to be the case, and the monarchy is to raise the whole tone of the nation, then a heavy burden is imposed upon the King. Charles I and Queen Victoria purged their immediate circle of the scandals by which it had been sullied in the years preceding their accession, and the results of what they did were felt to the farthest parts of the kingdom. Amid the storms of the post-war years the quiet home life of King George and Queen Mary shone like a beacon.

Napoleon spoke truly. A King is always on the stage, and this is especially so in a monarchy with the traditions of the British. The people look to the throne for guidance in their own lives, and so they examine the conduct of its occupant the more closely. They feel, too, instinctively that he sympathises with their difficulties, and they are right, but it is not easy for him to bridge the gulf that must necessarily lie between him and them. That four successive generations of our rulers have done this is a fact almost without parallel in the history of the world.

In one respect alone has the Royal Family of late years tended to keep out of touch, and that is where the thought of the country is concerned. Amid the crowd of statesmen, sailors, soldiers, financiers, and captains of industry who frequent Buckingham Palace men of letters are extremely rare. Of all the activities of his subjects at the present time King George VI is probably most ignorant of the intellectual, and it would be well for the monarchy if his advisers would see that he is brought into the same close and informal contact with those who are moulding the thought of the nation as he is with those who influence it in other directions. It is not enough for an occasional professor, or a novelist of established reputation, to be asked to dinner by one of the younger members of the Royal Family, or for the Presidents of the various Royal Societies to be invited to a garden party once a year. What is required is that the throne should associate itself with literature in the same way that King Edward VII associated it with the commercial and industrial activities of the kingdom. The Court of England to-day is simplicity itself compared with that of Versailles in the days of the *Grand Monarque*, but Louis XIV was on far more intimate terms with men of letters than has been the case with any modern English King.

The social influence of the Crown is not difficult to assess, but when one turns to its place in the Constitution one enters very debatable ground. The powers of a King of England are far more extensive than is commonly supposed, and they have not been diminished by statute since the Revolution settlement. They are, then, legally the same as when William III personally conducted the country's relations with its neighbours, and commanded its armies in the field. Anne often attended the meetings of the Cabinet as well as the debates in the House of Lords, and always claimed the right to appoint ministers according to her own choice, and from any party. We have seen that George III and William IV did not hesitate to dismiss governments, but that during the reign of Queen Victoria the Crown ceased to interfere directly in political matters.

Nevertheless the old powers still remained, and Bagehot wrote: "It would very much surprise people if they were told how many things the Queen could do without consulting Parliament, and it certainly has so proved, for when the Queen abolished purchase in the army by an act of prerogative (after the Lords had rejected the Bill for doing so), there was a great and general astonishment. But this is nothing to what the Queen can by law do without consulting Parliament. Not to mention other things, she could disband the army (by law she cannot engage more than a certain number of men, but she is not obliged to engage any men); she could dismiss all the officers, from the General Commanding-in-Chief downwards; she could dismiss all the sailors too; she could sell off all our ships of war and all our naval stores; she could make a peace by the sacrifice of Cornwall, and begin a war for the conquest of Brittany. She could make every citizen in the United Kingdom, male or female, a peer; she could make every parish in the United Kingdom a university; she could dismiss most of the civil servants; she could pardon all offenders. In a word, the Queen could by prerogative upset all the action of civil government within the government, could disgrace the nation by a bad war or peace, and could, by disbanding our forces, whether land or sea, leave us defenceless against foreign nations." These observations are equally applicable to King George VI.

The conventions of the Constitution are very different, and Gladstone did not exaggerate when he declared: "It would be an evil and a perilous day for the monarchy were any prospective possessor of the Crown to assume or claim for himself final or preponderating, or even independent, power in any one department of the State." Neither King Edward VII nor his son departed from the practice of Queen Victoria, and it is quite inaccurate to describe the events which led up to the abdication of King Edward VIII as causing a constitutional crisis. Neither the letter nor the spirit of the Constitution was threatened by the monarch or anyone else.

If Great Britain alone had been concerned, it is possible that in course of time the sovereign might have become a mere cipher, but the existence of the overseas empire has reversed the tendency which has been operating in the British Isles for a century. The Crown has always been the strongest link in the Imperial chain, but since the Statute of Westminster it has become the only connecting link between the Mother Country and the Dominions, as well as between the Dominions themselves. In consequence of this, a recent writer, Mr. Alport in his *Kingdoms in Partnership*, has gone so far as to say that the influence of the monarch is greater to-day than at any time since the accession of the House of Hanover. "In fact, it is the newest and most extraordinary of the paradoxes of an Imperial Constitution that the more democratic it becomes the greater grows the influence of the Crown." There is considerable truth in this contention.

The British Government has no voice in the affairs of the Dominions. The Governors-General are appointed by the King on the advice of the Government of the Dominion in question, and if ever a clash came between the Dominions, or between one of them and the Mother Country, he alone could decide what course to pursue. This personal responsibility has already been tested, and both Irish and South

African ministers have consulted the monarch on matters which were not discussed with the British Government. It will also be remembered that two of the Dominions approached King Edward VIII direct during the last days of his reign.

Where the theory and the practice differ so widely as they do with regard to the power of the Crown in the British Constitution, it is clear that the deciding factor must be the personality of the reigning monarch. The influence of King George V during the last years of his life was considerable, quite apart from his direct intervention in 1931. He played, for instance, no small part in bringing about the Irish settlement in 1921, and it was his speech at the opening of the Ulster Parliament which made possible the commencement of negotiations between the British Government and the rebels. Not the least of the advantages of hereditary kingship is that the sovereign is always there, while ministers come and go. He represents continuity, and can cite precedents which might otherwise be forgotten. Such being the case, the influence of a King of England is likely to increase with the passing of the years, as his memory grows longer and his experience comes to exceed that of his ministers. He is, too, like the chairman in one of the larger industrial undertakings. When all goes well there is no need for him to do a great deal, but when a crisis does arise he must be prepared to see that it is the national interest which is served.

One is inclined to take for granted the smooth working of the Constitution in normal times, and to forget that this is only achieved by eternal vigilance, not least on the part of the Crown, which often has to moderate the asperity of party strife to achieve this result. For example, when Mr. Balfour's Government resigned in 1905, King Edward VII asked the retiring Chief Secretary for Ireland, Mr. Walter Long, to see his Liberal successor and discuss the problem of Irish administration with him. "I know," said the King, "when Governments change, the outgoing ministers do not treat their successors in the same way as they would if it was a mere change of office under the same Government,

and they were to be followed by members of their own party.
This is, of course, natural, and as a rule, no doubt right, but
the case of Ireland is an exceptional one." Mr. Long readily
fell in with the King's suggestion, and spent two long morn-
ings with Mr. Bryce. On the other hand, the King must
exercise the greatest care that he does not even appear to take
sides in any of the questions that may from time to time
divide his subjects. As Charles I rightly observed, "The
English nation are a sober people," but there are moments
when they lose their heads, and it is on such occasions that
their monarchs have to be most careful. The great strength
of the throne is the belief of the ordinary man-in-the-street
that its occupant is an impartial umpire.

It is one of the fundamental doctrines of the Constitution
that justice, mercy and honour derive from the Crown.
Justice is administered by the King's judges, those condemned
to death may be reprieved in the name of the King, and it
is the King who ennobles and rewards his subjects. This
is indeed a magnificent conception of the monarchy, and it
recalls the days when any weakening of the Royal power
meant confusion and oppression. Changes there have been,
but to-day it is still the King's judges who dispense the King's
justice in the King's courts, and so carefully are the old
traditions preserved that, as has been shown, if a subject
wishes to obtain redress from the Crown he must proceed
by Petition of Right. If all this seems absurd to the sceptic
and illogical to the foreigner, as it well may, let them compare the administration of the law in some of the leading
republican countries, and then ask themselves whether the
impartiality which characterises it in Great Britain is not
in a large measure due to the practical application of the
principle that the Crown is the fountain of justice.

If the criminal can be punished in the name of the King,
mercy may also be accorded to him in the same way, and
this Royal prerogative is a very old one. The King is
theoretically prosecutor in criminal cases; all indictments
are drawn up as being "against the peace of our Sovereign
Lord the King, his Crown and Dignity"; and as it is the

"King's Peace" that is broken by a violation of the law, he himself, being the offended party, may forgive the transgressor. Formerly it was the duty of the monarch to consider every death sentence personally, and, in cases where a reprieve was not granted, to sign the warrant of execution addressed to the sheriff. The last occasion on which an English ruler acted on his own initiative was in 1830, when George IV, without consulting his ministers, ordered the Lord-Lieutenant of Ireland to reprieve a man who had been sentenced to death in Clare for arson. The King was, however, subsequently induced to let justice take its course on being informed that the individual in question had committed perjury as well as arson.

The personal responsibility of the monarch was abolished when Queen Victoria came to the throne by an Act of Parliament which provided that no report in regard to persons sentenced to death should be made to the Queen or to her heirs and successors. The onus is now placed on the Home Secretary; but although he is responsible the prerogative of mercy continues to be exercised, as of old, in the name of the King. "We, in consideration of some circumstances humbly represented to us"—so runs the order for a free pardon, addressed to the governor of the jail where the prisoner in question is incarcerated—"are graciously pleased to extent Our Grace and Mercy unto him, and to grant him our Free Pardon for the offence for which he stands convicted." Few, one imagines, would like to see it otherwise. At the present time there is a publicity attaching to criminals and their deeds which renders it most undesirable that the King should in any way be personally implicated in their condemnation or reprieve.

On the other hand, in the conferment of honours the monarch has always taken the closest interest as, in a very special sense, they emanate from the Crown. Direct evidence that can be quoted is lacking as to the practice in the last two reigns, but King Edward VII jealously guarded this prerogative. It is an incorrect assumption that the Prime Minister of the day can do what he likes in respect of the

Honours List, for such is not the case either in theory or practice. When Disraeli was Prime Minister for the first time, but in a minority, the Queen refused to sanction any new creations, for, to quote Disraeli himself: "It was deemed expedient that I should treat the exercise of the prerogative with great reserve." Nor is it only with the quantity of honours that the monarch is concerned, for the quality of their recipients cannot be indifferent to him, for the prestige of the Crown will be affected if the latter are unworthy. Recent sovereigns have paid great attention to this matter, and King George V was notoriously opposed to the conferment of a rank which he considered too high. It was almost certainly due to him that no dukedoms, apart from Royal ones, were created during his reign. Had effect been given to the Liberal proposal to use the prerogative to swamp the House of Lords at the time of the constitutional crisis in 1911, a blow would have been given to the reputation of the Crown from which it would have been extremely difficult for the latter to have recovered.

The somewhat mystical conception of the throne as the source of justice, mercy, and honour is still emphasised in other ways which have their origin in the remote past. The distribution of Maundy Money on Holy Thursday is a survival of the ceremony in which, following the example of Our Lord, the Kings of England used to wash the feet of beggars, and until the Revolution this was performed by the monarch in person, James II being the last to do so. Touching for the "King's Evil" was another sign of the divinity that attached to the Crown, and it is not uninteresting to note that Cromwell tried his hand at this. It was probably last done on English soil by Anne, to Samuel Johnson among others, though Prince Charles Edward, as Regent for his father, is said to have touched during the Forty-Five.

Thus the ideal of the Crown as something more than a mere part of the machinery of government has always existed in this country, as the elaborate ritual of the Coronation abundantly testifies. The Crown is not, as is so often supposed, one of the Three Estates of the realm, but it stands above them. Perhaps the best definition of its position was given by Elizabeth herself: "To be a King and wear a crown is a thing more glorious to them that see it than it is pleasant to them that bear it. For myself, I was never so much enticed with the glorious name of King or Royal authority of a Queen, as delighted that God had made me His instrument to maintain His truth and glory, and to defend this kingdom from peril, dishonour, tyranny, and oppression." That so many of our rulers have interpreted their position in this way is why the English monarchy is to-day so firmly rooted in the heart of the nation.

WAR
BY
J. F. C. FULLER

WAR

THOUGH, when measured by Continental standards, we are not a military nation, quite clearly does our Empire prove, not only by its size, but more so by the diversity of its parts, that we possess a genius for war; a genius lurking deep down in the English character, which has been both tempered and blunted by the English spirit. As we do not understand ourselves, little wonder is it that others misunderstand us. So fixed in our opinions are we that we look askance at every novelty and innovation; yet we are the most handy improvisers on earth, our very Empire being one huge improvisation. We abhor originality, it almost frightens us to think that Englishmen can change; it is an insult to the permanence of our institutions. Therefore, we love committees and are ruled by a committee, the most impossible instrument of rule, because no one in a committee, anyhow in ours, can be dominated by the individuality of another. We do not love able men, and in a great crisis, when they save us from our impossible system, we accept them only as we would an umbrella in a downpour. Such is the scaffolding of our history, which has so largely been built by war.

Sitting as we do on the rim of Europe, our insularity has enabled us to pick and choose as we like. What pleases us we take from Europe, what displeases us we leave to Europeans; for only accidentally do we consider ourselves as such. For eight hundred and seventy-two years no foreigner has set foot on our shores, except as a guest; for eight hundred and seventy-two years our little island has, but for a few baronial skirmishes and Roundhead–Cavalier affrays, slumbered in solid peace. From this secure base we have percolated throughout the world, and wherever we go we carry England and her spirit with us. We do not establish law and order to improve others; but because without it we are put to personal inconvenience, and for an Englishman to be so placed by a foreigner is something which really shocks him.

We are a dominant race by birth rather than by intention. Many times have I noticed this both in history and in actual life. For instance, in 1882, at the time of the bombardment of Alexandria, the mob looted and set fire to many of the buildings in the European quarter. The Hotel Abbat was, however, saved by the ruse of a Berberine doorkeeper; for, when the mob hammered at the door, instead of appealing to Allah, he appealed to something far more concrete and terrible—the prestige of the Englishman. Placing his lips to the keyhole he shouted: "You b—— b——s; what the b—— h—— do you want?" Coarse though these words are they are plainly those of the dominant race. They acted like a spell, for their effect was magical. The ring-leaders looked at one another, and then awestruck they whispered: "Why, the house is full of Inglesi!" This was too much for the rabble, which hurriedly retired, and instead burnt the Portuguese Consulate.

During the World War this same spirit may be seen in our unconscious almost instinctive contempt for both the enemy and our allies. It led us into many difficulties; because of it we lost more than one engagement, and beyond a doubt it added thousands in killed and wounded to our casualties. Yet without it we should have ceased to be English, and had such a calamity been possible, in my opinion the Germans would have won the war. This contempt made us indifferent to our own security. We did not hate the enemy, but we loathed digging trenches to protect ourselves from his fire. Protection shows some form of fear, and so we loathed it not for itself but for what it symbolised. When the trench peri-scope was invented, a War Office general turned it down, saying: "It is contrary to the traditions of the British officer to seek information from a position of security by means of a mechanical device." When, on the first Christmas of the war, the unofficial armistice took place, and the Germans and our men fraternised in no-man's-land, a safe opportunity presented itself for both sides to strengthen their wire entanglements. In front of one English trench it was noticed that, whilst English soldiers were holding the pickets, German soldiers were hammering them in. This incident, small though it is, is typical of our dominion. It explains many otherwise incomprehensible things, such as that our Empire covers one-fifth of the globe, or our control of India and her three hundred and sixty million inhabitants by some fifty thousand armed Englishmen.

Most of my life, fortunately and unfortunately, has been spent amongst soldiers. I say fortunately, because close contact with my fellow-countrymen has given me insight into their character; and unfortunately, because in England the soldier is despised, for he is under the discipline of some one man, and that is a horrid crime. Yet he remains an Englishman with the Englishman's outlook on foreigners, which is that of the classical Greeks. Nearly twenty years ago now I wrote of him as follows:

"I have watched him in two long wars struggling against odds, and I have learnt to appreciate his virtues, and his failings, and his indomitable courage. He is a man who possesses such natural pride of birth that, through sheer contempt for others, he refuses to learn or to be defeated. He divides humanity into two classes, Englishmen and niggers, and of the second class some happen to be black and others white. He only condescends to differentiate between these sub-classes by calling the latter dagoes. To him all white folk outside his own little island are such. From these he has learnt nothing, yet he is tolerant, tolerant as he would be to his dog; he has, in fact, raised the vice of contempt to a high virtue, and on this virtue is the British Empire founded.

"Having nothing to learn, through sheer power of domination he has become the prince of rulers, and through sheer refusal to be defeated by niggers, the master of improvisation. He is always there; for the sun never sets on his Empire, but he is never ready. For readiness would presuppose fear, and what has he, as an Englishman, to be afraid of?"

Nor is there anything new in this, for nations at heart do not suffer rapid changes, and what we are to-day we probably shall be hundreds of years hence, as we were hundreds of years ago. Listen to what Andrea Trevisano, Venetian Ambassador in England, wrote in 1498:

"The English are great lovers of themselves, and of everything belonging to them. They think that there are no other men than themselves and no other world but England, and whenever they see a handsome foreigner they say that 'he looks like an Englishman,' and that 'it is a pity that he should not be an Englishman.' "

Such, then, is the vehicle of our genius in war, which circumscribes it, reinforces it, limits it, delimits it, and is both its friend and its enemy. From it I will turn to those few great men it has allowed to rise above its complacence, and with the blood and sweat of Englishmen, and through their toilings and their pugnacity has made us what we were, and what I hope we still are.

Of these men and captains of men I shall select three. Each was a great and typical Englishman in his own way; yet each was very different from the other. They are: Cromwell, who founded our standing army; Marlborough, who first led it against a foreign foe, and Wellington, who matched it against the greatest military genius of his age, possibly of any age, and won.

All three came from out of the earth of England: Cromwell of yeoman stock; Marlborough from the squirearchy, and Wellington from the English–Irish bog-lands. Yet all three were smiled upon by Fortune. The first in that his family emerged from out of chaos a veritable military clan—Ireton, Hampden, Walton, Whalley and others—the very proton in the soul of the Great Rebellion. The second in that he had a frail sister, Arabella, mistress of James II; also his wife, his "dearest soul," bosom companion of the Princess Anne, daughter of James and heir to the throne after William and Mary. And the third—the blue blood of the landed aristocracy, a mother who thought him "food for powder and nothing more," and a brother who was Governor-General of India, or rather what India represented in those days. Thus fortune released from our English earth the three greatest generals in our history: a fiery-tempered man, full of the wrath of the Old Testament; a tactful and courteous man, who could suffer fools gladly, and a cold and cynical man, who could suffer them not at all.

These men, each in his turn, was called upon to work out of chaos towards some little-imagined cosmos; for as Cromwell said in one of those Isaian flashes of wisdom: "A man never mounts so high as when he does not know where he is going." In 1642 it was that feeling of an "insupportable all-pervading *Falsehood*," as Carlyle says, which precipitated the Great Rebellion, the first of the modern class wars. Again was it so in 1789, for as Hobbes says of the former, and his words may equally well be applied to the latter: "the people in general were so ignorant of their duty, as not one perhaps of ten thousand knew what right any man had to command him, or what necessity there was of King or Commonwealth." So Cromwell found himself among "a rabble of raw and poor rascals," Wellington in command of "the scum of the earth," and Marlborough, more fortunate, in control of a disciplined army, which affectionately called him "Corporal John"; yet his was a mixed host of which but a fraction was of British blood.

Wellington's method was direct and simple, for he lashed his rabble into soldiers, and, strange as it may seem, as he says himself, they "could go anywhere and do anything"; for as he also informs us: "There is but one way—to do as I did—to have a hand of iron." Yet turn to Cromwell, and how magically the picture changes. To John Hampden he wrote, after the battle of Edgehill, October 23, 1642:

"At my first going out into this engagement, I saw our own men were beaten at every hand. . . . 'Your troops,' said I, 'are most of them old decayed serving-men and tapsters . . . their troops are gentlemen's sons . . . do you think that the spirits of such base mean fellows will ever be able to encounter gentlemen, that have honour and courage and resolution in them. . . . You must get men of spirit . . . or else you will be beaten still.' "

This was his grand idea: that leadership is useless without *disciplined* followership, and that discipline demands not only that officers and men know what they are fighting for, but "love what they know." He therefore sought out men who had the fear of God before them, "and made some conscience of what they did." So it came about that a year later he was able to write to Friend Oliver St. John Esquire: "I have a lovely company; you would respect them, did you know them. They are no Anabaptists, they are honest sober Christians; they expect to be used as men!" In these last seven words lies the secret of his whole system of discipline.

Whilst Wellington would at times order up to twelve hundred lashes, Cromwell restricted flogging to sixty, and Marlborough fed and cared for his men. Read Parker's description of the march to the Danube in 1704. He writes:

"We frequently marched three, sometimes four days, successively, and halted a day. We generally began our march about three in the morning, proceeded about four leagues, or four and a half each day, and reached our ground about nine. As we marched through the Countries of our Allies, Commissaries were appointed to furnish us with all manner of necessaries for man and horse; these were brought to the ground before we arrived, and the soldiers had nothing to do, but to pitch their tents, boil their kettles, and lie down to rest. Surely never was such a march carried out with more order and regularity, and with less fatigue both to man and horse."

All three systems are different; yet that in itself is typically English. Cromwell, living in an as yet religious age, aiming at substituting the rule of honest men for that of a worn-out

kingship, demands warriors of God steel-girt in the principles
of the Old Testament. Marlborough, living in a more
settled age, an age of wigs and flounces, was more orderly
and polished; whilst Wellington relied upon the brutality
of the rising industrial epoch, which sanctified child labour
and the stove-pipe hat—the coronet of the newly fledged
steam-power aristocracy. All three were true Englishmen, improvisers and creators of invincible armies which,
according to the characters of their leaders, were used as
circumstances permitted—Parliaments, Field-Deputies and
Juntas allowing. What then in themselves were these great
soldiers like?

They were totally different men, linked together by one
supreme quality—the dominance of the Englishman. As a
boy Cromwell loved boisterous games; Marlborough read
Vegetius, and Wellington played the flute, or was it the
harpsichord? Baxter describes the first as being "naturally
of such a vivacity, hilarity and alacrity as another man is
when he hath drunken a cup of wine too much." To his
Parliament he certainly could talk forcefully, and when
weary of the bickerings of the Rump, striding into the House
he dismissed its members with such epithets as "whoremasters," "drunkards" and "corrupters." It was then that
he muttered, as his eyes glanced on the mace: "What shall
we do with this bauble?" Yet, should reality replace falsehood, his self-control was firm. When, in 1645, serving under
Waller, that general reports on him: "Although he was
blunt, he did not bear himself with pride or disdain. As an
officer he was obedient and did never dispute my orders or
argue upon them." Nevertheless, the clearest insight into
his character is to be found in his own words. In 1658 he
said, addressing his last Parliament: "I would have been glad
to have lived under my woodside, to have kept a flock of
sheep, rather than undertook such a Government as this is."
And upon another occasion: "I am a man standing in the
Place I am in, not so much out of hope of doing any good as
out of a desire to prevent mischief and evil; for truly, I have,
as before God, often thought that I could not tell what my

business was, nor what I was in the place I stood in, save comparing myself to a good Constable set to keep the peace of the Parish."

How different were Marlborough and Wellington, not only when compared to him, but when brought face to face with each other. Though a deeply religious man, Marlborough did not possess the volcanic faith of Cromwell, and though more imaginative than Wellington, he lacked his loyalty and integrity. Nevertheless, like him, his self-control was phenomenal: as plan after plan was ruined by the Dutch deputies, with a smile he pushed their debris aside and started on another. Nothing escaped his observation. The day before the battle of Blenheim we find him examining the enemy through his "prospective-glass" just as Wellington did at Salamanca. "The real reason why I succeeded," said Wellington years later, "is because I was always on the spot —I saw everything, and did everything for myself" . . . and so also did Marlborough. However, he had not Wellington's antipathy to humbug—falsehood, nor his biting sense of humour. For instance, in 1815, when at the Court of the Tuileries some of Napoleon's generals, who had become Royalists, turned their backs upon Wellington, and Louis XVIII attempted to excuse their rudeness, his Majesty received the following reply: "Sire, ils sont si accoutumés à me tourner le dos qu'ils n'en ont pas encore perdu l'habitude."

Wellington was an aristocrat to his finger-tips; Marlborough a courtier cap-à-pie, and Cromwell an Old Testament prophet dressed in "a plain cloth suit which seemed to have been made by an ill country tailor"—so says Sir Philip Warwick.

To understand these three men as soldiers, and to grasp how their war-craft expressed their genius, it is necessary first of all to examine them as statesmen and politicians; because, as war is an extension of politics, generalship, and more especially that of a general-in-chief, is in consequence an extension of statecraft.

When, in 1702, William III died, Marlborough assumed

quite naturally the position of national leader, yet not so much in the form of a statesman as in that of a diplomatist, working through the machinations of Sarah his wife and the financial abilities of his son-in-law—Godolphin. Unwittingly he followed in the steps of his great predecessor—Cromwell, whose policy was that of Elizabeth and Gustavus Adolphus: the establishment of a *Corpus Evangelicorum*. It was in fact this Corpus, or union of Protestant Princes, which William III had been compelled to create and which Marlborough directed. And so it came about that he and Cromwell anticipated the work of the elder Pitt, without which there would have been no Wellington as we know him.

Thus it was Cromwell who started the ball of Empire rolling, and, like Marlborough and Wellington, his genius lay in his ability to see into the heart of every question. He saw the events of his day as a whole event, and not in separated parts as did lesser men. So also did Marlborough see the war of the Spanish Succession as a whole, and Wellington the Peninsular War as a vital part of one vast combination. Like Wellington, Cromwell was an indifferent politician because he was a leader of men and not a follower of opinion. Though Wellington, in his younger days, displayed a wonderful grasp of Orientals; as one writer says: "Had his career ended at this time, his Indian dispatches alone would have proved him to have been one of the wisest and strongest heads that have ever served England in the East"; yet he had little understanding of the English temperament, whilst Cromwell possessed a profound insight into it. Though living in a narrow, intolerant age, Cromwell had an acute sense of the nature of British freedom, as the following two cases well illustrate. Once, writing to the Scottish clergy, he said: "Your pretended fear lest error should step in is like the man who would keep all wine out of the country lest men should be drunk. It will be found an unjust and unwise jealousy to deprive a man of his natural liberty upon a supposition he may abuse it. When he doth abuse it, judge." Also: "I had rather that Mahommedanism were permitted among us, than that one of God's children should be persecuted." Yet it seems strange that a man holding such liberal views should have perpetrated the atrocities he did in Ireland. There, in the barbaric fury of the Old Testament, he cried: "You are a part of Anti-Christ, whose kingdom the Scripture so expressly speaks should be laid in blood, yea in the blood of the saints." Mahomet II sacked Constantinople for twelve hours; Tilly, Magdeburg for twenty-four, yet Cromwell sacked Drogheda and continued the massacre of its inhabitants and garrison for days. It would appear that in fact there were two Cromwells; Dr. Jekyll was the squire of Huntingdon, whilst Mr. Hyde was the Sword of the Lord.

Strange as it may seem, whilst Cromwell fought against a legitimate King and Wellington against an upstart Emperor, both firmly disbelieved in "the collective wisdom of individual ignorance," as Carlyle puts it. To Cromwell universal suffrage tended "very much to anarchy," and to Wellington, for Members of Parliament to be elected "to obey the daily instructions of their constituents, and be cashiered if they should disobey them, would destroy," so he said, "the race of English gentlemen." The fact is, both were autocrats, body and soul.

Wellington misread the French. When Napoleon escaped from Elba he imagined that Louis XVIII would without difficulty destroy him "in a short time." Whilst Cromwell so profoundly read the inner meaning of the Europe of his day, that he became known as "the world's protector." Yet both dominated foreign affairs—Wellington by becoming the most influential personality in Europe; and of Cromwell, Clarendon says: his "greatness at home was a mere shadow of his greatness abroad." Nevertheless both ended by being detested by their own people, Wellington because he was tolerant to the Catholics, Cromwell for being intolerant towards them.

Turning from their influence on politics to their influence on war, a common bond between these three great soldiers was "audacity," or otherwise put: the moral courage they displayed in breaking away from the conventional and turning

circumstances to their advantage. From the outset of the
rebellion, Cromwell grasped the fact that as both sides were
undisciplined, the one which became disciplined first would
win, hence the creation of the New Model Army, which in
spirit was his child. Realising that cavalry was the dominant
arm of his day, and, as Gustavus Adolphus had recently
shown, that its supreme power lay in shock action, the
charge, his grasp of cavalry tactics was so profound that,
paradox though it may seem, he realised the essential truth
that the first duty of cavalry is not to gallop, but instead to
learn how to stand still. If at any moment he could halt his
horse, even in the middle of a charge, he could turn every
circumstance of the battle to his favour; if he could not, then
each charge was no more than a one-shot operation. We
see this from the very opening of the Civil War, and long
before the New Model appeared. At Edgehill, his troop was
one of the few not routed by Rupert's wild charge, and in
May the following year, at Grantham, he turned the tables
on his enemy.

At Marston Moor, July 2, 1644, it was the same, it
was because he could rally as well as charge that he
defeated Rupert's hitherto unconquered horsemen. It was
power to keep his horsemen in hand, the supreme test
of efficient cavalry leadership, which rendered so many of
his victories annihilating, the most decisive in its results
being that of Naseby, fought on June 14, 1645, in which
Charles I's last army was utterly destroyed.

In this battle the forces engaged were insignificant: those
of Charles numbered no more than 7,500 and those of Fairfax
13,500, and Cromwell's part in it was all but an accident,
for with his 600 horse he joined Fairfax only on the 13th.
Nevertheless, it was he who selected the Roundheads'
position on Mill Hill, taking command of the cavalry of the
right wing, while Ireton commanded that on the left. Rupert
charged, and Ireton's men were scattered. In *Memoirs of a
Cavalier* we read: "The inconsiderate courage of Rupert was
not equal to compete with the cool and masterly conduct of
Cromwell. Had he, at this critical juncture fallen in on the

rear of the foot, the daye had been secured; but accordinge
to custom, following the flying enemie, he never concerned
himselfe with the safetie of those behinde." "Whichever
leader," writes Professor Gardiner, "could [now] bring a
preponderant force of horse to bear upon the confused struggle
of foot-men in the centre would have England at his feet."

That leader was Cromwell, who, at the head of 3,600
horse, moved down the slope to meet Langdale's regiments
toiling up it. He charged, struck his enemy, drove two of
his divisions back, and then instead of, like Rupert, following
up his success with a headlong pursuit, he ordered three
regiments forward against the beaten enemy horse, and,
wheeling the rest of his command to the left, he fell upon
the Royalists' exposed left flank. The victory was complete,
Charles losing in killed and wounded 1,000 men and 5,000
in prisoners.

Turning to Marlborough we find that conditions have
changed, highly organised armies meet, the matchlock has
been replaced by the flintlock, and the pike by the bayonet;
besides, John Churchill is a soldier by profession, having
seen service under Marshal Turenne, and he had fought both
on land and sea. Yet we find the same aggressive spirit; the
same desire to push on and bring his enemy to action, to
battle with him and annihilate him. He also relies on
cavalry, because cavalry is still the decisive arm, and as we
are told: "He would allow the horse but three charges of
powder and ball to each man for a campaign, and that only
for guarding their horses when at grass, and not to be made
use of in action." Like Cromwell, he also is an unconventional general, but more crafty and subtle. He did not
believe in what may be called the "strategy of evasion,"
which consists in manœuvring rather than fighting; nor
in the "tactics of impregnability" as expounded by Monte-
cuculi: "The secret of success is to have a solid body so firm
and impenetrable that wherever it is or wherever it may go,
it shall bring the enemy to stand like a mobile bastion, and
shall be self-defensive." Instead, he returned to the offensive
strategy and tactics of Gustavus, of Condé and of Cromwell;

hence as an unconventional soldier he was most perturbing
to those who followed the doctrines of a highly conventional
age.

For instance, take his Blenheim campaign, the outstanding
example of English genius in war. Balked by the obtuse-
ness of the Dutch deputies in 1702 and the self-seekings of the
Dutch generals in 1703, in 1704, realising that the French
plan was to knock out the Emperor, he secretly decided to
transfer the decisive theatre of the war from the Low
Countries to the Danube, and on May 20, 1704, he set out
from Bedburg for the Moselle. On the 25th he entered
Coblenz, and instead of marching up the Moselle, his long-
proclaimed objective, he headed for Mainz. All were
dumbfounded, as Parker relates, and not least so the French,
who now conjectured that he was making for Philippsburg,
because bridges had recently been built there. Yet he passed
them by, and Paris was thrown into consternation. Moving
on Donauwörth, by a most audacious and skilful assault he
seized the heights of the Schellenberg, and gaining a crossing
over the Danube he penetrated into Bavaria, which he
devastated. Then he turned about and linked up with
Prince Eugene at Donauwörth, who was faced by Marshals
Tallard and Marsin and the Elector of Bavaria, at that time
moving forward from Höchstädt to a position a little west
of the village of Blenheim.

Here two things happened which shaped events. First,
these three generals decided *a priori* that they had victory
in their hands, victory of the bloodless type, because they
imagined that Marlborough would be compelled to retire,
for all three were incapable of believing that he and Eugene
could be so neglectful of the rules of war as to deliver a frontal
attack upon a numerically superior force in position.
Secondly, instead of preparing to attack their enemy, they,
according to the rules, took up a defensive position, and this
in spite of the fact that they had decided that Marlborough
and Eugene would not attack them. It was protected in
front by a marshy stream—the Nebel, behind which were
three villages, Blenheim on the right and on the Danube,

Oberglau in the centre and Lützingen on the left: a veritable
fortress—a moat and three bastions.

On August 12 Marlborough reconnoitred it, and then
made up his mind. He saw that the Nebel was weakly held,
and that, if he could cross it and contain the garrisons of
Blenheim and Oberglau, he would be able to open a path
for his cavalry, because these villages were too far apart to
permit of their fire covering the ground in between them.
Early the next morning he advanced at the very time when
Tallard was writing to Louis XIV that his enemy was with-
drawing. He drove in the enemy outposts, whereupon there
was pandemonium in the Franco–Bavarian camps. The
surprise was complete; thus before the battle had opened it
was already half won.

Whilst Eugene's columns were toiling over the broken
and wooded ground on the right flank, Marlborough cleared
the Nebel, and at half-past twelve o'clock, hearing that his
ally was then in position, he turned to his officers and said:
"Gentlemen, to your posts." The assault on Blenheim was
next launched, and though it was repulsed, so fiercely was
it renewed that the Marquis de Cléambault called to his
support eighteen battalions, and in consequence immobilised
Tallard's right flank. The same happened at Oberglau after
a desperate and critical fight, with the result, as Campbell
says, the Allies could now "march before it and attack the
cavalry of the enemy with great liberty." Thus the field
was prepared for the decisive stroke.

It came at about half-past five, whilst Eugene was at
grips with the Elector. "With trumpets blaring and kettle-
drums crashing and standards tossing proudly above the
plumage and the steel, the two long lines, perfectly timed
from end to end, swung into a trot, that quickened ever as
they closed upon the French." Tallard's troopers fired
wildly and broke . . . the battle was won. At seven o'clock,
Marlborough scribbled to his wife the following pencil note
on the back of a tavern bill: "I have not time to say more
but to beg you will give my duty to the Queen, and let her
know her army has had a glorious victory. Monsieur

Tallard and two other Generals are in my coach and I am
following the rest." It was the death warrant of the
ambitions of the *Roi Soleil*.

And so I come to Wellington, the last in my trinity. For
him circumstances were vastly different. Not only was he
faced by armies which had broken all conventionalities, but
armies fired by the genius of the greatest captain of war,
certainly since the days of Cæsar. And to accomplish his
main task, the reconquest of Spain, he was given the
scourings of the jails and the gutters, and was ordered to
work with Spanish Juntas, soviets of factious men, even
more ignorant of war than the Dutch field-deputies. Nearly
always outnumbered in the field, and generally meagrely
reinforced, supplied and paid, critics have written him down
as a defensively minded general, which, in fact, is an absurd
calumny. Wellington knew when to hit and when to guard,
and how to hit and how to guard—therein lay his genius.
He could be, when circumstances permitted, as offensive as
any general who has ever fought; witness his attack at
Assaye. There, on September 23, 1803, with 9,500 men he
routed Sindhia and Berar at the head of 40,000. Again,
when he landed in Portugal, in 1807, he at once assumed
the offensive, winning the battle of Roliça on August 17,
and that of Vimeiro on the 21st. But generally his army
was so small and always his problem so immense that wisely
he was cautious, realising, as he did, that a small army which
can adequately be fed is tactically superior to a larger army
which is reduced to foraging: in other words, that there is a
definite relationship between bread and bullets.

"All the business of war, and indeed all the business of
life," he once said, "is to endeavour to find out what you
don't know by what you do," and that was what he was
always doing. He invariably looked to his supplies, and he
never wasted his men, because he mistrusted the future. His
long-sighted calculations even outpaced those of Marlborough. Before taking over his second Peninsular command,
in 1809, he placed before Castlereagh an appreciation entitled "Memorandum on the Defence of Portugal," which

Sir Charles Oman rightly acclaims to be "a marvel of prophetic genius"; for in it he predicted the whole course of the six years' campaign. He stated that the war would be a long one, and that his task was to keep it going as long as possible, and that ambitious schemes should be set aside. Further, that by using Portugal as a fortress supplied by the sea, with no more than 30,000 men backed by Portuguese levies he would be able to operate against the flank of the French armies in Spain, and by paralysing them gain time for the Spaniards to develop a formidable guerilla war on their communications.

Of his strategical undertakings, it has always seemed to me that his masterpiece is his planning of the Torres Vedras campaign, and certainly not that of Waterloo, during which he was caught napping. This he thought out a full year in advance, as he did his move on Badajoz in 1812. Though Messéna did not appear before the famous lines which protected Lisbon until October 14, 1810, he had ordered their construction on October 26, 1809. Foreseeing that Napoleon would reinforce his armies in Spain, and that, when this happened, the British army would be compelled to retire, he built the lines of Torres Vedras, and ordered that the neighbouring country should be devastated, so that, whilst the fortifications protected his men, Masséna would be "attacked" by starvation. That is what actually happened, the French were starved out of Portugal and the road to Spain and to final victory was opened.

These three generals—Cromwell, Marlborough and Wellington, expressed the English genius in war each in his own way, and all according to the conditions in which they lived and fought. If there was one common conception between them it was not so much their pugnacity, clear-sightedness or courage, as their power to improvise and build up from one common and unchanging foundation, the fact that England is an island. All three grasped the meaning of sea power and its relationship to land power. Cromwell appreciated this fully when he said in January, 1658: "You have accounted yourselves happy in being environed by a great

ditch from all the world besides. Truly you will not be able to
keep your ditch nor your shipping unless you turn your ships
and shipping into troops of horse and companies of foot, and
fight to defend yourselves on terra firma." And what was the
result? "From the Baltic to the Mediterranean," writes
Frederic Harrison, "from Algiers to Teneriffe, from Newfoundland to Jamaica, was heard the English cannon."

On this naval supremacy, founded by Cromwell, all
Marlborough's plans were based. In his strategy the Mediterranean coincided with the Danube, with the result that,
in 1704, Rooke seized and held Gibraltar, and the Treaty
of Utrecht, in 1713, gave us Nova Scotia, Newfoundland
and Hudson Bay: the expulsion of the French from North
America thus began. On this supremacy, Wellington's
campaigns in Spain were also founded, not only because the
English fleet commanded the seas, but because he realised
how Nelson's victory at Trafalgar could be exploited on land.
He looked upon Portugal as nothing more than a coastal
fortress, linked to England by that great flexible road—the sea.
To him his army was a projectile fired by the navy, and above
all supplied by it, it was in fact its umbilical cord.

Looking back upon what I have now written, and having
set about this study of a great and vital subject with no
preconceived idea, it seems to me that the key to English
genius in war, and consequently also in peace, is to be found
in the word "dominance." That sense of exclusiveness and
superiority which our geographical invulnerability has engendered in our bones: dominance of the individual Englishman over foreigners, and the dominance of Englishmen in
mass over the individual Englishman. If the individual can
by some manner or means—religious fervour, soft words or
brutal actions, break away from the dominance of the mass
and impose his will upon it, then there can be no doubt that
he is a genius. But as the individual is mortal and the mass
everlasting, the test of genius is to be found in the degree of
eventual revulsion against its dominance. If the Berberine
doorkeeper received any acknowledgment at all, then, I
warrant, it was a well-aimed kick for daring to be original.

Therefore the measurement of genius among Englishmen can best be obtained by equating results with martyrdom.

Cromwell changed the direction of our political thought, for when the head of King Charles fell from the executioner's block in Whitehall, democracy shot green from his scarlet blood, and the echoes of its thud swelled onwards into the boomings and thunderings of the cannon of the American Rebellion and the French Revolution. He made England the Golden Oceanic Despot, hence it comes about that Carlyle brackets him with Napoleon in his *Hero as King*.

Marlborough, a soldier not to be judged by the slippery softnesses of succeeding ages, and traduced alike by Swift and Winston Churchill, the one skinning him alive and the other gilding him post-mortem, "changed," as Mr. Churchill says, "the political axis of the world," and by doing so smote into the dust, not the divine right of kings, but the temporal power of the last of the really great monarchs. Blenheim was the greatest English victory on foreign soil since Agincourt; as great as Breitenfeld, as great as Rocroi, and in results as world-changing as Naseby itself. Lastly comes Wellington—the Iron Duke, typical of the rising iron age. He beheaded a theory and sent Bonaparte to St. Helena. The theory was that all Englishmen are born free; the fact was that the age of iron had got them.

Yet in these three cases, and there are others, the English spirit remained what it was and always had been: the detester of changes and the abhorrer of changers. So they dug up Cromwell, spiked his head on Westminster Hall and his body they tumbled into a ditch at Tyburn. . Marlborough they called a "traitor" and a "thief", and that great know-all, Macaulay, daubed him with splashes of white and black, the white to persuade the black to become more noticeable. Wellington they hooted on the anniversary of Waterloo, and compelled him to protect the windows of Apsley House with iron shutters. Since then, metaphorically speaking, they have never been taken down; hence, whilst the English spirit lives on, English genius in war still lies imprisoned in its steel-bound St. Helena.

THE SEA
BY
ALFRED NOYES

THE SEA

TACITUS, in his life of Agricola, remarks with his usual vivid
suggestiveness of phrase that the sea not only surrounds
Britain, his remote Thule, but penetrates its inland fastnesses,
striking into its very heart by firth and tidal estuary. The
bearing of this remark is more than geographical. Beyond
its author's intention, there is a symbolism in it which, nearly
two thousand years later, was consciously elaborated by a
great English poet. Incidentally, in the italicised line of the
quotation below, the English poet himself unconsciously
translates the remark of Tacitus, and suffuses it with the
splendour and beauty of his own art.

> O, thou clothed round with raiment of white waves,
> Thy brave brows lightening thro' the grey wet air,
> Thou, lulled with sea-sounds of a thousand caves
> *And lit with sea-shine to thine inland lair;*
> Whose freedom clothed the naked souls of slaves,
> And stripped the muffled souls of tyrants bare,
> O, by the centuries of thy glorious graves,
> By the live light of the earth that was thy care,
> Live! Thou must not be dead!
> Live; let thine arméd head
> Lift itself up to sunward . . .

That is the idealised personification of Britain which,
however far it may surpass the reality, has haunted the
imagination of her poets from Spenser, Shakespeare and
Milton, to Wordsworth, Tennyson, Browning and Swinburne. It is associated with sea-imagery, not merely for
pictorial purposes, but for reasons of character, intellectual
and spiritual. When Wordsworth says of Milton:

> Thy soul was like a star and dwelt apart.
> Thou hadst a voice whose sound was like the sea,

he is using the physical imagery to depict intellectual and spiritual qualities of what may be called an isolated rather than an insular character. But the isolation is regarded by Wordsworth as one of centrality, with power to make itself felt throughout the world, in waves of light or thought that break upon a thousand shores. This symbolical use of a geographical fact stands out in English literature as in no other. The life of England and indeed the life of the whole British Commonwealth of Nations has been fostered and fed by the sea in the past; and it lives by the sea to-day almost as the human frame lives by the air it breathes. The geographical fact and the material consequences have been the text of a thousand volumes, from those which describe the various sea-faring tribes who raided or settled the island in the dawn of its history to those which trace the effect of "sea-power" on the course of modern civilisation. The strategical advantages of an island to which—as Shakespeare remarked in a famous passage, the sea is like "a moat defensive to a house," have been discussed by a thousand military and naval historians. Salamis and the defeat of the Spanish Armada have been made to illustrate one another as instances of the decisive value of a sea-position. But the subtler influences suggested and symbolised by the fact that this island is "lit with sea-shine to her inland lair," the subtler influences on the mind, heart, and character of an island people, and its daughter-nations defy analysis, and are therefore too often passed over, though they are by far the most important of all. It would be futile in a mere chapter like this to attempt to recapitulate the naval history of England, or even the names of her great sea-captains and discoverers from Raleigh to Frobisher, and Nelson to Jellicoe. These things are familiar to all English readers; and it seems preferable, therefore, to dwell here upon the less obvious aspects of that sea-history. They defy analysis; but analysis is not the only method of approach.

Mr. Fisher, in his history of Europe, has some striking sentences about the effect of geographical position on the character of nations. He attributes the depression, the despair, the dull fatalism of great sections of the Russian population to the monotony of her vast inland plains in which it might seem possible to travel for ever and find nothing but the same dead level of indifference. It is no idle imagination to suppose that the sparkling coast-line of Greece, with its adventurous possibilities and beckoning horizons, had a very powerful influence upon the Greek civilisation. Certainly, it helped the creation of the Odyssey; and that statement again is a mere summing up, a symbol in a nutshell, of a whole series of analogous truths. There is a profound truth hidden in the Greek myth of Beauty rising from the sea. The art and literature of a nation are obviously affected by the physical environment; and this does not, as materialists have often assumed, support a materialistic philosophy of art. The environment is only one of the factors. It is made up of physical instrumentalities, which are secondary causes, not originating powers. The influence of environment, there-fore, may be regarded as the influence of the Shaper of the environment and its beauty. In other words, the environ-ment is a medium of inspiration, the intermediary physical language through which spirit communicates with spirit. The magnificent use of sea-imagery in Wordsworth's "Intimations of Immortality" is only one of a thousand instances in our own literature.

In the case of Britain, those who believe that the destinies of nations are not entirely in their own hands, and that there is indeed a Power above the State, to which every State on earth owes allegiance, may well feel that a people so situa-ated, so led, and so developed, by the "logic of events" owes a special allegiance to that Power, and has a moral responsi-bility for its own actions which should be pondered by every man and woman in the British Commonwealth of Nations.

The "natural League of Nations," as the self-governing British Dominions have been called, occupies a very different position from that of the mother-island; yet this, too, has been fostered by and depends upon the sea. The sea which divides us from one point of view is, also, from another point of view, the great maker of contacts. Long before railways existed, and while the overland roads of the continent were few and could take the traveller only to a very limited number of pre-determined destinations, the island possessed a broad sea-highway leading to the ends of the earth in every direction; a highway that had its dangers, but needed no labour to repair its surface, and was barred by no impassable mountains; an open road that endowed a sea-faring race with a boundless freedom of movement. Sails went out over the horizons of the known world; and sails would bring strange visitants, not all of them welcome, but all at least stimulating and provocative of curiosity and the kind of thought that looks beyond its own frontiers. The sails of the islanders were the wings that made them more than islanders; for there never has been, and probably never will be, any means of transport, on a large scale, so efficacious as that provided by ships and the sea. Thus it came about that a striking contradiction was reconciled in a synthesis which might have provided Hegel with an object-lesson in his own philosophy of history. The very conditions which made the British the most characteristically insular people in the world, led them also into the widest world-relationships and gave them the most deep-set outposts and far-ranging frontiers. The nation which is, characteristically, the most single-languaged, does also possess, in its various specialists, and in its official ranks, a greater range of practical acquaintance with every tongue spoken by every branch of mankind than has ever belonged to any other nation. The English who may usually be put to shame, linguistically, in the pleasure-resorts of Europe, are the same people whose representatives may be found grappling with real problems in all the languages of the civilised world, or administering the law and acting as their own interpreters among remote tribes that never heard of Pentecost. The insularity, and the world-wide relationship are complementary; and the sea is responsible for both.

One of the inspired songs that come to the lips and rise from the heart of this island people in moments when it desires to celebrate these great facts of its history, and to keep them free from the terminology and spirit of "imperial-ism" is the great challenge of Blake:

> I will not cease from mental fight
> Nor shall the sword sleep in my hand
> Till we have built Jerusalem
> In England's green and pleasant land.

The City of God may be built in every land. It can never be comprehended in one alone; and it is only according to the degree in which each nation builds up that city, that the world can draw nearer to the harmony in which "all is for each and each for all." There is no other road to the only peace worth having. It may come eventually as many other great things have come, by way of the sea. It is in no spirit of imperialism that the British Commonwealth of Nations may lift up its eyes and see the vision of the prophet Isaiah.

> "All these are gathered together. They are come to thee. Thy sons shall come from afar, and thy daughters shall rise up at thy side. Then shalt thou see and abound, and thy heart shall wonder and be enlarged, when the multitude of the sea shall be converted to thee, the strength of the Gentiles shall come to thee."

The key to my meaning here is not the idea that "sea-power" means the "ruling" of the sea; but that the sea is a great international means of communication, which enables an island to act as a special mediator, with certain initial advantages.

It is through the sea that the peace of the world may eventually ensue, though the first essential is a profound and far-reaching change of heart, which can only be brought about by religion, and the moral law based on religion. But, on the physical side, there is only one set of conditions which is likely to induce or compel the abolition of warfare among nations. Peace would almost certainly reign if something could be discovered which gave a decisive, or even a very great initial advantage, to purely defensive armament.

The British Commonwealth of Nations and the United States do actually enjoy this great initial advantage by virtue of their geographical positions. The island itself may indeed be more vulnerable than hitherto from the air; but, with adequate defensive measures, it is absurd to argue that the seas which divide her from the continent have ceased to give her an immense initial advantage in war. What would not France and Belgium have given for even twenty miles of sea between themselves and the enemy in the last war? The "sea-power" whereby the British Commonwealth of Nations was developed and linked together is as important as ever, though in a different way. Rightly used, it does give just that initial advantage, that immense defensive advantage which should at least enable a great section of the world to stand outside the mad chaos in comparative security and, if only by giving an object-lesson of the benefits of peace to its own people, create a new kind of desire for those benefits elsewhere, from which a general peace would be more likely to ensue than if—on all possible occasions—as the League sought to provide—we all went mad together and set ourselves to slaughtering by the million. This initial advantage indicates, unmistakably, the true policy of this country, and its continuity with her old tradition of the sea. It lays an immense responsibility upon us in an age when war seems to involve a reversion to bestiality which sickens the heart and soul, and appals the conscience of all thoughtful men and women. Our initial advantage should enable us to make our defensive armament so strong that no aggression would be worth while. Britain and the United States owe a certain duty to their own younger generations, and their governments may rightly feel that they cannot gamble with millions of lives of their own children in the mad welter of cross-purposes and contradictory ends which they are asked to espouse elsewhere. Nothing may be more noble than that a man should lay down his own life for a high cause; but it cannot possibly be right for a few men to lay down the lives of others by the million (many of them hardly more than children) for all kinds of uncertain ends which the victims certainly cannot understand; ends which, in a few brief years, will be coldly repudiated by the historian.

Never again, by this country, should a million young lives be flung away on a continent where their bones have hardly time to rot before everything that they died for is either forsworn, or sneered at, or shown to be utterly beside the real question. A war involving twenty nations, under modern conditions, may easily be brought about by a campaign of lies, or a single act of individual wickedness, whether it be a pistol-shot or a leading-article.

A distinguished modern historian (Mr. Fisher) is compelled, again and again, in dealing with modern Europe, to write sentences like this:

> "It is eloquent of the international neurosis of these times that *two second-rate men, Aehrenthal, the half-Semitic Austrian Foreign Minister, and Isvolsky, a vain, empty, fire-eating Russian diplomat, were able not only to bring Europe to the edge of a general war, but*" etc., etc:, etc.

The italics are mine; but no conclusion seems to be drawn, or even indicated, by the appalling fact so coolly set down in black and white. No judgment seems to be delivered on the crazy system under which millions of young lives may be sacrificed to a purely personal quarrel, or to the whim of a single remote individual whose proper place is in the criminal under-world. When a fire breaks out, or a ship is wrecked at sea, we are quick enough with our life-saving apparatus. But many people seem to be curiously indifferent to the thought of life-saving when millions upon millions of the young are menaced in this Bedlamite manner. We still suffer from the old romantic illusions about war, and are half ashamed to consider the value of human life in the face of it. Yet, in circumstances of this kind the first duty of every responsible British or Imperial statesman is to their own younger generations. Never again should it be possible for a historian to say that the youth of this great Commonwealth could be flung into a blind welter of savagery on the continent, and an entire generation slaughtered to make a Balkan

holiday.   It is not a question of the courage of our youth, as
our sickening romantics would suggest.   To make the appalling problem turn on that is a mere trick of the music-hall and
the white-feather brigade.   One might as well taunt the
captain of an Atlantic liner into sailing through fog and ice
at full speed in order to confirm the courage of those for
whom he is responsible.   The courage is there all right.
The question is, whether it is better to let those who possess
it be exterminated wholesale at the beginning of their lives,
or whether we can make better use of them by taking full
advantage of our sea-position.   To "win a war" and lose those
lives may be infinitely less beneficial to the world in general,
as well as to our own Commonwealth, than to concentrate
all our energies upon making it impossible that those young
lives should be sacrificed in that brutal fashion.

The air has not robbed us of our power to do this.   We
are not impregnable to incidental outrage; but we can
easily, *with our initial advantage*, make it absolutely certain
that nothing can be gained by an attack which is in the least
comparable with the extermination of a whole generation
of our children.   Moreover, by such a concentration of our re-
armament energies on a defensive sea-position (co-ordinated
with air defences) we should accomplish several other things
which belong to the true fulfilment of our history.

(*a*) As soon as it became clear that we were freeing ourselves from the conditions in which we were committed to a
general holocaust, perhaps at the whim of some "second-rate
individual" (I quote the historian again) inspired by
"fantastic reasons" of his own, there would be an immense
strengthening of the bond between all the members of our
own Commonwealth.   The only weakness in that mighty
bond is caused by the doubt, overseas, whether "continental
entanglements" may not drag us into a useless war.   Nothing
would so knit together the English-speaking peoples as the
removal of that doubt.   It would probably draw the United
States and Great Britain together in a league of peace such
as the world has never seen; and, if it were then menaced, in
those defensive conditions, there would be an instant reply

of that ultimate kind which Chesterton foresaw in one of his
finest poems, none the less fine for its reminiscence of
Kipling:

> Seas shall be red as sunset
>   And kings' bones float like foam,
> And heaven be dark with vultures
>   The night our son comes home.

(b) The policy would again set first things first by pro-
viding against interruption of sea-borne food-supplies for the
island population.

(c) The return to the sea-tradition does not mean an impossible isolation from European interests. It means rather
that, in our own way, and in our own time, we may exert a
more effective influence; that we do not depend for the
"balance of power" on the success with which we play off
one gang of contract-breakers or criminals against another;
but that we retain the balance of our own power in our own
hands, and cannot be rushed again at five minutes' notice
into the sacrifice of a million of our own children, perhaps
at the whim of some "second-rate fire-eating individual"
(again I quote the historian) in the Balkans. If it be necessary to promise to support a continental ally, in certain
circumstances (a very doubtful necessity, since all such
circumstances nowadays are suspect, and never really satisfy
the later historians), if it be necessary, however, then our
contribution should be that of a sea-power only. If the
support of that greatly strengthened British sea-power is not
enough for any continental ally to make a friendship worth
having, then we had better not make the bargain. It is
literally true that if our own country had attempted to fulfil
all its commitments in the last few years, we might easily
have found ourselves at war in four continents at once, and
in four entirely different causes. In fact, there was a time
at which Great Britain seemed to be on the verge of promis-
ing (in the interests of peace) to engage in every war that
offered itself. This is not unselfishness: it is mere madness.
A combination is quite conceivable in which our Commonwealth might deliberately be drawn into a trap for its

betrayal and destruction. It is not only charity that must begin at home. It would not be helpful to humanity in general if we all insisted on tying each other's boot-laces. We are isolated, as human beings, each in his own frame, for a very good purpose; and we need not insist on the splendour of the isolation when we affirm that the sea-position of Great Britain is an asset to the world as well as to herself. It is no virtue of her own, and there is therefore no arrogance in saying that it may help her to save the world by her example. She is fortunate enough to be in a position where she can set that example. It is possible that by deliberately setting herself to demonstrate that those who preserve the lives of their children give more than those who (nominally) win a war, she may initiate a new era for Europe itself. There is at least a chance that those who are at present weltering in a political Bedlam may begin to hunger and thirst for the benefits which must so clearly accrue to those who keep out of it.

Finally, over a large part of the world to-day the word "law" has lost its authority, and the altars of God, upon which, ultimately, that law depends, have been ground into the dust. One of the obvious consequences of this is that no contract, no agreement, no treaty, no pact, is really worth much more than the paper it is written on. Why should it be? Our young intellectuals of the "anti-God" school have certainly no answer. The ensuing confusion of thought out-Bedlams Bedlam. The British Labour Party, in its protest against the recent executions in Russia, described them as fiendish reversions to bestiality. It was a courageous protest; but, in the very next paragraph, it invited the very men whose actions it described in those terms to adopt methods which would receive a better press, and become the leaders of democracy throughout the world. We have come to a pretty pass when British Labour leaders can invite Russians whom they themselves describe as fiendish and bestial to become their leaders. But the British Labour leaders did not, of course, mean it in that way. They were merely carried along in a huge jostling welter of blind confusion. The fact remains that—in the confusion—agreements and commitments on the continent of Europe cannot be trusted, because the moral law has gone, and the altars have been shattered. In our own country, almost the last of the secular codes that survive is that of the sea. Even this, on a famous occasion, was attacked by Mr. Shaw, when he remarked that the death of the captain who went down with his ship (the *Titanic*) moved him no more than the drowning of the ship's cat. It is true, however, that the British code of behaviour at sea does still shine out like a signal-flare in a black night. The life-saving activities of the British fleet in recent years have shown a truer kind of humanitarianism than any political party has yet been able to practise. Certainly no land-army has ever played so beneficial a part for humanity in general in time of war. It is not mere pietism to say that those who "go down to the sea in ships and occupy their business in great waters" are sometimes nearer to the great realities than landsmen. It is good to remember that one of the watch-words used by the ships of Frobisher as they plunged towards the West was a quite simple statement of the fact upon which the law of men and nations depends—*Before the world was God*. On this note, therefore, I may be permitted to end with some lines written for Nelson's birthday, a year or two ago:

> Of old, when Europe reeled thro' war's red night,
>   The pilot-stars in heaven for all men shone;
> Even when they sinned, they knew that right was right,
>   And wrong was wrong, whatever wrongs were done.
>
> Now, Europe grinds her altars into dust;
>   Her gods are dead. Her very soul grows blind.
> Is there a word, out there, that men can trust?
>   Is there an oath, out there, can hold or bind?
>
> There is no peace on earth till truth returns!
>   Guard then our own, while Europe learns anew
>   That law whose service only keeps men free.
> One light at least above this island burns,
>   One steadfast ocean-covenant still holds true;
>   And Nelson's watchword thunders in her sea.

MORAL INDIGNATION

BY
ROSE MACAULAY

MORAL INDIGNATION

Far be it from me to suggest that moral indignation is a British monopoly: it is, on the contrary, like immoral indignation, one of the most widely diffused of human attributes. Nevertheless, as one leans one's ear to catch the echoes of that great accusing chorus that surges and booms from the infuriate past, one does discern among the incantations of a displeased world a note perhaps peculiarly British (I do not say English, for England's Celtic fringe has always supplied its full quota of moral disapproval). "It's not right," the chorus swells. "Cruel, unfair, irreligious, immoral, inhuman, lying, treacherous, mean, lazy, atrocious, doesn't seem right. . . ." And no more, to be sure, it does: impossible not to notice it, and perhaps (one can only say perhaps) the British have noticed it most and said so loudest, from first to last.

At the present moment (considered, I believe, an unfortunate one in world history; though, really, when one looks at that horrible affair, world history, I do not know that one moment in it seems so much more unfortunate than another)—at the present moment, there seems to be going about a great quantity of indignation of all the various kinds. I was surprised to read lately in a letter to one of our graver magazines, that "it seems sometimes that the capacity for moral indignation is passing from the modern world." The writer of this must lead a sheltered life. I, on the other hand, who do not, meet eddies of moral indignation all about the place; they swirl round me, with a noise of waves and thunder. For, as usual, nay even more than usual, foreigners are being oppressed. Habeas corpus does not run in their lands, and they languish in jail, are persecuted, slain, beaten for an indiscreet word or thought, for desiring freedom, for being of the wrong race or class; in brief, they are dictated to, and, contemplating their slavery and their anguish, the free Briton cannot contain his rage.

> That man should thus encroach on fellow man,
> Abridge him of his just and native rights, . . .
> And doom him for perhaps a heedless word
> To barrenness, and solitude, and tears,
> Moves indignation,

as Cowper, a hundred and fifty years back, remarked. His own native nook of earth, he added, has a very rude climate, replete with vapours, and its manners are rather rude too, and less plausible than social life requires, "yet being free, I love thee." In the British patriot, self-congratulation and indignation with persecuting foreigners furiously rage together; his blood boils over with them. Nazis, Fascists, Bolshevists, dictators in every part of the globe, all doing their stuff—there are enough of them to have meetings against on every day of the week, and to fill Hyde Park with stands for a year of Sundays. Out of their ivory towers the indignant writers dash, like doves from a dovecot, or like those police officers who emerge to express disapproval of peccant motorists from that tower on Constitution Hill where they have their being; they defend culture against fascism (that is to say the writers do, not the police), they defend intellectual liberty, civil liberty, personal liberty, they fulminate against racial tyranny, political tyranny, tyranny over the Press, and the great Nordic Nonsense; they get so indignant that the very pacifists among them are almost ready to fly dropping bombs over the tyrants' domains. They are, of course, a minority, I suppose a very small minority, these indignant moralists; were they a majority, I presume that, since Britain is a democracy, they would long ago have persuaded their rulers to join in their protests against these so atrocious foreigners, whereas their rulers, on the contrary, hardened and made cynical by much experience of atrocities, and only concerned to keep safe and prosperous their native nook and its possessions, endure foreign domestic tyrannies with the utmost blandness. The

majority, in all lands, will always feel, concerning the
troubles of foreigners, that

> the noise
> Concerns us not, nor should divert our joys;
> Nor ought the thunder of their carabines
> Drown the sweet airs of our tuned violins.

It is the small, indignant, highly vocal minority whose cries
of protest rend Heaven. During recent years, they have so
rent it that Heaven shows a peculiarly tattered and crazy
pattern, being rent also by the usual multitude of the other
missiles aimed at it by humanity. Still, however rent and
riddled, Heaven retains its customary impervious Olympian
calm; humanity, it seems to say, must really manage its
affairs for itself: there is quite enough indignation on earth,
without troubling Heaven to be indignant too; even in the
rage said to be occasioned in it by robin redbreasts in cages,
its self-control remains admirable. So Britons and others,
but very largely Britons, get together and hold indignation
meetings. Yesterday they were about Abyssinia, Italian
treaty-breaking, Italian brutal aggression, and the suggestion
by an English and a French foreign minister of a plan for
accommodating aggressors and aggressed together in the
disputed land. This plan roused, as Mr. Baldwin startled
into retraction observed, deep moral emotion in the hearts
of the British public, led by its *Times*. They would not have
it; they held meetings, they barracked their M.P.s, they
wrote to their newspapers, they put, in brief, their feet firmly
down, and crushed the plan out of existence still-born, not
without blood and tears. Not because it was, as intelligent
people always perceived it to be, a silly and impossible
plan, and not because, as Italians always believe and always
will, it was against British interests to have them in Abyssinia
(this is the sort of consideration that goes with rulers, not
with the great simple), but because the English thought it
a dirty deal, immoral, not cricket, a swiz. They would not
have it. They would have, instead, sanctions; they would like
the Suez Canal blocked, the selling of oil to Italy forbidden.

No Government, of course, would do that, it would have been immoderate, excessive; still, public indignation did succeed in cramping the export of Italian olives, macaroni, and Chianti, which was like perching a small gadfly on a bull's neck, to inflame but not impede his rage. To-day our indignation for the poor Abyssinians has smouldered down to sulky embers, and all we can do is to pray for their souls. One last spurt of anger concerning them was the other day, when at Geneva Britain threw them publicly over as part of a bargain with their conqueror; and small and muted, though disgusted, were the protests raised.

Abyssinia was yesterday: to-day our moral indignation sprays the sultry Spanish Peninsula, the Japanese fighting their war of self-defence in China, Germany annexing Austria and bullying clergymen, Jews, liberals, democrats, and the Czechs. About the Spanish business, we are, on both sides, particularly hot. Clergy and laity attend meetings and condemn in no measured terms such atrocious deeds as have, they are credibly informed, been committed by the side with which their informants are not in sympathy. So great is the indignation that practically everything gets believed; Spain is obviously, from the reported behaviour of its denizens and of its invaders, a country only fit for Spaniards to live in, and not really fit even for that. Our indignation rages not only, possibly not even mostly, at the committers of atrocities in Spain, but at those of our fellow-countrymen who approve of the wrong side in this acrimonious dispute, and who invent such malicious and ignorant falsehoods about the other. "We cannot regard with any other sentiment than indignation," as Dean Liddon so truly said, "the propagation of what is known to be false." Indeed, no; and of course they know it to be false, the liars, so naturally we are indignant.

Meanwhile, animals are being ill-treated, hunted, inhumanely butchered, beaten, starved, caged, put into arenas to serve as dartboards for matadors or goring-targets for bulls, instructed by sinister methods to perform tricks in circuses. All over Europe, all over Asia, the Americas,

Mexico, and darkest Africa, indignant English ladies start up in the best Ouida tradition, crying, in all languages at their command, but usually relapsing in their excitement into their own humanitarian tongue, "Stop beating your mule. Do not goad your horse. Six huge Mexicans on one poor little donkey! Don't you see the poor dog is starving? How dare you prick your elephant's trunk? The poor bull, the poor horses, *sin duda quejaré al consul ingles.* Tying up a dear little kid for leopard-bait—you ought to be leopard-bait yourselves."

But the indignation that has for so long surged around the crimes committed against our dumb friends is too vast a sea to embark on here. So also is the indignation aroused by the shocking behaviour of our foes in wartime, for this tends to merge into patriotism, and to lose its pure altruistic flavour: even those emotions caused to the less patriotic by the shocking behaviour of their own side is less moral indignation than pro-enemyism, that well-known disease that afflicts an ardent British minority in every war, and that inspired, it was said, Miss Emily Hobhouse in her campaign against the concentration camps in which female and infant Boers languished during our war against their husbands and fathers. In our quest after British moral indignation, we must, then, pass over wars in which Britain has been a combatant; the emotion, in its purest form, should rage in the breasts of neutral onlookers at wickedness. Such emotion shook Mr. E. D. Morel, Sir Roger Casement, Mr. Henry Nevinson, and all their readers, at the relation of such atrocities as were wont to be perpetrated by Portuguese, Belgians and Colombians on those who gathered for them cocoa and rubber in São Tomé, Putumayo and the Congo. Many high-minded Britons renounced cocoa and rubber, as a century earlier they had, on account of the Jamaica slave trade, given up sugar in their tea. I am not sure what they gave up from Russia during the years of British indignation with Tsarist tyranny—possibly vodka—but when the Tsar was to visit London in 1909, a mighty crowd assembled in Trafalgar Square to forbid the approach of this little knout-wielding, duma-suppressing emperor from whose land refugees had for so many years escaped to England with their horrid tales of woe. Russia has always supplied us with plenty of fuel for our displeasure, what with sending liberals to Siberia, knouting mujiks, ill-treating Poles, wanting Constantinople, going home during the European war, making ill-timed revolutions, assassinating their Royal Family, abolishing capitalism, liquidating kulaks and bourgeois, starving mujiks, trying British engineers, executing Trotskyites, and a hundred similar barbarous habits.

Where have we arrived, in our backward glance down the indignant centuries? I think nearly at Alfred Dreyfus, anger at whose treatment is said to have made the books by his champion Zola the bedside reading of many a virtuous and prudish Briton who had hitherto banned them even from his smoking-room. Then we come to Parnell, whose notorious solecism English and Irish, Protestant and Catholic, politicians and people, all joined to reprehend. Meanwhile, the Turks were continually shocking; whether their behaviour to Armenians or to Bulgarians excited the more censure in Great Britain, is a near thing. There have, indeed, been occasions since then, such as the Great War in which Bulgars were found on the wrong side, and encounters with Armenians selling rugs, when the Turkish atrocities on both these races have been by Britons partially condoned: but in the nineteenth century, a more moral age, no excuses were found. Gladstone, whom the horrors of the slave-trade left placidly unmoved, proclaimed that "there was not a criminal in a European gaol, nor a cannibal in the South Sea Islands, whose indignation would not rise" at Turkish cruelties. Lord Derby sent a message to the Porte through the British ambassador that the atrocious crimes of his people had roused the righteous anger of practically all ours: Carlyle announced that the Unspeakable Turk must be turned out of Europe: and at a huge meeting at St. James's Hall such authors and artists as Trollope, Morris, Browning, Ruskin, and even the gentle, unpolitical Burne-Jones, rushed out of their ivory towers with the strongest expressions of disapproval.

A few years before that, Mr. Gladstone, always most indignant when out of office, had been much annoyed by the prisons of the Kingdom of Naples, which were, as he rightly remarked, fitter for hell than earth, but, one infers, worse than hell in that their inmates were confined there for far less reason. Imprisonment for what appear to Britons to be poor reasons has always roused in our liberty-loving islanders the most vehement indignation: to-day the name of Pastor Niemöller will stir the most placid English tempers to the boil; no longer in these days, however, the blood of cabinet ministers, who have become more tactful and discreet; one imagines them murmuring, with Wordsworth,

> through the nation spread a moral heat
> Of virtuous feeling. For myself, I own
> That this particular strife had wanted power
> To rivet my affections; nor did now
> Its unsuccessful issue much excite
> My soul. . . .

which was much the feeling that Mr. Gladstone, scion of Liverpool West India merchants, would appear to have had about the slave trade. All of us have our tolerant and good-tempered spots: but Gladstone's were smaller than those of his modern successors, and the notion that the ill-treatment of his (white) fellow-creatures abroad was no concern of his simply because they were subjects of another state, was alien to the Grand Old Man. It is probable that the thunder of his righteous wrath over Nazi inhumanity and injustice would either diminish it or plunge us into war, and the mild and fitful disapproval we express to-day would have scandalised him by its inadequacy. So also would our weak-kneed tolerance of irreligion. Mr. Gladstone was a stern spokesman of a generation of churchmen which thundered its horror at the defiance of the Book of Genesis implicit in the researches of our major biologists; that man should be declared kin to the ape creation wounded the haughty biped's every instinct of piety and pride, and stirred storms of which those in more recent years at Dayton, Tennessee, are but faint echoes.

Still, such moral rages as this are not more English than continental, indeed cosmic, and we will turn from them to anger of a more British hue.

The first half of the nineteenth century, looked back at from the twentieth, wears an air of grim annoyance and disturbance. So many shocking social wrongs, so many people endeavouring, not without dust and heat, to right them, so many politicians, philanthropists; novelists, poets, rushing into the fray, so much indignation about the treatment of the poor, the treatment of children, factory conditions, chimney sweeps, underpaid seamstresses, votes, machinery, liberty (perpetually violated nymph, whose shrieks rang out at this period even more freely than usual), religious equality, black slavery, foreign tyrannies—one would say that our ancestors and our ancestresses never enjoyed a quiet moment, except when one reads their letters and diaries, and the novels of Jane Austen, when one realises that their moral indignation, though vocal, was never, endemic. It got a good deal into poetry, poets being, as a rule, indignant people. Shelley was rightly angry with the world through pretty well most of his short life. All round him the most immoral outrages were being perpetrated; women were being immured in convents, undergraduates expelled for writing atheistic pamphlets, poets slain by the spiteful reviews of carrion kites, other poets turning Tory in their middle age, the marriage laws abominable, the subjection of women a disgrace to humanity, the political and economic system a disgrace to Britain. After the Peterloo massacre he pictured the Government riding by in a grim cavalcade of murder—

> I met murder on the way—
> He had a mask like Castlereagh.
> Very smooth he looked, yet grim;
> Seven bloodhounds followed him;
>
> All were fat; and well they might
> Be in admirable plight,
> For one by one, and two by two,
> He tossed them human hearts to chew.

> Next came Fraud, and he had on,
> Like Lord E——, an ermined gown. . . .

And so on. Liberty was foully crushed, and as for the poor, he bade them

> Arise, arise, arise!
> There is blood on the earth that denies ye bread!

Shelley's and Cowper's were perhaps the purest, the most altruistic moral indignations in English literature. Byron's can scarcely be called either; it had always a gamy, cynical, wounded-vanity flavour, which is not really very English. Wordsworth's was nobler, and, always highly correct in tone, changed its direction as he grew older, soberer, and Toryer. The other poets—Southey, Coleridge, Moore, Blake, and the rest—each expressed his anger against iniquity according to his temper and talents, from Southey's early Jacobin and late Tory wrath, to Blake's robin redbreast in a cage that so enraged a humanitarian Heaven.

Meanwhile, side by side with all this public and large-scale indignation, there was the moral reprobation poured out on the juvenile population. Children had always, of course, been known to be dear little vessels of wrath, and been treated accordingly; they were probably much less severely dealt with in the eighteenth and early nineteenth centuries than in earlier ages, when hell was always just round the corner for them and they were not allowed to forget it. But there had been little literature specifically for them, except books of instruction in manners, morals and grammar, until the eighteenth century, when the good Dr. Watts wrote for them charming little poems about their sins, their duties, and where they would, if they were not careful, go when they died. Against those who tell lies he was particularly stern:

> Have we not known, or heard, or read,
> How God abhors deceit and wrong?
> How Ananias was struck dead,
> Catch'd with a lie upon his tongue?

> So did his wife, Sapphira, die,
> When she came in and grew so bold
> As to confirm that wicked lie
> That, just before, her husband told. . . .
>
> Then let me always watch my lips,
> Lest I be struck to death and hell,
> Since God a book or reck'ning keeps
> For every lie that children tell.

The doctor, kindest of men, must have kept on his desk always a list of such useful words for poetry as tell, dwell, well, fell.

> There is a dreadful hell, [he told the nursery]
>   And everlasting pains,
> There sinners must with devils dwell,
>   In darkness, fire, and chains.
>
> Can such a wretch as I
>   Escape this cursed end? . . .

And,

> What if his dreadful anger burn,
>   While I refuse his offer'd grace,
> And all his love to fury turn,
>   And strike me dead upon the place?
>
> 'Tis dangerous to provoke a God!
>   His power and vengeance none can tell;
> One stroke of his Almighty rod
>   Shall send young sinners quick to hell.

The habit of invoking divine moral displeasure against the young went inexplicably out of fashion in the mid-nineteenth century, and the persecuted, preached-at little Rosamonds, Sandfords and Mertons, Fairchildren, and the rest, gave place gradually to the perkier and freer model of to-day, at whom no one dares preach.

But was it specifically English, this displeasure with the young? Probably not. Mr. Harvey Darton has pointed out that the "moral urge" in children's books came largely from France; and certainly no English child that I remember had a career so beset with penalties and wrath as the unfortunate

Sophie of the *malheurs*. But adult impatience with children has always and everywhere required such vent; its absence to-day is said to be causing alarming complexes and warpings of the soul among parents, who now face the world with a nerve-ridden lack of tranquillity less usual among our ancestors, who could cleanse their stuffed bosoms of that perilous stuff by giving their little ones a beating and damning them to hell. Serenity to-day is found mainly among the childless.

Nor, of course, can we maintain that other forms of moral indignation throughout the centuries are peculiarly British. The most morally wrathful man of the eighteenth century was probably Voltaire; but France is a land of extremes, and the sentiment appears to have been more widespread in the British Isles. Dr. Johnson, of course, was seldom free from it. Unbelievers and Whig dogs (equally children of the devil), dissenters, Scots, women (though not men) who had fallen from virtue, readers of *Tom Jones* ("I am shocked," he said to Miss Hannah More, whom it had entertained, "to hear you quote from so vicious a book. I am sorry to hear you have read it: a confession which no modest lady should ever make. I scarcely know a more corrupt work") —canters, pretenders, prigs, Americans, libertines, republicans—those who would pass his moral tests and escape the judgment must tread funambulously indeed the narrow path of virtue. John Milton, that acrimonious and surly republican, failed to tread it; if these two contemptuous and contentious scholars walk now the same Elysian fields, the asphodel must wither and burn up beneath the streams of moral reprobation poured out by each upon the other.

Passing lightly over Pope, Swift, Jeremy Collier, and a great orchestra of angry, noisy, and moral eighteenth-century politicians and theologians, all angry and noisy and moral about different, often opposite things, we come to the century of Milton, Cromwell, Clarendon, and Prynne, malignants and rebels, canary-bibbing, swan-devouring prelates, bloody regicides, sabbath-profaners, maypole dancers, crop-eared precisians, witches, Quakers, blasphemers,

and a hundred other objects of virtuous odium. The stormy
seas of English moral disapproval in this century thundered
and boomed, or so it seems to us who listen from our distant
beach, with an even more than customary loudness. Surely,
we think, continental civil wars were not waged with so
much righteous contumely on both sides. And who but
those whom Milton called God's Englishmen protested with
such altruistic fury, and sent out such eagerly irate com-
missions of inquiry, when the unfortunate Waldensians were
slaughtered in the Alpine valleys cold and rolled down the
rocks by the bloody Piedmontese? Nothing since the Massacre of St. Bartholomew had made the English send such
indignant, interfering protests.

But those vociferous packs of infuriate opinions which
modern journalists love to call ideologies were now in full
cry. Religion and politics joined to damn their opponents,
and one faction was not morally hotter and sterner than
another through the turbulent sixteenth and seventeenth
centuries. A visitor from some other planet, or even from
Lapland, would not have been able to guess, after listening
to all they had to say about one another's iniquities, which
side in those tremendous arguments was the more depraved
and lost. Hear the angry young Oxonian Stephen Gosson
on the idle wantonness of his age:

> "Our wrestling at arms is turned to wallowing in ladies'
> laps, our courage to cowardice, our running to riot. . . .
> We have robbed Greece of gluttony, Italy of wantonness,
> Spain of pride, France of deceit, and Dutchland of
> quaffing. . . ."

Let everybody, he exhorts, get to work for his country,
for no man is born to seek private profit, but all to work for
the public good. As for all this play-going with lady friends,
which includes

> "such giving them pippins to pass the time, such ticking,
> such toying, such smiling, such winking, and such manning
> them home when the sports are ended,"

well, the more said the better about these goings-on, and
Gosson says a lot of it. For of courting he cannot approve:
nor of "pipers, poets, players, jesters, and such like cater-
pillars of the commonwealth."

Nor can his contemporary (from Cambridge), Philip
Stubbes, who was especially fussed by women's clothes, that
time-honoured cockshy of godly and angry men (Stubbes
particularly detested starched ruffs and the gentlemanly-
looking doublets for a time a smart female fashion), and by
maypoles, of which he gives a pretty account that shows
very ill-repressed enjoyment.

> "They have twenty or forty yoke of oxen, every ox
> having a sweet nosegay of flowers tied on the tip of his
> horns, and these oxen draw home this may pole (this
> stinking idol rather) which is covered all over with flowers
> and herbs. . . . And thus being reared up, with hand-
> kerchiefs and flags streaming on the top, they straw the
> ground about, bind green boughs about it, set up summer
> hauls, bowers and arbours hard by it; and then fall they
> to banquet and feast, to leap and dance about it, as the
> heathen people did at the dedication of their idols. . . ."

Worse still, he had heard it "credibly reported, and that
viva voce, by men of great gravity," that there were dreadful
goings-on in the woods all the night before, and that of the
maids who went there scarcely a third part returned as they
went out.

Such sinful merry pastimes as these were, of course, an
old story, which priest and parson had told since maying
began; probably the druids had thundered it to British maids
and lads, and medieval sermons and poetry resound with it,
as with the wickedness of Sunday games, piping, dancing,
and secular plays. The Elizabethans, less domestic and
devout, and getting about more, shifted the emphasis to
some extent, and much of their moral indignation was with
the outrageous foreigners: with the Spanish devils, "abhorred
of God and man," who persecuted the poor Indians so and

stole their treasures before the English could get there; with
the odious Dutch who fell foul of us in the East Indian seas;
with the false French, the whoring, poisoning Italians, the
thieving Portugals and lascivious idle Greeks. There was
plenty left over for political and theological opponents at
home; but the grand English game of baiting the foreigner
absorbed much of the indignation that had been in the
medieval centuries poured on to the devoted heads of clergy
and laity by those moralists who disapproved of either or
both; of, in fact, human nature.

Entering the Middle Ages in our backward stroll, we begin
to realise what moral indignation can be. Such a clamour
of voices rises, such deadly sins are rebuked, such earthquakes
warn us to beware, such heavy allegories load poetry and
fable, such corruption is unmasked in church and state. On
the continent, of course, a similar clamour resounded; but
it seems to have been less long sustained, and on the whole
a less heavy business, than ours. No continental archbishop
has been quite so stern with his erring sovereign as was our
Dunstan with the tenth-century Saxon monarchs; and, as a
poet's magnificently indignant vision of a corrupt society,
our *Piers Plowman* has no rival but the diatribes of the
Hebrew prophets. It echoes and amplifies Roger Bacon's
complainings of a century before:

> "Let us see all conditions in the world, and consider
> them diligently: we shall find boundless corruption. . . .
> Lechery dishonours the whole court, and gluttony is lord
> of all. . . . See the prelates, how they hunt after money
> and neglect the cure of souls. . . . The whole clergy is
> intent upon pride, lechery and avarice. . . . None care
> what is done, or how, by hook or by crook, provided only
> that each can fulfil his lust."

So Wycliffe and the Lollards were saying a hundred years
later; so the poets and homilists all through the Middle Ages.
"Sinners Beware," "Signs of Death," "The Eleven Pains of
Hell"—such grim names as these for their works poets

favoured, and the seven deadly sins revel hand in hand to suitable retribution through many an epic. Minstrelsy, tournaments, games, dancing in churchyards, large and late suppers, females and all their ways, the clergy and most of theirs: with what heat, what puritan passion, these are rebuked! It must not discourage us in our quest after English indignation to note that the most moral and indignant works are often adapted from the French. For human wickedness was, we must admit, a universal theme. English literature, when it began, was but another voice in the great chorus of Christendom, which sang perpetually of sin, Satan, and the Christian attitude towards both. The first English poets (whom for brevity's sake and to conceal our ignorance we call Caedmon and Cynewulf) bore their part in this world concert by monks, which, started by Avitus and his *De Originali Peccato*, continued with the utmost monotony down the centuries; but their righteous wrath cannot be called specifically island, it was the great complaint of Christendom, concerning which one's only surprise should be that it has been, in more recent centuries, so tepidly and perfunctorily delivered. Still, when we consider the British part in the concert, we do perceive one point in which it outdid its continental models: it went on longer. When the French, wearying of the great theme, were addressing themselves to livelier topics, such as war, wine, women, and song, and their poetry rang with chivalric shouts from Roncesvalles and gay amours from Provence, the English poets, bogged in tradition, still complained in long epic poems, riddles, animal fables, and even mathematical treatises, of man's sin. In fact, their moral indignation proved itself, if not flashier, more enduring.

Leaning an attentive ear to Ancient Britain, before she was disturbed by irrupting Saxons, one seems to hear there, too, the indignant chorus swell. Gildas, for instance, the first Briton whose comments remain for us *in extenso*—what acid comments they are! What sins the British had committed, how vicious were the Devon and Cornwall princes, how corrupt (already) the clergy! Of the heathen invaders

themselves he can scarcely say worse; but his anger against
these is, one presumes, less moral than patriotic (if one can
ever disengage such close-embracing twins). Behind this
bitter Briton loom remoter British beings—Cymbeline,
Arthur, Lear, Boadicea—of whom our records are slightly
sketchy, but their historians have put into all their mouths,
I dare say quite rightly, fine gusty diatribes about the ill
conduct of others. Nor is it for us with any fullness to
know what our Anglo-Saxon ancestors were saying about
misconduct before they came to England: something immoderate, doubtless, for they were an immoderate people in all
their ways, and we must leave it at that.

We are arrived at the end of our somewhat casual backward stroll down the story of our race; or, rather, we are
arrived at a blank wall, behind which no voices (perhaps it
is as well) can be heard. Turning back to where we took
off we find ourselves again in an uproar; all kinds of new
sins have been perpetrated since we left. Here is a hot-coal
father, there inhuman foreigners, while, towering above
both, an insolent bureaucracy infringes the privileges of our
members of Parliament. . . . It's not right: no, it's not
right. . . .

DISSENT

BY

BRIAN LUNN

DISSENT

THOSE who concern themselves with bridging the differences between Christian Churches divide their problem into the two main headings of Faith and Order which correspond to the older distinction between heresy and schism. Since the declaration of papal infallibility in matters of faith and order any act of schism is necessarily an act of heresy in the authoritarian Roman Catholic Church, but the distinction is still useful in considering the motives which prompted Christian communities in England to dissociate themselves from the Anglican Church, for the characteristic of English Dissent which distinguishes it from sectarianism on the Continent has been, especially in its later manifestations, a preoccupation with questions of church government and the practice of worship rather than with points of doctrine. The dissenting Churches have contributed their distinctive colours to the social fabric of England in which they are now firmly interwoven, and English Nonconformity has a character as peculiarly national as the British Constitution, or the public school system or the Anglican Church itself.

The aim of Queen Elizabeth was to make the national Church acceptable to the greatest possible number of her subjects, and it is due to her sagacity and that of the able draftsmen who assisted her that in a period when Europe was devastated with religious war from the Meuse to the Alps so few Englishmen were faced with the necessity to die for their beliefs. The issues in our civil war, when it came, were political rather than religious.

The Articles of Religion "agreed upon by the archbishops and bishops of both Provinces and by the whole clergy," and published with her Majesty's Declaration were such as to satisfy even exacting Protestants. Three Articles laid down the authority of the Bible over tradition or Councils; Original

Sin, Free Will, Justification, Good Works, Predestination are all dealt with in accordance with the teaching of Geneva.

But, whereas the Articles, which concerned mainly the experts, were thoroughly Protestant, the Rubrics defining the Order of Service were so designed that congregations in country districts should not be sensible of any sharp break with the cult of their forefathers. Moreover, while she made the doctrine and worship of the Church as elastic as possible, Elizabeth had no patience with "prophesyings." She was determined to maintain the authoritarian rule of her father within the Church, and not to tolerate religious worship outside it. The Church of England was governed by bishops appointed by the sovereign.

The removal of one authority leads men to question all authority before they will accept the substitution of another; a democratic and individualist spirit was stirring, and those who felt they had the gifts of the spirit were not willing to refrain from pastoral work merely because they had not been ordained by a bishop, while congregations of earnest men and women claimed the right to worship in their own way with the pastor of their choice. Many felt too that the reformation of church abuses should be speeded up, that vestments, church ornaments and "popish" practices should be radically suppressed, and above all that clergy who neg-lected to preach should be dismissed. "Reformation without tarrying for anie" was the slogan of the first Independents and Congregationalists, and the Separatist movement might have become dangerous even under Elizabeth, had not religious enthusiasm become discredited by the freakish excesses of antinomians in Germany, so that the name Anabaptist affected many Englishmen much as the name Bolshevik does to-day. Thus, although there were a few heroes who spent many years in the foul jails of that time, one or two who died on the gibbet, more who emigrated to Leyden and thence to America when they fell out with their Dutch co-religionists, the movement did not develop suffi-ciently to engage the close attention of a queen who had to steer her way among so many other difficult problems. As she passed the place where Barrowe and Greenwood had lately been hanged she asked Dr. Reynolds what he thought of them. The learned divine answered "that he was persuaded if they had lived they would have been two as worthy instruments of the Church of God as have been raised up in this age." Her Majesty sighed and said no more. Then she turned to the Earl of Cumberland who was present at the execution and asked what end they had made. He answered, "A very godly end, and prayed for your Majesty and the State."

Such was the loyalty of the Separatists to Queen Elizabeth, but between James I and the English there was never that mutual confidence which the three great Tudor sovereigns had inspired. The zealous reformers had been nicknamed Puritans by their enemies in Elizabeth's time; when James I said "I will make them conform, or I will harry them out of the land," Puritanism became a national movement which brought his son to the block and founded an empire beyond the Atlantic.

Early in the seventeenth century Puritanism received the doctrinal stiffening which it needed to carry the movement to success on its political side. Arminius, a Dutch professor of theology, shocked the Protestant world by propounding from his chair at Leyden that: "The providence or government of God, while sovereign, is exercised in harmony with the nature of the creatures governed, i.e. the sovereignty of God is so exercised as to be compatible with the freedom of man."

As Erasmus had foreseen, Luther's doctrine of the helplessness of the will had been made the corner-stone of the new theology, the doctrinal rallying point of the Reformation. The doctrine was original to Luther only in the sense in which any doctrine is ever original—he had come to it through his own spiritual experience. It was his way of expressing the truth that the wind bloweth where it listeth, that inspiration cannot be induced by effort, that the kingdom of heaven is within you, that good works cannot produce faith, they are the fruit of faith. Calvin, an uninspired doctrinaire, had made this doctrine with its corollary of pre-destination the central point in his dialectical system. It enabled him to enlarge upon the awfulness of the Almighty, whereby he was exalted as the Almighty's agent on earth. It was, he explained, "a very sweet and savoury doctrine, for it shews forth the glory of God and promotes true humility," that divine justice should have predetermined a small number to share the joys of heaven, while the vast majority have been consigned as vessels of wrath to roast in everlasting fire. Sensitive minds were tormented even to madness by this doctrine, but the generality of Calvin's followers felt safe and comfortable in the tutelage of this ruthless servant of a ruthless god. Justified by faith in Calvin, they found it easy to believe themselves the elect, and as easy to believe all non-Calvinists reprobate.

Above all, the doctrinal system centred on predestination was not yet stale, and the main result in England of the Leyden professor's defiantly "heretical" proposition was to provide orthodox Protestants with a term of abuse for those whom they suspected of doctrinal weakness. The term arminian came to have much the same flavour as the term bourgeois used by a Marxist. Still, the reign of James passed without much trouble from the Puritans who may have felt that the Catholic plot to blow up Kings, Lords and Commons indicated that the government was theologically sound. But when Charles I became king, the politico-religious revolutionary movement developed rapidly. Laud, the Archbishop of Canterbury, was an avowed arminian, and announced that it was not necessary for a clergyman to believe all the articles of the prayer-book. He prepared a list of clergy for the King in which he marked the names O for Orthodox and P for Puritan. He worked in close collaboration with Strafford to whom he wrote: "As for the State, I am thorough," but the result of his totalitarianism was to stimulate Puritan emigration to the New World and to multiply sectaries at home, so that in 1641 a bishop asserted that there were in London "no fewer than four-score congregations of several sectaries, instructed by guides fit for them, cobblers, tailors, feltmakers and such like trash."

In August, 1642, the English Civil War began; in the following January, from his window in the Tower, Laud blessed Strafford who was going to execution, following him to the block a few days later, and in due course their royal master suffered the same fate. Under Cromwell's rule the chief dissenters from the official religion were the Episcopalians and the Roman Catholics, but it cannot be said with any precision what the official religion was. The Presbyterians, who had developed an autocratic form of church government, were strong in Parliament, and when Cromwell proposed a motion for religious freedom (amongst Protestants) Presbyter Baillie said that it would lead to amsterdamnation, Amsterdam having a bad reputation for doctrinal looseness.

After the battle of Naseby Cromwell did not need to suffer the pedantry of Presbyterian divines. His secretary Milton pointed out that that new presbyter was old priest writ large, and Cromwell's psalm-singing Ironsides were either Independents or adherents of one of the many eccentric sects which flourished for their brief day. It was indeed a period of extraordinary religious confusion during which the committee for Plundered Ministries was the most characteristic organ of church government.

While he treated with indulgence the enthusiastic fancies of his soldiers, outside the army Cromwell found it more difficult to restrain Protestant heresy hunters, and it is not easy to ascertain how far "the great dissembler" really tried to do so. There has survived, for instance, the following pitiful letter written in 1656 to the future Charles II by an Anabaptist:

"We must confess that we have been wandering, deviating, and roving up and down, this way and that way, through all the dangerous and untrodden paths of fanatic and enthusiastic notions, till now at last, but too late, we find ourselves intricated and involved in so many windings, labyrinths and meanders of knavery, that nothing but a divine clue of thread, handed to us from heaven, can be sufficient to extricate us, and restore us. We know not, we know not, whether we have juster matter of shame or sorrow administered to us, when we take a reflex view of our past actions, and consider into the commission of what crimes, impieties, wickednesses, and unheard of villainies we have been led, cheated, cozened and betrayed by that grand impostor, that loathsome hypocrite, that detestable traitor, that prodigy of nature, that sink of sin, and that compendium of baseness, who now calls himself our protector. . . . He answers us, 'You are factious, you are factious; if your burdens are heavy, I will make them yet heavier.' Thus do we fly, like partridges hunted, from hill to hill, and from mountain to mountain, but can find no rest; we look this way, and that way, but there is none to save, none to deliver. . . . When we looked for liberty, behold slavery; when we expected righteousness, behold oppression; when we sought for justice, behold a cry—a great and lamentable cry—throughout the whole nation."

Even the founder of the Society of Friends, commonly called Quakers, for whom Cromwell had a personal affection, spent some time in prisons during the Protectorate. George Fox is the only Englishman after Wycliffe who may justly be called a heresiarch, since the other founders and leaders of sects either took their doctrine from the Continent, left their parent church from schismatic motives, or founded ephemeral esoteric groups. Blamelessness, courage and intelligent sincerity are the outstanding characteristics of George Fox; his *Journal* is a landmark in the Christian practice of introspection, whence autobiographical writing has developed. He is perhaps the first man to have put on record his memories of early childhood:

"In my very young years I had a gravity and stayedness of mind and spirit not usual in children; inasmuch that when I saw old men carry themselves lightly and wantonly towards each other, I had a dislike thereof raised in my heart, and said within myself, 'If ever I come to be a man, surely I shall not do so, nor be so wanton.' "

George Fox was not what the Catholic Church calls a scrupulant; he was not started upon the road to heresy or sanctity, as were so many Christians, by a sense of inexpiable guilt, but by perplexity regarding the conduct of others. He was disillusioned in his first employer: "that was a shoe-maker by trade, and that dealt in wool; and a great deal went through my hands. While I was with him, he was blessed; but after I left him he broke, and came to nothing." But he was even more disillusioned in two professors, who may be defined as lay members of the Puritan party, who said to him after a glass of ale that for additional glasses "he that would not drink should pay all." After this episode, at the age of nineteen, he left his parents and wandered for three years about the country, hoping that he would find a pastor or professor to answer the questions which were troubling him. But one was like a hollow cask, another told him to sing psalms and take tobacco and then "told my troubles, sorrows, and griefs to his servants, so that it was got among the milk-lasses, which grieved me that I should open my mind to such a one." Another professor flew into a rage when Fox stepped into his flower-bed, while most sickening of all was the discovery that the one who had seemed to be most helpful had been pumping him for sermons: "What I said in discourse to him on the week-days, that he would preach on the first-days, for which I did not like him. This priest afterwards became my great persecutor."

When at length Fox realised that priests and professors could not help him to become happy, he became happy himself. He began to have "openings" of which the first which his *Journal* records is "that being bred at Oxford or Cambridge was not enough to fit or qualify men to be ministers of Christ, and I wondered at it, because it was the common belief of people. But I saw it clearly as the Lord opened it to me, and was satisfied, and admired the goodness of the Lord who had opened this thing unto me that morning." The truth of this opening was not new, but original truth exists only for those who suppose that truth can be thought out, and that it is variable. The characteristic of men of insight is that they see the same truths as one another, but seeing them independently they clothe them with words which give them the force of a new discovery. Fox's simplicity has the force of humour; he called churches steeple-houses, because for him a church was merely a house with a steeple on it.

There were, however, already enough Ranters and Seekers going up and down the land, who preached that religion was not in need of trained experts or of sacred buildings. The multitudinous sects battened on the fact that the Bible had not long been substituted for the Church as the authority in doctrine, and its authority had as yet been little impaired by practical use, especially as any kind of printed word still had immense prestige with the bulk of the population. The practical result of the teaching that justification was by faith alone had been to make those on whom the wind of faith did not list to blow seek refuge in words instead of works. Having mastered the jargon of the Calvinist dialecticians they felt secure as they babbled to one another their mantras of prevenient grace, the sin of Adam, imputed righteousness, election, reprobation. Instead of reciting paternosters they bandied texts from Scripture, and instead of going on pilgrimage they listened to three-, four- or five-hour sermons delivered by a professor, or delivered them themselves.

George Fox attacked the practice of weaving "windy doctrines by which they blow the people about this way and the other way, from sect to sect"; as Luther was led through denying the value of "holiness by works," to repudiate the holder of the keys to the Church treasury of merits, so Fox through his attack upon holiness by words was led to qualify the authority of Scripture: "All Christendom possesses the

Scriptures," he wrote, "but lacks the power and spirit of the men who gave the Scriptures, and this is the reason why Christians are not in fellowship with the Son, nor with the Father, nor with the Spirit, nor with one another." Here George Fox came near the teaching of the Catholic Church, and Cardinal Newman says much the same thing: "It may be objected that inspired documents, such as the Holy Scriptures, at once determine Christianity's doctrine without further trouble. But they were intended to create *an idea* and that idea is not in the sacred text, but in the mind of the reader."

Fox set up the authority of the "Inward Light," the light which lighteth every man that cometh into the world, and his followers were first known as Children of the Light. After reciting his acceptance of the general Christian verities he says—rather like Paul who preached Christ for three years after the vision on the road to Damascus before he went to see any of the disciples—"These things I did not see by the help of man, nor by the letter, though they are written in the letter, but I saw them in the light of the Lord Jesus Christ, and by his immediate spirit and power, as did the holy men of God by whom the Holy Scriptures were written." An ingenious doctrine, very widely preached, laid down that it was a grievous sin to strive after perfection, since it was an affront to the divine majesty to suppose that the creature had any power for good in itself. At Duckingfield Fox records that "the professors were in a rage, all pleading for sin and imperfection, and could not endure to hear talk of perfection, and of a holy and sinless life."

Contemptuous of windy doctrine, Fox was uncompromising in the application of the moral precepts contained in the Gospels. Not for him Calvin's easy principle to choose the more convenient injunction, where the New Testament conflicts with the Old. Oaths, for instance, were justified by Calvin from a passage in Exodus, while in the teeth of Christ's teaching about the Sabbath, he introduced the Puritan Sunday, whereby the minister's authority over his congregation was increased. The Beatitudes may be counsels of perfection to which men can only approximate, but the injunction, "Swear not at all. Let your communication be yea, yea; nay, nay: for whatever is more than these cometh of evil," is one that can be practically applied. However, when nearly all men believed in a miraculous religion, they felt there was all the difference between merely telling a lie and forswearing themselves, so that the oath, whether to king or covenant or in a court of law was regarded as an indispensable prop in the machinery of government. The Quakers suffered far more for their refusal to take the oath than for their refusal to take up arms which, in our time, became for all except those sects which had acquired a prescriptive right in pacifism, a serious cause of persecution.

Fox would have sympathised with the feelings of those who resent the corruption of English in the misuse of words such as awfully, decent, nice. It followed from the obligation to be perfectly accurate that the Quaker was forbidden to haggle in business. Having named his figure as buyer or as seller, he must stick to it; no splitting the difference was permissible. When this became known as a Quaker principle of business, it assisted many Quakers to become wealthy.

All founders of Christian societies have had a text which specially corresponded to their message, and there was no precept which George Fox impressed more assiduously upon his followers than that their communication should be yea, nay. He condemned polite manners, and it is a measure of his refusal to compromise that the Quakers refused to uncover before the magistrate, although the country was full of spies eager to report persons guilty of acts or omissions which might be construed as hostile to the government.

As nowadays on the Continent, the second person plural was used in the time of Fox to indicate respect for the person addressed. Fox condemned the use of "you" to a single person. Fox might have said "you" to all, as a twentieth-century egalitarian may say "Mister" to both master and servant. Fox's practice was the more difficult, and it may well have disconcerted Vice-Admiral Penn, when his sixteen-year-old son William, returning from college, where he had become a Quaker, greeted the Admiral with the words: "I am much pleased, friend, to find thee in good health"; but when the currency of social intercourse has become inflated, it needs to be strengthened with the precious metal of sincerity. In the over-ceremonious eighteenth century Voltaire expressed his great pleasure in the deliberate and accurate speech and the natural manners of an old Quaker on whom he called.

George Fox believed in the value of communal worship, but that such worship should be perfectly free and spontaneous. He would have no paid preachers. Friends met in a convenient meeting-house and spoke, or refrained from speaking, as the spirit moved them. A friend might pray, tell a story, perhaps two friends would speak at the same time, each continuing so long as the spirit moved him, while other friends sat quiet, looking before them. Or they might all sit half an hour or more in silence, when of a sudden the spirit would come upon some of them, and they would be seized with tremors.

Other religious societies of such loose organisation have either evaded the principles of their founders and introduced a machinery of organisation, or they have failed to survive. The Quakers, however, have preserved their constitutional anarchy unimpaired, and the sect shows every sign of vitality. The most distinctive of the nonconformists, they make little effort to gain proselytes, but a member of a Quaker family rarely leaves the sect, and until recently a Quaker would rarely marry a non-Quaker. The absence of a salaried ministry specially marks them off from other sects, and whereas many chapel-goers will readily transfer their allegiance from the Baptist to the Methodist or from the Methodist to the Congregational chapel, they consider the Friends' meeting-house, like the Jewish synagogue, as something quite different, scarcely to be entered without an introduction.

The absence of a professional ministry saved Quakerism from the Jesuolatry which has characterised evangelicalism. The Protestant minister, being no sacrificing priest, has had to justify his office by his powers of oratory. Even here his field was much restricted by solofideist doctrine, for if good works are useless for salvation, hortatory injunctions lose much of their force. The preacher could, however, enlarge upon the torments of the damned, for thus a state of mind is induced, especially amongst a crowd, to which there readily succeeds "une sorte de pâmoison provoquée par le sentiment de terreur," as Father Piette calls it—the agony of terror is followed by a purging wave of contrition, and this again by a beatific calm, in which the poor sinner feels that he is forgiven, that he is saved. "I've got it," he shouts; he dances for joy; he twitches all over; he faints in a rigid trance. But the memory of the *pâmoison* grows dim; the saved sinner slides back into the old ways, and begins to doubt the reality of a salvation which has not changed his conduct. *The Pilgrim's Progress*, which became a children's Bible in evangelical homes, has dramatised in unforgettable imagery these alternations between hope and despair which Bunyan has detailed in his autobiography, the record of an almost weekly soaring into bliss or plunging into despair according to the text upon which his eye lit when he opened his Bible.

Bunyan worked out his salvation alone with his Bible; many found comfort in the assurances of a favourite preacher, or sought to recapture the ecstasy of an early *pâmoison* in rousing hymns:

> There is a fountain filled with blood
>   Drawn from Immanuel's veins;
> And sinners plunged beneath that flood
>   Lose all their guilty stains.

Evangelistic preachers became salvation salesmen with the technique of the quack doctor, their business being, as an American life-changer recently put it, to sell Christ. Instead of the Sermon on the Mount, they offered men their specific, Jesus-on-the-Cross who had made a bargain (Calvin's *contrat*) with his father that his suffering should be placed to the credit of all sinners who believed in him. The Protestants who had charged Catholics with the worship of images, substituted the single idol of a miraculously redeeming Jesus.

The absence of professional teachers soon caused "the preaching of the blood" to decline amongst the Friends. Their worship approached more closely to the Hindu ideal, being contemplative rather than personal; or, in terms of Christian theology, they did not exalt the Second Person of the Trinity to the neglect of the Third. Thus, at an early stage some Quakers showed a tendency towards Unitarianism. It was the heresy of Arius with a difference, for while Arius denied that the Son was of the same nature as the Father, these Quakers held that Jesus merely manifested in a high or a supreme degree the divine which is in all men. Such doctrine was more than heresy, for it touched the fundamental Christian verities. When, therefore, James Nayler, a former quartermaster in Cromwell's army, entered Bristol on horseback attended by seven followers who shouted, "Hosanna! Holy, holy! Lord God of Sabaoth!" he and his followers were brought before Parliament charged with blasphemy. The proceedings of this long trial show that the accused was neither a fanatic nor a madman. The sincerity of his answers, having the unseizable quality of truth, produced upon the court the same kind of disintegrating effect as had been produced upon the Jewish tribunals by the blasphemy trial recorded in the Gospels. Asked whether he claimed to be the son of God, he replied: "I do not deny that I am the son of God, and have many brethren!" Asked whether he had accepted the worship of his followers, he replied: "Not as a creature, but if they give it to Christ within me, he hath a kingdom of which thou wottest not." The Presbyterian divines were maddened by answers which cut the ground from institutional religion, but Nayler's sincerity affected individuals much as the answers of his prototype had done. Like the Roman governor and the soldier at the cross, one or two military members of the Parliament saw no fault in him, and it was nearly two weeks before Parliament reached the finding that Nayler was guilty of blasphemy. He was sentenced to be whipped from

Westminster to the City, to be branded in the forehead with "B" for blasphemer, to have his tongue bored with a red-hot iron, and to be whipped through the streets of Bristol before serving a sentence of two years hard labour.

From the Restoration of the Stuarts until the Hanoverians were firmly seated on the throne, men of any definite religious views, especially those in holy orders, could hardly escape a period of discomfort, if they lived long enough. Loyalty to the Church of England as by law established became synonymous with loyalty to the governing power, and an oath of loyalty to the Church was exacted from the king no less than from the least official. "No Popery" was still a powerful slogan, but hatred of Puritan tyranny was nearly as prevalent as the fear of a Catholic reaction. Cromwell's saints had been as intolerant as violent ideologues always are of all communal festivities rooted in the past. Christmas itself had been suppressed for a time on the pretext that it was popish.

With the restoration of Charles II the Puritan party naturally suffered most. Test Acts excluded from public employment those who would not conform to the usages of the Establishment; clergymen ejected from their livings for unorthodox teaching were not allowed to come within five miles of any town where they might have gained a living by teaching. James II, whose genuine spirit of tolerance has scarcely received justice on account of his Catholic sympathies, would have been willing to end this persecution if he could have struck a bargain giving the Roman Catholics liberty of worship, but most Dissenters preferred to suffer persecution themselves rather than agree that Papists should be exempt from persecution. For a long time they nourished resentment against the Quakers, the first religious sect to advocate tolerance, because the Quakers expressed approval of James's Declaration of Indulgence.

When the bloodless revolution of 1688 set a Calvinist upon the throne, the Puritans expected to come into their own; but in all the vicissitudes of the previous hundred years the

Church of England had been growing in strength. While Englishmen would have found it difficult to explain what their Church was, they knew very well what it was not. It was neither Papist nor Ranting. The fine Elizabethan English of its prayers and collects gave it dignity, and had won for it a place in the affections of the people. What could be more sweetly reasonable, more calculated to inspire loyalty in the hearts of those who heard them Sunday after Sunday than the invocation at morning prayer to the dearly beloved brethren followed by the general confession of pastor and people. Besides, the Church of England did not hector people with its doctrine. Before the days of Cromwell Bishop Chillingworth had laid down what was involved in accepting her Articles: "For the Church of England I am persuaded that there is no error in it which may necessitate or warrant any man to disturb the peace or renounce the communion of it. This, in my opinion, is all that is intended by subscription." As Edward Dowden has put it, the Church "had a unity of life, if not an absolute unity of idea. . . . It was of the nature of a federal union between groups of believers in a common Christianity, whose diverging opinions in detail are wholly incapable of logical conciliation." Just as in 1928 millions of Englishmen who never went to church rose up to prevent the bishops from changing their prayer-book, so by the reign of William III Englishmen were already beginning to feel, even if they were dissenters, that the Church of England was their Church. Of the seven bishops who went to prison under James II because they were not Catholic enough, five refused the oath to his successor because they were not Calvinist enough, and with some hundreds of clergy lost their employment as non-jurors.

During Anne's reign anti-Puritan feeling still ran high. Dr. Sacheverell, a sort of Pemberton-Billing, roused nation-wide enthusiasm with the cry, "The Church in danger," and Daniel Defoe wrote—probably with his tongue in his cheek, but it answered to a prevalent sentiment—the pamphlet *The shortest way with the Dissenters*:

"The time is come which all good men have wished for,
that the gentlemen of England may serve the Church of
England, now they are protected and encouraged by a
Church of England Queen. . . . If one severe law were
made, and punctually executed, that whoever was found
at a conventicle should be banished the nation, and the
preacher be hanged, we should soon see the end of the
tale. One age would make us all one again. . . . It is
cruelty to kill a snake or a toad in cold blood, but the
poison in their nature makes it a charity to our neighbours
to destroy these creatures."

Such violent sentiments were largely induced by fears
concerning the future government of the country. Anne had
no children; many High Churchmen were Jacobite, while
Dissenters were believed to be covenanting republicans. As
the Hanoverian dynasty became secure, the feeling against
Dissenters and Catholics relaxed. A Toleration Act was
passed and the harsher laws were allowed to become
obsolete. Moreover, in the eighteenth century men adopted
the convenient practice of distinguishing philosophy from
religion, and metaphysical speculation became almost free,
so long as it was not introduced into the pulpit. Those
who might have troubled the Church with doctrinal conun-
drums worked out their wisdom in university chairs. The
Church was left free to develop its own rhythm as an
integrating element in English rural life, while the sects,
each pivoted about a favourite text from which they derived
their particular mantras of salvation, were becoming
atrophied, as narrowing groups of peculiar peoples.

Meanwhile the first stages in the mechanisation of life
were causing new towns to spring up in the neighbourhood
of coal and iron. The owners of this new wealth lived far
from districts rendered hideous by its production; those who
got it from under the earth came to be regarded as a sub-
human species. Methodism, which now numbers more
adherents than all other English sects combined, achieved
its success because it met the needs of this new population,

but its founder, John Wesley, was the antithesis of a non-conformist preacher. Devoted to the Anglican Church into which he was born, John Wesley resembled the religious zealots whose names appear in the Catholic calendar of saints, and, like most Catholic saints, John Wesley had parents who were both of ancient lineage, for while few men of genius or heretics have been of gentle birth, the majority of the canonised have family trees which would please any college of heralds. Unquestioning loyalty to his prince was a mark of the medieval gentleman, and the single-minded devotion which leads to sainthood is more often to be found in the highly bred, while the wide and intimate relation with reality which is the mark of a genius is more likely to be found in the man of the people. It has been suggested that if the Catholic Church should select a Protestant for canon-isation, the man to be thus honoured would be John Wesley, and most Catholics believe that if John Wesley had been born a Catholic he would, like Loyola, whom he so much resembled, have formed an Order within his own Church.

Indeed the movement which Wesley launched was essen-tially a counter-reformation to Puritanism within the Church of England, and Methodism would not have broken away from the parent Church if Anglican prelates had been gifted with some of the sense for reality shown in the deliberations of the Council of Trent. John Wesley was the Father of the whole movement of social progress which was inspired by the Evangelical Revival within and without the Church of England, "the modern watershed of Anglo-Saxon history," as Dr. Bready has called it.

The abolition of the slave trade at a cost to England of over £20,000,000, prison reform, the great Protestant missions, popular education, factory and child welfare legislation are some of the benefits directly attributable to the movement initiated by Wesley. Even in his day the Church was stung into initiating Charity Schools, but felt it necessary to defend this action: "Because Providence has thought good to place some in a helpless and forlorn situation, shall we deny them the consolation of knowing from the operation of their own minds that they are reasonable creatures? . . . The objectors need be under no fears lest, by the operation of these schools, there should be no dregs in the community, no bottom class to do the labour and drudgery of the public."

Above all, by his gospel of divine love, by preaching that the children of a heavenly father are brothers, Wesley gave the first impulse to the co-operative spirit of the wage earners, so that they achieved social progress by peaceful means instead of by revolution which has always substituted a new tyranny for the old.

The son of High Church[1] parents, Wesley was brought up on the Arminian Jeremy Taylor and the Catholic Pascal. "Whatsoever thy hand findeth to do, do it with all thy might," became—despite its context in the Book of Ecclesiastes—his favourite text. When he became the leader of the "Holy Club" at Oxford, visiting prisoners and the relief of distress formed at least as large a part of their activities as Bible-reading and prayer.

By the impulse which has so often prompted the enemies of a movement to invent the name under which it has become famous, Wesley's contemporaries derisively nicknamed his religious society the Methodists. The Oxford of the Wesleys was, indeed, more than usually zealous in observing the university statutes inversely to the sense in which they are printed, and according to Amhurst's account the many theological students played their part in maintaining the prevalent tone:

"I have observed a great many of these transitory foplings, who came to the university with their fathers, rusty old country farmers, in linsey-wolsey coats, greasy sun-burnt heads of hair, clouted shoes, yarn stockings, flapping hats, with silver hat-bands, and long muslin neckcloths run with red at the bottom. A month or two afterwards I have met them with bob-wigs and new shoes,

---

[1] The name was just coming into use, but it should be remembered that it did not then imply belief in Transubstantiation or in a sacrificing priesthood.

Oxford-cut; a month or two more after this, they appeared in druggett cloth and worsted stockings; then in tye-wigs and ruffles; and then in silk gowns; till by degrees they were metamorphosed into complete Smarts, and damned the old country putts, their fathers, with twenty foppish airs and gesticulations.

"Two or three years afterwards, I have met the same persons in gowns and cassocks, walking with demure looks and holy leer; so easy (as a learned divine said upon a quite different occasion) is the transition from dancing to preaching, and from the bowling-green to the pulpit."

These young products of a cynicism which had followed upon a bloody conflict of ideologies were soon to be rulers in church and state. That Wesley's movement broke from the Church which he loved was due to the sceptical spirit in which the prelates regarded his work, until he was driven to "take the world for his parish."

When, after a brief visit to the new colony of Georgia, Wesley preached from London pulpits and founded Societies similar to the Oxford Holy Club, he soon fell foul of the bishops who had extremely sensitive noses for "enthusiasm," which they defiantly declared to be incompatible with the practice of revealed religion. The statesmanlike prelates avoided the step of pronouncing judicial sentence against John Wesley, but he gradually found the Anglican pulpits closing to him. Early in 1739 he took the step which marks the beginning of Methodism as the greatest missionary effort since the early middle ages.

The most eloquent member of the Holy Club had been George Whitefield, in many ways Wesley's counterpart. Wesley was short, spare and ascetically handsome; Whitefield, son of a country tavern-keeper, was tall, full-bodied and radiantly handsome. Wesley was an Arminian touched with Lutheran fervour; Whitefield was pure Calvinist, and although he gave of his eloquence to the crowds he was best known as principal private chaplain to the Countess of Huntingdon, "whose sole purpose in life," says Canon

Overton, "was to bring about a revival of religion among the upper classes." In her London house Chesterfield, Horace Walpole and members of the Hell-Fire Club appraised Whitefield's descriptions of hell fire, and in her chapel at Bath bishops listened to his sermons from a curtained recess nicknamed Nicodemus's corner.

Whitefield, less nice than Wesley in his methods, had preached in the open air at Moorfields, and just when the churches were definitely closing to the Wesleys he was preaching to the miners near Bristol. He invited John Wesley to Bristol, and Wesley went reluctantly, being never in full sympathy with Whitefield's doctrine or practice. If Whitefield's teaching were true, he wrote in 1740, "All preaching is useless; with or without it the elect are saved. The non-elect are infallibly damned. . . . Man is led by this doctrine to treat with contempt and indifference those whom he supposes to be reprobate of God." Of imputed righteousness he wrote: "The imputed righteousness of Christ is a phrase not scriptural. It has done immense hurt. I have had abundant proof that the frequent use of this unnecessary phrase, instead of 'furthering men's progress in vital holiness,' has made men satisfied without any holiness at all; yea, and encouraged them to work all uncleanness with greediness." Of the open-air preaching he wrote: "I could scarcely reconcile myself to this strange way of preaching in the fields . . . having been all my life (till very lately) so tenacious of every point relating to decency and order, that I should have thought the saving of souls almost a sin, if it had not been done in a church."

When Wesley saw the tears make white gutters on the miner's cheeks—Whitefield's phrase—he consented to carry on this work of Whitefield who was called to London. We are now approaching that dark time of the Industrial Revolution when the average age of a worker (reduced by the high mortality amongst child-workers) was twenty-two years, that of a pauper being more than twice as long. When Wesley told the English untouchables that Jesus had loved each and all of them to the point of dying for their sins on

the cross, the tears ran nearly as easily as when Father
Claver met the shiploads of African slaves with the same
message on their landing at Carthagena. We live in a
country whose industrial areas were re-Christianised by
Methodism, and it is difficult to realise that the wretches
who had been removed for two generations from the land
knew less about Christ than an average council schoolchild of
to-day knows about Buddha. "Wretch" is the word by which
they were called in a period when a young lady returned
from church to her mother crying with anger because the
parson had said she was of the same race as the labourers.

Wesley rode hundreds of thousands of miles on horseback,
preached tens of thousands of sermons, an average of 3.3 per
diem for fifty-five years. Methodism went multiplicando;
more than ten thousand chapels, millions of souls and millions
of money for missions, schools, Sunday-schools, halls and
chapels. In due course there were Methodist millionaires.
For Wesley had what is called a business sense, the gift for
picking up and applying those suggestions for organisation
which are always forthcoming, when a movement has been
launched.

The basis of Methodist organisation, its unit-cell, is the
class of ten plus a leader, which originated in money difficulties at Bristol. The leader has to collect a penny each
week from the members of his class, a duty which gives him
an opportunity for checking up on their general conduct.
Methodist organisation is non-elective. "As long as I live,"
said Wesley, "the people shall have no share in choosing
either Stewards or Leaders. . . . We are no republicans and
never intend to be." Methodism attracted the frugal man
with a taste for business; its machinery reflected the spirit of
the commercial age which was beginning, and Wesley had
misgivings before he died: "In the nature of things," he
wrote at the age of eighty-three, "a religious revival cannot
be lasting. For the practice of religion necessarily implies
industry and frugality; and these cannot but produce riches.
Now when riches increase, they are accompanied by pride,
anger and love of the world in all its forms."

Almost before Wesley's body was cold, Methodism began to split into groups. In the middle of the nineteenth century there were some thirty churches calling themselves Methodist; there are less of them now, for Methodism has proved to be almost as easily coalescive as it was at first fissiparous.

The most important Methodist schism, now healed, was that of the Primitive Methodists who split on the attitude of the parent Church to the working-class movement.[1] The Chartists and Luddites both adopted the Methodist system of penny a week contributions with class-leaders to collect the funds, as well as the post-Wesley Methodist practice—which became a leading feature of American negro Methodism—of camp meetings whose participants maintained their religious or political fervour for days in the open. Moreover, the political class-leaders, at a time when Methodism provided the only culture available to the wage-slave, were often practising Methodists who opened the political meeting with prayer and closed it with a hymn. Thus Methodist organisation provided the proscribed workers' associations with the necessary *esprit de corps* when their members were still liable to be carried to Botany Bay on the word of an informer that they had taken an oath of association.

The attitude of Methodism's autocratic oligarchy, the Conference, to the preachers who assisted the Chartists shows how by the time a generation has grown up within a movement the movement has little left but the name. It takes but three generations, they say, to make a gentleman, and the members of a Church have almost as much the sense of belonging to a traditional body after one as after twenty centuries. A Methodist child would feel indeed that he was living amongst people who had a higher standard of holiness than the indifferent Anglicans, most of whom could never get to heaven, whereas he had a ninety-per-cent. chance, if he observed the practices of the warm little world about him with its pleasant Sunday afternoons for men, its sewing-meetings for women. While the injunctions to temperance

---

[1] See *Methodism and the Working-class Movements of England: 1800–1855*, by Robert F. Wearmouth.

and frugality retained their force, those relating to the more
inconvenient virtues were so much stretched by human
ingenuity that, like perished elastic, they soon hung long and
limp. Moreover, while Wesley's message was essentially to
the down-trodden poor, the offices of Methodism soon
provided employment for the new industrial magnates.
These, having no part in the government of a landed church,
could exercise spiritual patronage on their election as choice
laymen to Conference, while Methodist practice trained
them in the new technique of pluralities, whereby they
amassed directorates in railways, buildings and finance
instead of prebends and lay rectorships.

Thus we find that while the field-preachers were guiding
the first halting steps of the Labour Movement, Conference
was wearying Home Secretaries with resolutions condemning
"those who fear not to speak evil of dignitaries," expressing
more than Podsnapian "zeal for the support of our unrivalled
Constitution," gratitude for "unexampled civil and religious
privileges," and "attachment to the person and family of
our beloved Monarch." Many of the Radical preachers
were expelled by Conference; others voluntarily severed their
connexion with men whose parrot-cry, "Render unto
Cæsar," covered the fact that they had nothing to render
unto God, and who "not content with patching up Toryism,
throw the blame on Divine Providence for the widespread
depression." But Wesley's impulse was not yet spent, and the
Radical preachers formed the Primitive Methodist Church.

The work of the Primitive Methodists has been done, and
led by their wealthiest member, the late Sir Robert Perks,
they recently became re-united with the Wesleyan Methodists.

There is one offshoot of Methodism which must probably
remain an organisation of militant Christianity outside any
church. It was appropriate that William Booth who was
converted in Wesley Chapel, Nottingham, and was for a
time a Methodist minister should, with his wife, have been
the subject of the following minute by the Annual Methodist
Conference of Cornwall: "The perambulations of the male
and female Booth were considered, and it was resolved to

pray Conference to forbid the use of their chapels to Mr. and Mrs. Booth." The prayer was granted, and soon afterwards the Primitive Methodists followed suit, so that the houses of God built as the result of a similar religious revival little more than a generation before were now closed to the spiritual descendants of John Wesley. Nor was it long before the Salvation Army invented "the Freezer," as their second general, Bramwell Booth, playfully called his device for extinguishing uncomfortable enthusiasts. In all organisations relating to the activities of the human mind the problem is the same; Vincent van Gogh wrote to his brother, when he was dismissed his employment as preacher to Dutch miners:

> "I must tell you that it is with evangelists as with artists. There is an old academic school, often detestable, tyrannical, the accumulation of horrors, men who wear a cuirass, a steel armour of prejudices and conventions; those people, when they are at the head of affairs, dispose of positions, and by a rotary system they try to keep their protégées in their places, and to exclude other men."

The coalescive movement within the Free Churches has extended to the Anglican Church; committees of prelates and divines have passed resolutions tending towards mutual recognition, and it is not unlikely that if another sovereign is crowned at Westminster a Free Church dignitary or two will handle certain articles of the regalia. The average nonconformist minister could probably subscribe to the thirty-nine Articles more heartily than the average ordinand.

But the real difference between church and chapel has little to do with such matters; it has to do rather with the manner in which different types of Englishmen like to express their religious life. Revivalism, for instance, is alien to the Anglican Church, for it depends upon the essentially Protestant idea of an instantaneous conversion when, at the sight of the Crucified in the moment of faith, the burden of guilt drops from Christian's shoulders into the pit behind him. The Anglican, like the Catholic, keeps worship and preaching distinct. To the worshipper he is the impersonal priest; as preacher he does not play upon the religious emotions. To the evangelist preaching, prayer and hymn are all alike means of bringing the penitent to the mercy-seat.

It might gratify some Free Church clergy that their Orders should be recognised by Anglicans who are themselves recognised by eastern bishops who, in turn, are recognised by Rome as possessing valid Orders. But if their nonconformist congregations suspect that their religious practices may be interfered with, any amalgamation of Churches would be followed by a fresh schism.

SNOBBERY

BY

REBECCA WEST

SNOBBERY

SNOBBERY is the eternally comic attempt of humanity to solve an eternally tragic problem. It is eternally comic because of the vast disparity between the complexity of the problem and the simplicity of the means man has at his disposal for solving it. The problem is eternally tragic because its existence argues that the universe is not favourably disposed to man, that when he lives he is working in a medium detached from him and hostile to him, and that the purpose of creation is not plain.

It is asked that a scheme should be devised for ensuring efficient leadership for a community which is more complicated than the peasant state. In a village a number of men work in identical conditions, which, since they are largely influenced by the weather, are for the most part unpredictable and make useful tests of initiative and endurance. Hence it is easy for ability to declare itself and gain a reputation in the surrounding countryside. In a nation made up of villages such ability will never find its own interests separate from those of the community; and when any particular exemplar of it comes to an end of usefulness the continuous process that had produced him is ready with a successor. But the minute society departs from this simplicity it becomes more and more difficult for it to choose leaders, guarantee their integrity, or procure their permanence.

The trouble begins when warfare becomes elaborate and a country must needs have professional armies under military leaders who are specialists. The leader must win his dignity by the possession of certain talents which can be demonstrated only on rare occasions, not possible to be witnessed by the whole community, and powerfully affected by mere luck. Once the dignity of leadership is won, the leader is bound to be tempted to blackmail the rest of the community, because he means security to them, and also to demand that it gives him wealth and privilege beyond his deserts. His interests, therefore, become distinct from those of the nation and even inimical to them. This creates a state of insecurity in which it is essential to eliminate all factors of disorder that can be attacked without causing still more disorder. Hence competition for leadership is forbidden, and power descends from father to son in the form of a monarchy far more alarming than the kingship of a simple tribe, where the temptations to loss of integrity are fewer and the calls upon ability less exacting. This is obviously a false step, considering that the prime necessity of leadership is ability, and that heredity is abominably capricious. The horrible researches of Mendel have shown that heredity is the victim of compulsion neurosis, just as Dr. Johnson was, and brings down its rod on this and that generation to strike it with favour or disfavour simply to gratify some arithmetical whimsy, instead of going about its business sanely and seeing that if a man is an admirable Chairman of the St. Pancras Borough Council he shall beget admirable Chairmen of the St. Pancras Borough Council. Therefore it appears that in the name of security we choose leaders whom we need only in order that they should bring us security, on a principle that makes it doubtful indeed whether they have the intelligence necessary for procuring us security. As Leviticus so tartly says of another matter, this is confusion. The situation grows alarming.

It is, indeed, very alarming by the time we come to Chairmen of the St. Pancras Borough Council. We are caught in the barbed-wire entanglement of the modern capitalist state, which is but a collection of hostile sovereign interests loosely united by a sense, which may become very weak indeed if international social and economic interests are sufficiently strong, that they are benefited by the continued existence of that state in its present form. The sovereignty in such a state is split up among townsfolk, country-folk, industrialists, landowners, workmen, politicians, bureaucrats, and a score of other orders of beings, as

well as among residues of other orders that have been powerful in the past, and still have enough prestige to make useful
bargaining counters. The cause that rendered suspect the
leadership of the first professional soldiers renders the leadership of these a thousand times more suspect. They gain their
successes in fields not open to the inspection of the community
as a whole, where luck, which in modern conditions is more
likely than on a medieval battlefield to take the form of
finding a fifth ace up one's sleeve, can play a decisive part.
Any mistakes that thereby creep into the system are per-
petuated with a unique firmness, for the hereditary nature of
power derived from monarchy is not nearly so adhesive as
the hereditary power derived from wealth. There are legal
reasons why a king can be removed from the throne, all
connected with the efficient prosecution of his job; and he
can of course be jockeyed into an abdication by any politician who is clever enough to appeal to the visceral prejudices of the mob. There are no legal reasons at all by
which a millionaire industrialist or banker can be separated
from his fortune on the grounds of inefficiency. Our leaders
therefore tend to be more and more obviously the casual
harvest, tares and all, gleaned from a number of historically
interesting beds. The rise of the Socialist movement
threatens this arrangement at least to the extent of changing
its personnel. But a Socialist leader is as open as any other
leader in the modern world to the objection that his interests
are not identical with those of the whole community. He is
fighting, and would be a fool if he were not, on another
field. He has to fight the employing class, which has to a
very large degree dismissed the welfare of the community
from its calculations; and it must be remembered that when
the Germans marched through Belgium the French and the
English had to trespass there too. The Socialist also, however much he desires to enforce order, provokes disorder,
because the insufferable prospect of new aspirants to
leadership coming to bring further confusion to our confused
society rouses the same panic in the ordinary man that led
to the invention of modern monarchy; and this time it

leads to the reckless exaggeration of the caution of conserva-
tism, the determination to stabilise all present conditions of
society, no matter how unstable, which is known as fascism.
The questions ask themselves: Dear God, is it possible that
we have got ourselves into such a hopeless muddle that we
permit ourselves to be led by persons who have other con-
siderations far dearer to them than our security? Is it
possible that this is not even our fault, that it was bound to
happen once we left peasant simplicity and embarked on
the enterprise of modern civilisation? A horrid question
this. If the answer comes out wrong it suggests that maybe
the universe was not made to be a soft cushion to the human
rump. But it is followed by a question more horrid still.
We learn in church what the heart teaches us in infancy,
that it is virtue and not strength which should be obeyed.
Our age has insisted on liberty to deride its leaders, if not to
depose them. We know what they are. Are we doing right
in obeying them?

These questions asked themselves in the last days of the
Roman Empire, that age which so strongly resembled our
own. At times the persistence with which they were silently
asked by its citizens and slaves and the other silence which
announced that they were not being answered seemed to
make the tottering edifice of Rome rock under the feet as if
there had roared forth some noise louder than all noise. It
was convenient that at this time an influx of captured
Asiatics spread among the people the religion of Zoro-
astrianism, and its offshoot, the worship of Mithras. These
explained neatly that no man need ever doubt his leaders.
According to these doctrines all souls existed before their
birth in the firmament and came down to earth after a tour
through the constellations, during which they absorbed the
qualities of whatever planets into whose orbits their destinies
led them. Those who passed within the influence of the
Sun, the Lord of the Heavens, naturally acquired divinity
and became Lords of Earth. After the Emperors accepted
these beliefs they officially took the titles of *pius*, *felix*, and
invictus. The Emperor had to be *pius* lest an outraged

Heaven should reverse his destiny; he was *felix* because
Heaven had chosen him for his high destiny; and he was
invictus because his defeat of the Imperial enemies proved that
Heaven had so chosen him. His legitimate authority came
to him not by birth or by a vote of the senate, but from the
divine powers; and the proof of that was that the divine
powers did not take it away from him. If they did, one was
not at a loss; it meant the signs of favour were transferred to
someone else. All this worked beautifully, except that not a
word of it was true, and that whenever reality took the not
uncommon form of failure and desolation it went up in
powder like a kicked toadstool. It was bound to be super-
seded by Christianity, which taught man not to hope for
order in any society here on earth, either in respect of leadership or anything else, but to establish order within himself
and trust in the kingdom of heaven. But it fulfilled a
purpose in the case of people who could not make that re-
nunciation, who could not resign themselves to the harsh
truth that man's reason is not powerful enough to control
his environment, and that therefore he cannot be certain
of material security.

To-day we have exactly the same kind of people, and
neither Zoroaster nor Mithras comes to aid them. We
know too much about the stars to believe that they bestow
virtue on souls that circulate among them, or rather we think
we do. Actually no astronomer is in a position to say that
they do not, but a general sense that it is improbable has got
about. Such people therefore have invented the religion of
snobbery, in which, in its purest form, the glory of the leaders
is certified as authentic and deserved, because grace and
greatness have been conferred on them by their ancestors'
gametes, which are held to be sacred because of their power
to confer grace and greatness. The elements of luck and
opportunity are dismissed; and the question whether
success cannot sometimes be commanded by anti-social
characters is not raised, even when the doctrine is expanded
and it is held that a man who is very rich deserves to be
honoured, because he would not be rich unless he deserved

to be honoured. This is a comfortable doctrine, if one is a leader or if one is not. The Duchess can shut her eyes and see glory and grace travelling from loin to loin of her ancestors, not with the usual dancing speed of pleasure but at the rate of a cortège. The Duchess's companion smiles in her doze, knowing that she will not be trodden down by the mob, since during the passing of a cortège the police have the streets under perfect control. As the loins are indelicate the endopsychic censors of both ladies blot them out and they are left enjoying the best kind of beatification, which is wholly without details and therefore cannot be criticised. But the doctrine is more than comfortable, it is useful, both to the individual and to the state. It is best, of course, to learn the grim lesson of the saints: that to be fortunate is an accident, that to be obscure is an accident, that never can one make a satisfactory design out of such temporal matters, that always one must steel oneself to live according to certain principles certified by tradition and our hearts as making for grace, even if they make for earthly disgrace. It is better than nothing, however, to feel that one should do well because one is who one is, and for the same reason will be able to do well. It saves the well-born and the well-to-do from the obvious ingratitude of not repaying the community for the sweets it has thrust upon them. But it also tempts the idiot to set up his lack of wits against the standards determined by culture. Ozymandias is not in it for insolence compared with the British Minister's wife and her water-colours.

The blackest score against snobbery is, however, that it is not true. Zoroaster was telling fairy-tales, and so is the Duchess. The constellations are not a rigid system pegging out the destiny of man. Not a gipsy, not a will-of-the-wisp, not a butterfly can match them in caprice. It takes a star to slip down half the universe in a hundredth of a second and exchange brilliance for blackness and annihilation. Neither are the aristocratic a solid framework of excellence over which the growing civilisation can be trained. Let us take Viscount Cecil, who though not a snob himself would be taken by any snob as evidence of his faith. When we regard his wisdom, stooping under the burden of his saintliness, it does not seem credible that in the passage of his line from the great Lord Burghley there were three centuries of obscurity which at one point darkened to such night that after a visit to Hatfield Mrs. Elizabeth Montagu pronounced that "All the noble Lord's noble delight is in horses and strumpets." This is perhaps even more remarkable than the behaviour of the shooting star. But not only is race uncertain in its issue, it is also true, as Lord Tennyson says, that "God fulfils Himself in many ways lest one good custom should corrupt the world." Jane Austen, who is the supreme morphologist of English snobbery as Proust was of French snobbery, often remarks this terrible contention between old and new sovereignties. Only the ass complains against her that she writes nothing of the Napoleonic wars which shadowed her age; she often sets down sentences which mirror the peculiarities of that age and none other. There is a deal of history in the remark of Sir Walter Elliott in *Persuasion* that the navy was offensive to him as "bringing persons of obscure birth into undue distinction, and raising men to honours which their fathers and grandfathers never dreamt of." There is a deal of history in his inability to recall the Mr. Wentworth mentioned by Mr. Shepherd, and his coolness when the right man came into his mind. "Wentworth? Oh, ay, Mr. Wentworth, the curate of Monkford. You misled me by the term *gentleman*. I thought you were speaking of some man of property: Mr. Wentworth was nobody, I remember; quite unconnected; nothing to do with the Strafford family. One wonders how the names of many of our nobility became so common." There is a deal of history in Mrs. Elton's complaint about the family at Maple Grove, upstarts who annoyed her brother and sister, who were themselves upstarts of a larger growth. "People of the name of Tupman very lately settled there, and encumbered with many low connections, but giving themselves immense airs, and expecting to be on a footing with the old established families. A year and a half is the very utmost that they can have lived at West Hall, and how they got their fortune nobody knows. They came from Birmingham, which is not a place to promise much, you know, Mr. Weston. One has not great hopes from Birmingham." In fact the nineteenth century was jostling the eighteenth century out of existence, and there is never an age that can be trusted not to devour its yesterday. Not only is the structure rickety, but the ground on which it is built trembles perpetually.

It is for this reason that the mark of the snob who is of the sovereign breed is rigidity. He stands as if he were already dead and had been stuffed; his female, it is to be noted, wears the tiara, of all ornaments the most difficult to balance. He does not speak or move if he can help it, so that he shall not consent to the passage of time to a lesser excellence. That is why there are so few good snob stories that are true. There is one perfect snob story, but it is so good that, while it is supremely comic, for the reason that snobbery itself is comic, because it reveals an imbecilely inadequate attempt to cope with tragedy, it is also horrible because the tragedy was so great. When the Archduke Franz Ferdinand and Sophie Chotek, the wife whom he had insisted on marrying morganatically since the Habsburg family laws forbade him marrying a mere Countess, were murdered at Sarajevo in 1914, the old Emperor Franz Josef, who had been greatly shocked by the marriage, remarked to his adjutant, "God cannot be flouted. A Higher Power has restored an order of things which I was unable to maintain." The Great War then broke out. But it takes circumstances like that, which are as unique as *King Lear* in the imaginative world, to surprise the snob into a demonstration of his essence. He can be more easily seen than heard, and every now and then he betrays by some action what he is thinking. The eighteenth century Marquis of Abercorn seems rarely to have said anything ridiculous, largely because he rarely said anything at all, but it was impossible to keep secret his practice of insisting that the housemaids who made his bed should wear white kid gloves. That practice speaks of terror, sister of hypochondria; and indeed fear is a characteristic of the snob, save when he is isolated from reality by an unusual degree of stupidity, which sometimes indeed induces a lovely content-ment, featureless like an unclouded summer sky. But the least degree of intelligence warns the snob of sovereign breed how much he has to fear from time, his own corruption, and rivalry; and that is why he calls into being the other sort of snob, the snob who is not by birth or fortune among the nation's rulers but finds his ecstasy in contemplating them.

This other kind of snob is as uneasy as the object of his worship. In this country we know a great deal about his unhappiness, because many of our writers have belonged to that category, and it is the strength and weakness of English literature that our writers think aloud in their writings. Hence those who have been snobs have not, as French and Italian and Spanish literary snobs have done, converted their entranced views of the rich and the great as the wise and delicate into works of art; they have carried on in print their internal debate as to the validity of the theory of snobbery. There is no foreign novel, I think, in which an author gets into such a sweat over the matter as Thackeray in *Vanity Fair*. In that book the case against snobbery, against both kinds of snobs, particularly from the moral point of view, is put with the extreme of savage wit. The Crawleys are put down for what they are worth, the lecherous and miserly old lout Sir Pitt, his two sons, one whole prig and one half fool and half rogue, Miss Crawley, the mean and bullying old heiress, and her circle of toadies. He is harsher still about the Steynes, and it is asked whether there can be any reason to give respect to such human rubbish as this. Not less forcibly did Thackeray describe exactly what sort of respect was given them. Of George Osborne's father he wrote "Whenever he met a great man he grovelled before him and my-lorded him as only a free-born Briton can do. He came home and looked out his history in the Peerage; he introduced his name into his daily conversation; he bragged about his Lordship to his daughter. He fell down prostrate and basked in him as a Neapolitan beggar does in the sun." But throughout the book he himself writes and feels as a snob; and his snobbish feelings are concentrated on the character of Becky Sharp. Whenever she comes into his story he cannot control himself. He is tormented as if she were a living and breathing flesh-and-blood hussy who had forced herself into his study and was tempting him with her reprehensible charms. In his excitement he betrays that his snobbery is twofold. It is in part derived from the noble and traditional sources which spring from an ungovernable desire for order. That is proved by his curious assumption that a woman of strong acquisitive instincts like Becky would feel no affection for her child. This offers a curious parallellism to Tolstoy's assumption that a mother who fell in love with a man other than her husband would lose her affection for her child; for Tolstoy also was a ferocious snob. When he was a young man he inscribed in his diary a vow not to waste his time at balls dancing with women whose company was not socially advantageous to him, and his insistence on the superiority of peasants over all other classes in the community was a case of snobbery to end snobbery, since it put him in the position of rejecting all recognised elements of aristocracy and going one better. This desire, common to Tolstoy and Thackeray, that women who were deficient in one admirable quality should be deficient in the most admirable feminine quality of all, is obviously part of a wider desire for a completely tidy universe, where black is black and white is white; the universe, in fact, where the theory of snobbery would come true. Actually, as any experienced midwife or governess would have told the two authors in the event (the improbability of which throws a harsh light on the nature of literature) of their attempting to verify their theory, a woman with acquisitive instincts may rejoice in a child as yet another and peculiarly personal possession, a woman with strong passions may find her most sensuous delight in a child. One recognises the fatally unamenable quality of life, its refusal to fit into categories and to be predictable, which is the snob's despair.

But Thackeray's snobbery is in part derived from another source, and that new and not pleasant. It is not really

Becky Sharp's greed and cunning he resents. These please
him in her, as they often please men in their mistresses.
What makes him want to strike out at her with his pen and
invent new degradations for her was her effrontery in making
her way into the society of respectable people when she was
the daughter of a drunken artist and a ballet-dancer.   In the
passages where he describes her suffering insult from the
well-to-do, or better still from her servants, there is an exalta-
tion of a quite dreadful kind.   One sees blows being rained
on a hand that grips the side of a raft, one sees the bruised
fingers loosen and slip back into the water.   There is a fear
here that is to raise its head in a great deal of nineteenth
century literature.   It is to be seen in a peculiarly naïve form
in that curious book, Dean Farrar's *Eric, or Little by Little*.
When Eric runs away to sea, to escape the extraordinary
complications of life in a school where education is more
honoured in the breach than in the observance, the author
takes up a strange terror-stricken attitude towards the sailors.

"And there, in that swinging bed, where sleep seemed
impossible, and in which he was unpleasantly shaken
about when the ship rolled and pitched through the dark,
heaving discoloured waves, and with dirty men sleeping
round him at night, until the atmosphere of the forecastle
became like poison, hopelessly and helplessly sick, and
half-starved, the boy lay for two days.   The crew neglected
him shamefully.   It was nobody's business to wait on him,
and he could procure neither sufficient food nor any water;
they only brought him some grog to drink, which in his
weakness and sickness was nauseous to him as medicine.
. . . He felt very ill—he had no means of washing or
cleaning himself; no brush, or comb, or soap, or clean
linen; and even his sleep seemed unrefreshful when the
waking brought no change in his condition. And then
the whole life of the ship was odious to him.   His sense of
refinement was exquisitely keen, and now to be called
Bill, and kicked and cuffed about by these gross-minded
men, and to hear their rough, coarse, drunken talk, and

sometimes endure their still more intolerable patronage, filled him with deeply seated loathing. His whole soul rebelled and revolted from them all, and, seeing his fastidious pride, not one of them showed him the least glimpse of open kindness, though he observed that one of them did seem to pity him in his heart. . . . The homeward voyage was even more intolerable, for the cattle on board greatly increased the amount of necessary menial and disgusting work which fell to his share, as well as made the atmosphere of the close little schooner twice as poisonous as before. And to add to his miseries, his relations with the crew got more and more unfavourable, and began to reach their climax."

This is quite an innovation. It would be interesting to know what Queen Elizabeth or Defoe or Fielding or Jane Austen would have said if they had been read this passage and told that the book which contained it was to be put by prosperous English people into the hands of their children for over fifty years. (It was published in 1858, and even in the last ten years before the Great War it passed through five new editions.) Miss Austen would have had something very crisp to say about that phrase, "It was nobody's business to wait on him." There is a double unwholesomeness in the passage. There is a lack of virility in the prosperous boy; there is an artificial division between him and his poorer fellow-creatures. That is to say, he is unnaturally subject to fear, and what he fears is not the enemies of his group, but other members of his own group. He felt this fear not for lack of information about these other members. Charles Dickens and Charles Reade and Charles Kingsley were explaining to him as fast as they could go that the workers of the world were decent folk who were doing well under harsh treatment. But there was a painful situation that prevented a great many people from using this information. A certain number of well-to-do and educated people lived in towns on incomes derived either from professional activities or from invested capital. They thus lost the vitality of country life

and the knowledge of their fellow-men which comes of living
in small groups. They only saw those who were socially
beneath them under the dreadful aspect in which urban
civilisation of the nineteenth century disguised its poor, and
never got to know them well enough to penetrate that guise.
They thought the poor a wholly disgusting alien race, but
they suspected that incomes derived from such resources as
their own were too artificial to be completely reliable, and
they were exceedingly afraid of being cast down from their
advantageous position into poverty. They dreamed of a
community to consist solely of the aristocracy and themselves;
and any attempt of the poor to make themselves less poor
seemed a vicious effort to prevent that dream coming true
and to spread the black and stinking area of poverty.

This was the attitude of Matthew Arnold. Too few read
his works now, but one of those Brocken spectres which are
so common in literature, those shadows made in the form of
a man but having nothing of his substance, stalks the common
consciousness bearing his name. This Brocken spectre is a
person of infinite fastidiousness, who preferred the observ-
ances of eternity to those of time, and produced works of art
that are like small classic temples, instant in their appeal to
all inheritors of the European tradition of culture. Some
such ideal visited the mind of the real Matthew Arnold from
time to time. But he was not a person of impeccable taste.
Few could be found to-day to defend his opinion that
Chaucer lacked "high seriousness" that Heine was blame-
worthy for "his incessant mocking" and his want of "moral
deliverance," and that Pope was nearly nothing at all.
Nor was he concerned with everlasting things; many of his
writings are so journalistic in the pejorative sense, so much
interventions in petty controversies of the day, that they are
now unintelligible except to those well acquainted with the
unimportant history of his period. His impressiveness lay
in his extreme hatred of poverty. It is thought that he hated
poverty because it was inimical to culture, but that is not so.
He showed extremely little concern for culture. He derided
the dowdy and snuffy little people who tried to bring culture

into the lives of the poor; he showed very little curiosity about the survival of English rural culture that the millions trapped by the industrial revolution must have brought into the towns. He showed, indeed, that he was repelled by the very notion of culture, that is to say the expression by a group of what it has been able to learn about reality, in a famous essay on the translation of Homer. There he declared that the conscientious translator should remove from any work of art which is his subject all the idioms by which the individual who created it and the group which produced him show their particular genius, and should substitute for them terms borrowed from a jargon acceptable to members of a class who received a prolonged and allusive education, thus insulating them from contact with anything they did not already know. It was not culture he loved, nor anarchy he feared; it was civilisation he loved, and poverty he feared. It is fair to him to say that it was civilisation at its height that he loved, its order and opportunities as well as its material comfort. But poverty he hated too absolutely, for, like Dean Farrar, he feared poor members of his group as in a healthy dispensation men fear only enemies of their group. Where this led the spirit of him and his kind, was betrayed by the ingenuous works of his niece, Mrs. Humphry Ward, who wrote popular novels in which she brooded over grave social problems like a clothed female version of Rodin's *Le Penseur*; but every now and then there burst through her clenched jaw a whoop of delight at the upper class's habit of dressing for dinner and having good furniture. In fact, people who were moved by emotions quite definitely not heroic, by dislike of those who were less fortunate and a determination not to join their ranks, thrust their allegiance on the snobs of the sovereign breed, who to do them justice were inspired by emotions quite definitely heroic, by a determination to care for the less fortunate and raise them up. It is true that if the less fortunate showed a critical attitude to that determination the snob of the sovereign breed might persecute him with the extremity of mean vindictiveness; the landed gentry of a West Country constituency have

been known to boast of how they boycotted a grocer who had
shown the Liberal colours in an election and had made him
a bankrupt in two years. But all the same he means to do
well by his brothers. Nevertheless he could not refuse these
new base allies drawn from the middle classes, because of the
fear that girded him also.

Those allies are in one sense not so offensive as they were,
largely owing to the efforts of one man. Rudyard Kipling
did much to give them an aristocratic virility. One of his
stories, *Captains Courageous*, takes the sad tale of Eric and his
sufferings among the rough, rude sailors and rewrites it as
the saving of a pampered little beast who falls overboard on
the Atlantic and is rescued by a herring-boat, whose hands
makes a man of him. He claimed, rightly, that the achievements of the landless men of moderate means who were
soldiers and sailors and colonial administrators, made them
just as valuable to the British Empire as landowners and
industrialists. But he also hated all of the poor that had not
settled down to be good doggies on the rich man's hearth.
He represented them as whimpering and undisciplined
cowards who cared nothing for their country. So they
should be, if life were logical. But then came the Great
War, and the poor kept excellent time as they marched out
to die for England. If courage and discipline could be
stolen one would have suspected theft. The doctrine of
Kipling was not what it had been for many years before he
died, but there is no comfort there even for those who disliked it most. He had no successor in lending dignity to the
middle class sense of insecurity. There is now an altogether
ghastly simplicity about the snobs of the second order, the
snobs not of a sovereign breed. They represent in the purest
form the passion people feel in an age of plentiful manufactured articles for possessing a large number of manufactured
articles, the panic they feel at the idea of possessing none;
their suffering lies in an anguished greed for superfluities,
knowing the artificiality of the situation to be such that when
superfluities fail them it is likely that essentials also will pass
from them. Those of our clerks who represent this phase

of our nation's consciousness are cruder by far than Thackeray or Dean Farrar or Matthew Arnold or Rudyard Kipling. They gain, far more easily than their more deserving predecessors, the bright shelter of the chandeliers in great houses, and in that radiance they speak plainly of their flimsy distress. There are eccentrics that are displeasing enough. Some startle the ear. Young Excelsur said to the woman next him at dinner, that it was difficult to be punctual for evening engagements when one's friends lived far away. "Yes," she said, "it is tiresome if one has to go up to Hampstead." "Well, one does not often go to Hampstead," Excelsur said coldly, "but sometimes one goes to Kensington Palace Gardens." Others amaze the eye, like dapper Archangelos, whose evening clothes are of such perfection that it seems to have stopped just in time to prevent a monstrous imperfection, such as a jewelled nose-ring or infibula from Cartier. But less pleasing still are those who do it better. The Creator has given us nothing worse than the plump, piggy little man who, in the words of Dr. Watts, constrains the rich to love him, and is meek when they reprove. Seen in a railway train travelling down to spend the week-end in a historic house, he is snug as a bug in a rug. When he eats his bird at dinner in the Great Hall he is performing with dreadful satisfaction a double function; he is dining with the Marchioness, he is not eating Sunday supper in the Highgate villa where he was born. He is not conscious of any of the graciousness of the occasion; he is only gleefully aware that he is somewhere where he has no natal right to be, where many people could never be. There is no sacrifice he will not make to keep his place in the rug. If piety is pleasing to the great he will kneel in the stately family pew; if they were infidels he would with as comfortable conformity deny his Lord. It is natural that he should dare to be so careless of his dignity, for he has his own means of keeping it. "Is our host the funny little man who smells of hair-oil?" he will ask another guest at the end of a luncheon party. But the real sourness of the situation lies not in his detestability, but in the fact that he is accepted. The Marchioness should not

have him as a week-end guest, she should not have him at
her table in the Great Hall, she should not admit him to the
family pew. But the excuse of fear is valid. The snobs of
the sovereign breed must have support. They say that it is
Moscow which terrifies them. But Moscow is where it was
twenty years ago. It has not extended its territory by a
yard. Worse enemy than Moscow is time. Worse enemy
than Moscow and time is reality, in which nothing is as it
ought to be, and heredity will not work as it should to suit
the theory of snobbery. A sorely beleaguered army can
refuse no ally, so the little pigs must make their trough with
the old wrinkled heroes in the Great Hall.

There is no help for it. Yet it will not endure. The
alliance itself sets marching forces which must change the
scene so fundamentally that nothing shall have quite the
same being. There are certain fields of activity which are
reserved to snobs of the sovereign breed, and one of them is
foreign policy. The other breed of snobs sees to that. But
the snob of the sovereign breed is less capable of acquitting
himself in that field than any other, because he has always
been and is increasingly liable to temptation to betray his
own group, from fear of the non-snob elements in it, and
form an international pact with the snobs of other groups.
For the sake of that fellowship the snobs of our sovereign
breed supported the dying Ottoman Empire; the Turkish
pasha was a gentleman, his Christian subjects had the gross
offensiveness of the extremely poor and showed a capacity
for rebellion that aroused fear. The Austrian aristocrat
also was a gentleman, and so the Austro-Hungarian Empire
was well regarded. Thus it was the Balkans flared to war.
A great many snobs there solved the problem of their being
in the grandest style. Since no system has ever been devised
by which snobs can be taught to distinguish between hubris
and the holy ghost there is no doubt that other exits will
be found for them in our time. But the very gravity of their
error assures us that up to the very end snobbery will be
comic from its sheer awfulness, up to the very last moment
in the consummation of its tragedy.

FOOD AND DRINK

BY

KENNETH HARE

FOOD AND DRINK

A LEARNED philologist, a short while ago, put forward this singular theory, that since the words "veal," "mutton" and "beef" are not Saxon English, but of Norman importation, the contemporaries of Alfred the Great subsisted exclusively upon bread and cheese! But I recall some words which are English of the native rock—words of which the Normans knew nothing—which denote either raw or cooked meat. "Lamb" is such a word. How odd if King Alfred the Great ate lamb because it was English, but eschewed mutton because it was Norman! Philology is no guide to gastronomy. The period A.D. 450 to A.D. 1066, was by no means deficient in culinary science. It is now generally agreed that even in the days before Julius Cæsar invaded Britain, Roman cooking-utensils—metal pots, cauldrons, and the like—were imported for their own use by the Britons, a quick-witted people, as Tacitus notes. The heroic achievements of the legendary hero Beowulf, after years of oral tradition, were given epic form at some period in the seventh century. King Alfred graced the latter half of the ninth—and as founder of the British Navy may well have opened the eyes of his subjects to the value of sea fish as comestibles. What was the culinary raw material upon which the cooks of Beowulf and later King Alfred had to draw? We shall see that the list is far from meagre. The chief crops were rye, oats, barley, beans, wheat, pease. The cottage patch yielded leeks and kale. It also produced herbs of many kinds, excellent for flavouring, and to-day very foolishly under-valued. There were beehives of course; the mead upon which the Beowulfians regaled themselves was prepared with honey. Beowulf, however, would seem to have known nothing or next to nothing of river- or pond-fish, and of sea-fish only herrings and sturgeons. Ancient Rome had been the Mecca of all the cooks in the world. Juvenal satirises the spendthrifts who race to Baiae for the oysters. Cicero deplores the crowd of gastronomically minded young gentlemen who give politics to the devil, and talk of nothing but fish-ponds.

But the Roman tradition in England would appear to have died out. On the other hand, to supplement his herrings and sturgeon, Beowulf would relish two aquatic animals which we of to-day would call in vain for at Sweetings, namely porpoise and whale, both of which retained their popularity so late at least as the days of Henry VIII. It was the whale's tongue that was considered the delicacy, and the uxorious monarch's chefs broiled it with pease. This was in the tradition. The wife of Simon de Montfort —died 1265—ate whale's tongue dressed with pease, and porpoise prepared with frumenty sugar and saffron. Connoisseurs in Continental cookery will recall the important part which saffron plays to-day in *bouillabaisse*. Generally speaking, King Alfred the Great's contemporaries preferred their fish boiled, with a sauce of wine, or vinegar and herbs. Flesh they roasted, or boiled and served with the broth, a practice which was still in vogue in Elizabeth's day —as we see from their "brewis"—and in all probability much later. To this day the Flemish dish *waterzoï*, where a fowl is boiled with herbs and served in its own liquor, will give us an excellent idea of an exceedingly old dish. Bread our Anglo-Saxons prepared from grain of various kinds, which their womenfolk ground in hand-mills, those little "querns" at which centuries later Shakespeare's Puck would labour, a slight compensation for frightening with his pranks Elizabethan country maidens. Baker and "bakester" were important persons in the houses of men of standing. Ale— that hopeless ale of our ancestors, long considered peculiarly beneficial to the national constitution—was extensively employed. As there were then, of course, no monopolies granted by the Government to limit its supply, every household of note brewed for its own requirements. Thus our remote ancestors enjoyed a privilege denied to their descendants of to-day, that of ensuring, by personal supervision, the purity of the beverage they drank. One thinks of the supper of pre-Conquest days as a bachelor affair. I suppose ladies were sometimes permitted to be present, but, in any case, the evenings were devoted not to small talk, but to harp-playing and improvisations. The Beowulfian evening meals had something in common with the symposia of Hellenic days. That a certain standard of proficiency was required is manifest from the legend of Caedmon who felt himself to possess no talent for such exercises, withdrew before it fell to his turn to play and sing his improvisation, threw himself down on the bare ground outside the hall, and wept bitterly. While he was thus abandoning himself to grief, an angel stood beside him, crying, "Caedmon, sing!" "I have no skill," cried the weeping man. "Nevertheless, thou shalt sing!" declared the angel, and from that hour Caedmon became the inspired father of English song.

The spread of Christianity throughout the island brought us back to the European tradition, to that stream of the old Roman culture, a minor characteristic of which was an appreciation of the value of fish as food. Lakes, pools, and fens began now earnestly to be explored by disciples who, being also men of the world, desired to render fast-days, not only not intolerable, but, if that might be managed, actively agreeable. Sea-fish, however, still enjoyed comparative immunity from sportsmen, a fact which has puzzled many, but which I personally ascribe to the ever-present menace from raiding Northmen. One reads of an English bishop kidnapped by these savages, and when the ransom was not forthcoming, pelted to death upon the beach with bones of oxen. Fishermen may be pardoned for preferring the Thames to a sea-coast which exposed a man to such unpleasant attention!

With the fusion—or shall we not rather say "absorption" of the Norman race, for with sublime pig-headedness we imposed our language upon those who too hastily assumed that they were conquering us—we note the more general importation of wine from the Continent. At King Arthur's Christmas feast, in the poem "Sir Gawayne and the Green Knight"—(?) 1360—the guests enjoy "good beer and bright wine *both*." If we take the fourteenth century as typical of the Middle Age at its best, we shall have no lack of material for a study of the English cookery of that day. Is not one of Chaucer's Canterbury Pilgrims himself a cook? Let us see what he is in the habit of cooking, as this will show us the type of fare provided for the "man in the street," of whom, with the possible exceptions of the Knight and the Squire, almost any of Chaucer's pilgrims will furnish an example. It is better to study the "Coke's" bill of fare than his story, which in the presence of ladies is embarrassing.

> A cook they haddé with hem for the nones,
> To boille chiknés with the marybones,
> And poudré-marchant tart and galyngale;
> Wel koude he knowe a draughte of London ale;
> He koudé rooste and seethe and boille and frye,
> Maken mortreux and wel bake a pye . . .
> For blankmanger, that made he with the beste.

Clearly this cook is an artist at his work. We are in an England which enjoyed its meals and took cooking seriously. "For the nones," it should be said for non-Chaucerian readers, means "for the occasion." I don't know whether the exact nature of "poudré-marchant" can be determined to-day. Its flavour was sharp, and that I believe is all that is known about it. "Galyngale" was the root of sweet cyprus; it is no longer used in cooking. "London ale" which has been famous as early as Henry III's days, was more expensive than that purchased in the provinces, but it was better esteemed. "Mortreux" or "Mortrews" could be either fish or flesh, and, like every dish of this curious period, was elaborate. The "mortrew" of fish was a soup which contained roe, and the liver of fish, bread, pepper, and ale. The meat kind was also a soup in which the principal ingredients were chicken, pork, bread-crumbs, yokes of egg, and saffron. Table manners would appear to be really good, although the fork is still undreamed of, and will remain so until Jacobean days. The fingers and thumb of the right hand alone may be used for eating. Diners wash meticulously both before and after the meal, although it is not thought bad form to throw whatever may be left over on one's trencher upon the floor rushes, for the benefit of those "houndés" whom the illuminators depict as gazing upwards with wistful anticipation and commendable restraint, while kings and great ladies dine. The plate or "trencher" (compare the French *trancher*, to cut), is not of wood but coarse bread baked especially for this use, and into this the gravy soaks, as though into a blotting-pad. The men of the middle age are very curious in the matter of bread. Chaucer's "Nonne" fed her "smalé houndés" upon "wastel breed," or fine cake-bread. He gives us a careful study of this lady's manners at table. They would not discredit good company to-day. Before every diner is laid his wooden platter or "roundel," on which he places that finer bread, which he will eat—for the "trencher," the meal over, will be thrown into the alms-basket for the poor. These roundels were often pretty, being inscribed with verses, or bearing designs of figures in sets: the twelve Apostles, the Seasons, or what not. Roundels of a later date may be studied in the Victoria and Albert Museum, South Kensington. Ordinarily so soon as a meal was over, the table, being an affair of planks laid along trestles, would be carried away, for the Great Hall of a castle is the centre of the communal life of the inhabitants; a great living-room which serves many uses besides that of meals. People still speak of "sitting by the board," although *planks* may be represented by a masterpiece of Chippendale. Chaucer's "Franklin" never removes these planks, nor suffers the trestles to be displaced.

> His table dormant in his halle alway
> Stood redy covered al the longé day.

This was in order that any traveller might enter and feast his fill. The "Franklin" is a substantial householder, a great gourmet, and sets the example of the proverbial "old English hospitality." Cleanliness and almost modern appurtenances characterise the banquets described in the charming medieval poem, "Sir Gawayne and the Green Knight."

> The sewers served him, seemly for to see.
> They set him up a table on trestles fair
> Beside the settle, and spotless everywhere,
> They spread upon the boards a cloth full clean.
> The napkin and the salt-dish they were there,
> And silver spoons . . .

The fault of gluttony is one with which the men of the Middle Ages have been charged, both by English and French writers. My personal impression, derived from much haphazard reading in medieval authors, is that the men of the fourteenth, fifteenth, and sixteenth centuries did unquestionably eat far more than we do to-day, but yet I hesitate to bring the charge of gluttony. One has but to reflect that even now a "farmer's appetite," and a "farmer's helping," are proverbial for a keen appetite, a large helping, and then to reflect upon the long hours of open-air exercise which travel in those days entailed upon all classes alike. Without commenting upon the violence of the sports, whether of knights at tilting, or 'prentice boys at wrestling, quintain and the like, think of the state of the roads, and the jolting to which that must have subjected a rider.

The Roman tradition of efficiently made roads had perished with the Anglo-Saxon influx. The highways along which our ancestors of the Middle Ages travelled were country tracks, which a season of heavy rains reduced to a condition differing little from ploughed land. Chaucer's poor parson had a "wyd parisshe," with houses "fer asonder." This did not prevent him from visiting the sick and every man or woman besides who needed his help or advice, at all hours, and in all weathers,

> Upon his feet, and in his hand a staf.

After "foot-slogging" half the night, by greasy stile-paths, through drenching rain, he was entitled to an excellent

supper, and I like to imagine him—like another country
priest several centuries later, Robin Herrick to wit—as
thanking God for his "jolly wassail-bowls"! The labourer
is worthy of his hire—and his supper!

It ill becomes us who travel along smooth roads in swift
cars, and who, if the windows be kept shut, do not even
receive the stimulus of fresh air, to arraign as gluttons a
generation which travelled under rougher, and manlier,
conditions. I have attempted to give something of the
"background," and "atmosphere" of the medieval dinner;
something also of the typical fare consumed by the "man in
the street." Chaucer's godlike sympathy with his fellows,
enables us to see not only those gorgeous feasts of princely
nobles, but also the frugal repast of his "poor widow," a
cottager advanced in age. This old body is a "maner deye,"
that is, a sort of dairywoman. The "deye" commonly
attended to the making of butter and cheese. She also
tended calves and poultry and did other odd jobs upon a
farm.

> Thre largé sowés hadde she, and namo;
> Three keen and eek a sheep that highté Malle.
> Ful sooty was hir bour, and eke hir halle,
> In which she eet ful many a sklendre meel.
> Of poynaunt sauce hir needed never a deel.
> No deyntee morsel passéd thurgh hir throte,
> Her diete was accordant to hir cote;
> Repleccioun ne made hire never sik,
> Attempree diete was al hir phisik,
> And exercise, and hertés suffisaunce.
> The gouté lette her no-thyng for to daunce,
> Napoplexié shenté nat hir heed;
> No wyn ne drank she, neither whit ne reed;
> Her bord was servéd moost with whit and blak,—
> Milk and broun breed,—in which she foond no lak;
> Seynd bacoun and somtyme an ey or tweye, . . .

"Seynd"—broiled. "Ey"—egg. The "whit" wyn, would
probably be "osey," as we then termed it, from Alsace.
The "reed"—probably that called "Mountrose," a highly
esteemed wine imported from Gascony. So Skeat conjec-
tures; but of course no particular wine may necessarily be

intended. What then, in a word, was this old peasant woman's daily diet? Remember we are considering the fare of one only a degree above indigence, a cottager who does odd jobs which require little skill. She has bread of two kinds, broiled bacon, milk in plenty, and sometimes eggs. Such a scheme of diet lacks variety, of course, the case of extremely poor people has always been hard; and yet for health-producing food I have come, in my perambulations about the English countryside, upon cases of cottagers —whom Chaucer's "wydwe" would have considered aristocrats—who fare no better, even worse. With such "tea" is the chief meal of the day—the *show* meal of the house, that to which guests are invited. The "tea" will be a rank liquid which has simmered half the day on the hob; it is bubbling tannin, and as like as not has a lump of washing-soda thrown into it to make it "stronger." There will be a cake bought from a shop, an object made not to nourish, but to catch the eyes of gulls, with tawdry decoration, and there will be tinned salmon, and tinned fruit salad. The grocer, in many places, has alm ost ousted the butcher, fishmonger, and fruiterer. I remember well the lodgings of my bachelor days, and the style of fare to which I was not seldom subjected owing to the sluttish laziness of landladies. How often have I been given tinned tomatoes when ripe were on the stalks! How often tinned fish when living within sound of the sea! I have even had tinned *vegetable* soup in the heart of the country, though every cottage patch can produce sorrel, lettuce, and potatoes which, together with the leaves of watercress, needs but a trifle of butter and hot milk or boiling water to make the most delicious and nourishing soup that one could wish. The notion that the English cannot cook has nothing in *tradition* to support it, and it must be borne in mind that it is to the manifest advantage of a host of Frenchmen and Italians to perpetuate the notion. They find their account in it. Why we are such more than indifferent cooks at the *present day*, I shall consider in its place. Breakfast in the Middle Ages was not a sit-down

affair, but consisted of a mere draught of "sops-in-wine,"
or wine into which cake has been crumbled. Thus does
"Gawayne" breakfast in the poem we have already cited,
and thus does another character we have mentioned,
Chaucer's "Frankeleyn." As a gourmet this man perhaps
is hardly to be considered typical, still a glance at the fare he
favours throws an interesting light on the then culinary
practice. He is distinguished by his hospitality and civic
sense; he keeps open house for travellers and others:

> Seint Julian was he in his contree

or district. (A few days back a rustic of whom I inquired
in what county he was born, answered me, "In Hereford,
the finest *country* in the world!") The saint with whom
Chaucer compares his Franklin, was that appealed to by
those seeking food or lodging. It is to St. Julian that Sir
Gawayne renders thanks, when he perceives the "Green
Knight's" castle, and presumes that he may now count upon
shelter. And it is again St. Julian to whom the traveller
appeals in one of the merriest of Boccaccio's tales, nor does he
appeal in vain. The Franklin's bread and ale are of the
highest quality, and his larder is never without pasties of
baked flesh and fish. Many a fat partridge has he in his
coops, and in his private fish-ponds bream and "luce," or
pike—"the tyrant of the fresh waters," as Isaac Walton terms
him. To-day, regarding pike as a scavenger, we doom him
to undue neglect. I have eaten pike in the Loire country,
with salad and a suitable sauce, and found him delicious,
but then the dish was prepared by a cook who understood
his profession. Chaucer's Franklin delights in "poynaunt"
sauce—something after the fashion of a *sauce piquante*, one
may suppose—and a sorry man is his cook if the sauce be
not "sharpe" enough to please his palate, or if aught be
amiss with the table appointments. And there is quantity
to be found here as well as quality: "It snewéd (snowed)
in his hous of mete and drynke," says Chaucer, happy as ever
in his choice of the vivid and picturesque. After all this it
seems superfluous to add that the Franklin's cellar was of

the choicest and that it was plentifully stored. What sources of supply were open to him? As many as are open to us to-day; one may add more, for everything points to a price in that England as reasonable as then obtained upon the Continent. To-day one is not taxed but fined for drinking. The Franklin might purchase wines from Alsace or the Moselle country or the Rhine land; from Gascony whence came some of the most esteemed; from Spain, Italy, Greece, Cyprus; and from many of the vine-growing islands which stud the Aegean Sea. Neither did the Church set the sorry example of water-drinking. When wine was acid, it was employed not only in sauces, but in the fabrication of any quantity of compound drinks, sweetened with honey and flavoured with all manner of spice, in varying quantities and combinations; there was little that the cellarer and cooks of Chaucer's England did not know about spice. Many compound ale drinks were also enjoyed. The mead of Alfred the Great and his contemporaries retained its popularity. Ale, the common drink of all, was prepared from barley or oat malt, and lacking the bitter hop (which only reached us in quantity in late Tudor days) was *sweet*. *Ale* and *cakes* therefore went suitably together, whereas in such connexion modern hopped beer would be disgusting. It is not certain whether "braggot" was ale concocted with spices, or a particular type of mead. "Metheglin" was composed of ale made with "hotte herbes" boiled with honey. It was said to taste "hotter than mead," and was at first associated with Wales. Roasting in modern England has practically died out. In Chaucer's England the cooks roasted with the spit at the open fire. The old illuminators show us their mighty fireplaces and Homeric hearths, before which, at the right hand side, a kneeling boy turns the handle which causes the spit to rotate, thus exposing to the action of the leaping flames, a whole colony of little birds. It is well known in those parts of France where the old style of roasting is still practised, that the choice of particular woods as fuel, imparts distinctive flavours to the meat. I have spoken with an old lady in Gloucestershire who tells me that her father never had his meat roasted otherwise than by the jack, and before a wood fire. He also, she informs me, was curious in his choice of fuel, and would touch no beef that had not been roasted before oak. Since the tradition of this choice of roasting fuel is even to-day, as we see, not quite extinct, we may surely assume that the cooks of Chaucer's England perfectly possessed this curious science, seeing that they lived in a country which was hardly less overspread with forest than it had been in the days of the legendary Robin Hood. (It has been asserted that so late as the reign of Elizabeth, a squirrel might hop from one end of England to another, without once setting foot to ground!) The "Luttrell Psalter," affords us a vivid picture of roasters at their work. Prominent amongst them is a man who would more fittingly be termed a *toaster*, for he has set the meat he is exposing to the flames, upon a fork as long as a hayfork, and with reason, for otherwise he might roast not his meat only but himself. I picture this fellow as the master-cook, attending himself to a collop destined for some epicure whose disgust will be manifestly apparent, if he be proffered second best. Perhaps Chaucer's "Frankeleyn" is expected to "soper." One gains some idea of the heat of the kitchen from the *toaster's* costume, which he has reduced, like the attendant at a modern Turkish Bath, to a mere rag about his middle. Two things appear clearly from the study of the cookery in England at this and the preceding period: (1) Cooks could draw upon a quantity of the purest material. (2) Cooking was a masculine art. The cooks whom the illuminators depict are all men, although boys commonly figure in the minor office of turn-spit. Ale, however, is sold and served by the "ale-wife," who fills the role of the later barmaid. The poets of the day never weary of describing feasts—a fact with which Milton will reproach them; banqueting inspires them. When men interest themselves in an art, and assume control of, and responsibility for it, it is a sign at least that it will be taken seriously. To-day, speaking generally, cooking is made over to

women, and is not taken seriously. What would the
men of Chaucer's England think of our precious meta-
morphosis of tavern into tea-shop, and ale-house into
milk-bar? Foodstuffs were health-giving. The doctor knew
little; the cook much. No need to preach a "national fitness
campaign" to the toughs who wrestled for the ram upon the
village green, and won the battles of Crécy, Poitiers, and
Agincourt. Such men knew nothing of our stucco em-
poriums, which—though, parenthetically, they cannot brew
coffee—are liberal in the supply of bottled this, tinned that,
and boricated and preserved everything else. You suppose
that it is only because they lived before the dawn of science
that those benighted poor devils of Chaucer's England were
so profoundly ignorant of the art of poisoning their fellows?
They would have been the Borgias that we ourselves are had
they had the benefits of modern education. It is possible,
of course, that those who did attempt to foist deleterious drink
or food-stuffs upon customers dealt in those days with a
public which "hit back." Witness the fate of John Penrose,
committed to Newgate with a colleague of his, John Rightwys,
for that "on the Eve of St. Martin, . . . in the Parish of
St. Leonard Estchepe, in the tavern of William Doget there,"
he sold "red wine to all who came . . . unsound and unwholesome for man, in deceit of the common people, and
in contempt of our Lord the King, and to the shameful
disgrace of the officers of the City," and, as though all this
did not suffice, "to the grievous damage of the Commonalty
etc". On the "Saturday following," the testimony of all witnesses having been taken, the case comes up in court, when
John Rightwys is declared "in no way guilty of the sale of the
said wine," so home he goes, this righteous taverner, restored
to citizenship, and the embraces of his Wife-of-Bath-like
spouse. But the jury find that "the said John Penrose was
guilty of the sale of such wine," and therefore they adjudge
"that the said John Penrose" shall be put on the pillory, and
that "the said John Penrose shall drink a draught of the same
red wine which he sold the common people"—similar cases
show that a culprit was ordinarily compelled to drink a

pint—and "the remainder of such wine shall be poured on
the head of the same John," who shall "forswear the calling of
a vintner in the City of London for ever." (John, however,
obtained a king's pardon, and was readmitted to the trade,
in the fourth year of Edward III.) Still, it had been a
dangerous game to play, and one that John Penrose will
never play again. To stand up there before that booing and
stinking mob which laughed itself almost into convulsions so
often as he puked in his efforts to swallow his own vinegar,
had been a horrible experience.

And so the Middle Ages merge at last into the first faint
dawn of the English Renaissance, with those fathers of all
the sonneteers, Wyatt and Surrey, and the impressionistic,
satiric Skelton, and—as symbols of the age—the over-
mastering personalities of the Great Cardinal, and
Henry VIII. Paulus Jovius, a contemporary Italian historian, gives us a vivid impression of the courtly banquets of
this day. "That people," says he—the English—"are more
devoted to feasting than are any other race of mortals. For
they prolong their banquets many hours together, and
intersperse their varied and exquisite repasts with music
and jesters, and when the meal is over, they fall to dancing
and indulge in the embraces of their ladies." Note, sceptics,
that we have here an Italian, one of that race from whom
the French themselves acquired the art of cookery, praising
as exquisite the dishes that are to be found in England.
The impression which the French critic Taine—1828–1893—
derived from his study of our Elizabethan age, has much in
common with that formed by the Italian Jovius several
centuries earlier. "That age," says Taine, in effect—I have
not read him for many years—"witnessed a great pagan
revival, when men drank, and sang, and tumbled the girls."
But England was by no means alone in manifesting queasi-
ness when confronted by austerities. A study of his nymphs
will persuade few that Rubens wore a hair shirt. Rabelais
preached no crusade against wine or women. But let
us study the methods of the masters, and see how the great
Cardinal prepares to entertain the French Ambassadors

to dinner, at his palace of Hampton Court.[1] "My lord Cardinal called for the principal officers of his house, as his Steward, Comptroller, and the Clerks of his kitchen, whom he commanded to prepare for this banquet at Hampton Court, and neither to spare for expenses or travail, to make them such triumphant cheer, as they may not only wonder at it here, but also make a glorious report in their own country, to the king's honour and that of the realm. His pleasure once known, to accomplish his commandment, they sent forth all the caterers, purveyors, and other persons, to prepare of the finest viands that they could get, whether for money or friendship among my lord's friends. Also they sent for all the expertest cooks, besides my lord's, that they could get in England, wherever they might be gotten, to serve to garnish this feast. The purveyors brought and sent such plenty of costly provision, as ye would wonder at the same. The cooks wrought both night and day in diverse subtleties and many costly devices; where lacked neither gold, silver, ne any other costly thing meet for the purpose. . . . Then the carpenters, the joiners, the masons, the painters, and all other artificers necessary to glorify the house and feast, were set to work." The "subtleties" had made their appearance long before in the Middle Age. They were pasties, or other edible stuff, fashioned to represent figures, buildings, ships and the like. We read of a subtlety of an Angel singing to Three Shepherds, an Abbey with a Bishop kneeling before the high Altar and so forth. The "subtleties" of the Renaissance were elaborate, castles and the like being represented, and furnished with figures, of course. Sometimes wax would be used to stiffen out such features as the spars of ships, which pastry alone was not strong enough to support. The "subtleties" were carried in while the meal was in progress, and since no one could divine what form they would take, constituted a surprise feature which was exceedingly popular. They had also a practical use. They closed and preceded courses, and in earlier days were called "warners." To exhibit his gold

[1] The particulars from Sir William Cavendish, Wolsey's Biographer.

plate, Wolsey's carpenters and artificers made a buffet six
stages high, which ran the entire width of the lower end of
the banquet-room. The plate was gorgeous yet tasteful,
"very sumptuous and of the newest fashions." It included
two prodigious candlesticks of silver-gilt, large enough to
hold wax-lights of the thickness and height of torches, which,
together with the curious workmanship, cost three hundred
marks in gold. Yet such store of gold and silver plate did
Wolsey possess, that that displayed upon the buffet was not
touched during the feast, there being sufficient without it
to serve the tables. So exquisite was the music that the
"Frenchmen were rapt into a heavenly paradise." Not
till the conclusion of the first course, a banquet in itself,
did the Cardinal arrive, and then in his hunting-costume,
"booted and spurred all suddenly." No one knew better
than he how to produce a *coup de théâtre*. He forbade the
company to rise, bade them "prouface"—Latin *proficiat*;
"May it do you good"—called for a chair in the midst of
the table, and "showed himself as merry as ever he had in
his life." There were above an hundred "subtleties" on
this occasion, and the guests were engaged in studying the
first instalment when the Cardinal made his dramatic entry.
Fowls and beasts figured in lively counterfeit. There were
soldiers fighting with guns and crossbows, and knights
jousting or dancing with ladies. One subtlety presented a
great chessboard complete with the pieces, and since the
French enjoyed a reputation for excelling at this game,
Wolsey had a case made *ad hoc*, that the Ambassadors might
carry it away with them, a not very endurable trophy of
the occasion. At another such banquet the King with a
dozen masquers more, disguised as shepherds—of a type
rarely encountered in the wilds, for they wore "princely
garments," and some of them stage-beards of gold or silver
wire—arrived incognito, and played dice about the ban-
queting-hall, the better to "peruse"—trust King Henry for
that! —the "incomparable beauty," of the "excellent fair
dames" there present. Having satisfied his curiosity on this
head, the royal shepherd approached the Cardinal's chair,

and pouring some two hundred golden crowns from a goblet, invited him to dice. In 1531 a fat sheep might, with luck, be purchased for 2s. 4d., a hog for 3s. 8d., and an ox entire for £1 6s. 8d. What eggs were selling at then, I cannot discover, but in 1314 they went at twenty to the penny; from all which we may safely deduce that a couple of hundred golden crowns was a respectable sum!

My lord Cardinal takes the dice-box in hand.

"At all!" cries he. And amidst tumultuous applause, wins the whole glittering heap!

"At all!" . . . Do not these two monosyllables breathe initiative, decision, courage? Do they not reveal the man's soul?

"*At all!*" Well, he had already won a higher stake— England, to wit—so what the devil mattered a few hundreds of beggarly golden crowns!

And what of the peasant? Princes, we know, commonly fare well. We have viewed through Chaucer's eyes the "merrie England" of tradition. Towns are small, and except in rare periods of famine, the crops supply abundance of all that is essential to life. The unenclosed common fattens the goose. From the king downwards, all men are archers. The very ploughman drives with his bow across the plough-shafts, that he may take a shot at the passing bird. The England of Henry VIII's day offers immense tracts of fen and forest, and the bird whether a flier or wader, is undiscovered, which the yeoman whose digestion Hercules might envy cannot relish. But there are signs of change. Tillage gives way to sheep-farming which employs few hands, and "hay-makers, rakers, reapers, and mowers," trudge from their ancestral fields to make way for a single shepherd. And where shall the ejected turn for relief? To the great house? The migration to town is beginning, and it is odds the Squire may be away from home. When "the new porter, John"—as a balladist sings who, years later, is to delight Mr. Pepys,

Relieves the poor with a thump on the back with a stone!

Then let the destitute wretch seek the monks. . . . King
Henry's agents have done their work well; jackdaws nest in
their broken walls. But those countrymen who still find
work, and they are still many, are hardly aware of the
change. As for the roving poet, his labour is not with
Justice Shallow's country estate, but with

> The wise and many-headed bench that sits
> Upon the life and death of plays and wits; . . .

with the "Fortune," or the "Globe," or the "Swan" play-
house; with the "Mermaid," or the "Devil" tavern. He
beholds the countryside with the eyes of a Renaissance
idyllist. He views forest tracts clothing the hills with purple
or with bronze, which imagination peoples with elves so
real-seeming that maids place cream-bowls for them, so
that, as for a fee, they will thresh wheat, grind corn, scour
harness. Fairies enter the thatched cottages by night, lured
by the grateful glow from the embers, to dance the "Hays,"
or other rustic dance, before the hearth. All this the
poet beholds with the mental eye, but with the physical
he contemplates the scene upon the greensward, the girls
who yet wear garlands in Roman fashion—clear-eyed, apple-
cheeked, so fresh after his London light-o'-loves. He sees
the Maypole with its ribbons and crown of blossoms, and the
old men, with ale-jacks, toasting its going-up. He breathes
the flower-sweet air, and finds it heady as the "Mermaid"
wine.

> Let the bells ring, and let the boys sing,
>   The young lasses skip and play;
> Let the cups go round, 'till round goes the ground;
>   Our learnéd old vicar will stay.
>
> Let the pig turn merrily, merrily, ah!
>   And let the fat goose swim;
> For verily, verily, verily, ah!
>   Our vicar this day shall be trim.
>
> The stewed cock shall crow, cock-a-loodle-loo,
>   A loud cock-a-loodle shall he crow;
> The duck and the drake shall swim in a lake
>   Of onions and claret below. . . .

Give me the Elizabethan dramatists; I will compose a menu from their lyrics alone. The first poor-law only dates from Elizabeth's reign, but as yet comparatively few feel the pinch of real poverty. If a reader distrust the evidence of the poets—although he need not, for the Elizabethan dramatists might be termed idealistic realists—let him hearken to the independent testimony of William Harrison (1534–1595), a Londoner by birth, but now parson of Radwinter, Essex, whose description of contemporary England prefaces Holinshed's *Chronicle*: ". . . Both the artificer and the husbandman are sufficiently liberal, and very friendly at their tables; and when they meet, they are so merry without malice . . . that it would do a man good to be in company with them. . . . If they happen to stumble upon a piece of venizon, and a cup of wine or very strong beer or ale . . . they think themselves to have fared as well as the Lord Mayor of London, with whom, when their bellies be full, they will not often stick to make comparison." All classes drank ale or beer, the last differing from the former by the addition of hops, which act as a preservative, and are thus of benefit to the trader. The country parson from whom I have just quoted, although his stipend was but £40 a year, yet brewed his own beer—or rather his wife did—in his own house. He reckons that it cost him 20s. the two hundred gallons. Beer was rationed out to seamen who drank water only in emergencies. The Armada was defeated by beer drinkers—a sufficient reply to the ass who tells one that "alcohol depreciates a man's value as man," a dogma with which some crank society were mendaciously placarding a hoarding which I happened to pass by yesterday. Harrison shows us that we, not the Americans, were the pioneers of that merry art of christening drinks with rococo names. "Such mighty ale" is to be had at fairs and markets as, "for the mightiness thereof" it is "commonly called, 'Huff-cap,' 'the mad dog,' 'Father Whoreson,' 'Angels' food,' 'dragon's milk,' 'go-by-the-wall,' 'stride wide,' 'lift leg,' etc." Drinkable wine was still cheap as it had been in Chaucer's day. It would be interesting to ascertain, if that were possible, what percentage of the wine then drunk was prepared at home. Drayton, in his *Polyolbion*, speaks of the "Cotswold vines, famed throughout all the world for their delicious wines." When a year back I was shown by a gardener, in this same neighbourhood, a sunny hill, which he assured me was still called in his boyhood, "The Monks' Vineyard," I thought at once of Drayton.

"Where did they get their plants from?"

"They were all brought over from France," said my informant.

This sounds circumstantial, and, personally, I am inclined to credit his tale. Many houses, in many parts of England, are still called the "Vines," and many streets, "The Vineyard." In any case, on a feast day at least, an Elizabethan labourer could afford to call for wine by the pint. "Faith, Joan," says Thomas, in Robert Greene's pastoral comedy, *Friar Bacon and Friar Bungay*, "I'll bestow a fairing on you, and then we will to the tavern, and snap off a pint of wine or two."

"Their food," says Harrison, still talking of the poorer class, of artificers and husbandmen, ". . . consisteth principally in beef, and such meat as the butcher selleth : . . mutton, veal, lamb, pork, etc., whereof he findeth great store in the markets adjoining, besides sows, brawn, bacon, fruit, pies of fruit, fowls of sundry sorts, cheese, butter, eggs, etc." This picture may appear highly coloured, but it is to be remembered that Harrison lived in the country, and as a parson would have ample means of ascertaining the habits and customs of those amongst whom his lot was cast. Perhaps other counties were less favoured than his Essex, but a point to be remembered is that this pre-Puritan England was first and foremost an agricultural country; towns were small, and food in one form or another was the product of the national industry, farming. "In their feasting also," it is still Harrison who speaks, ". . . especially at bridals, purifications of women, and such odd meetings, . . . it is incredible to tell what meat is consumed . . .

each one bringing a dish, or so many with him, as his wife and he do consult upon. . . . This also is commonly seen at these banquets, that the good man of the house is not charged with anything saving bread, drink, sauce, house-room, and fire." That last clause gives one to think; the host is charged with nothing *except* "drink"! This at the present day would be a crippling expense. In the Cots-wolds a labourer often works for ninepence an hour, some-times indeed for so little as sixpence an hour. Under the present punitive taxation, beer *costs* sixpence a pint. If a man drink three pints at this rate—no immoderate allowance for one who has lost bodily moisture by sweating on a hill-slope with a scythe throughout a summer's day—if he drink his three pints, he pays for them with hours of severe toil. So long as England was ruled by aristocrats, the labourer had a fair deal, but no sooner was he championed by Socialists and other "friends of the People," than he was forced down by his self-styled defenders, almost to the condition of a serf. To continue our list of articles of diet ordinarily consumed by countrymen of slender means, we find melons, pompoms, gourds, cucumbers, radishes, "skirets," the last an umbelliferous water-plant whose roots, or tubers, in appearance not unlike small carrots, were appreciated for their succulence. Common also at this time were carrots, parsnips, cabbages, "navews"—appar-ently some species of turnip—turnips proper, and any quantity of "salad herbs." The Elizabethan country popu-lation revelled in salads—the more so as they had, as yet, no acquaintance with the potato. When Sir Walter Raleigh introduced this last, it was the yam, or sweet potato, not that which we eat to-day. It was credited with aphrodisiac properties, and it is an agreeable fancy that an Elizabethan rake might surreptitiously consume *potatoes* in the hope of rekindling the fires of youth. Harrison reckons up "about fifty-six sorts" of small wines, and "thirty kinds of Italian, Grecian, Spanish, Canarian, etc." One regrets that "etc."; one would have liked the full list. All sorts of fish are now taken along the coasts, though fish-ponds for such fresh-water fish as carp characterise the gardens of the bigger houses. Lettuce which had arrived amongst us in Henry VIII's day is rarely mentioned; presumably its popularity is still to come. We read of orchards being cultivated to good effect. Apples, pears, plums, are common, as also the nuts: filberts, walnuts, and others. "Strange" fruit, to be viewed as yet only in the gardens of the rich, are apricots, almonds, peaches, cornels, figs.

The Cromwellian period witnessed a decadence in cookery, not destined happily to be lasting. The food in Cromwell's Whitehall is described as "ordinary and vulgar." There were no *quelque choses*. Scotch collops of veal appeared with monotonous regularity, and I have read, though I cannot give my reference for this, that the Protector's wife refused her lord an orange to mitigate the insipid dish when oranges were dear. Once, a poor peasant woman who had grown early peas in her garden, took a dish to Whitehall, refusing on the way an offer of a gold Angel for her little basket. The peas were taken in for "Joan" Cromwell's use, and a crown was proffered. At this, the peasant woman returned the money and stoutly refused to budge until she was given back her peas again. We find "leg of mutton," "pig collared like brawn," "liver puddings," and "hog's-liver sausages" mentioned as dishes which now obtain favour in what had been a royal palace. Spices are barred upon the supposition that they excite passion, and such Christmas dishes as contain them are regarded by the zealots with especial horror, as recalling the now-exploded "pagan" feast of the Nativity. So late as the eighteenth century, the refusal of a mince-pie at Christmas denotes the Dissenter. Butler in his *Hudibras* scoffs at the Puritan food taboos.

> . . . They [the zealots] will
> Quarrel with *minc'd Pies*, and disparage
> Their best and dearest friend *Plum-Porridge*;
> Fat *Pig* and *Goose* it self oppose,
> And blaspheme *Custard* through the *Nose*.

Many contemporary pamphlets bear witness to the misery of the poor, excluded by the suppression of Christmas from their customary mid-winter relief. The Protector's wife was ancestress to the nascent race of teetotal women. She drank "Punnado," a toast-water compounded with currants, rose-water, mace and sugar. How much better had she drunk the water clean, as it came from the well! When enjoying at the Palace the amenities of family life, Oliver drank the very smallest of small beers, a brewage called "Morning Dew"; perhaps we are to suppose the title symbolic. Everywhere the ale of "Old England" which had exhilarated alike the soul of pious monk and Elizabethan adventurer, is broken down. Cavaliers curse. Farmers make wry faces drinking. Farewell "Huffcap!" Farewell "Father Whoreson!"

When Count de Grammont dined at the royal table after the Restoration, Charles drew his attention to the serving-men who proffered the dishes kneeling, as "an extent of respect not observed in other Courts."

"I am obliged, your Majesty, for the explanation," de Grammont replied, "I thought they were begging your Majesty's pardon for offering so indifferent a dinner!"

The wit will have his say, but we are not obliged to take him over-seriously. Plenty has succeeded parsimony, but Puritanism *has* left its mark, even upon the banquets of the rich. One remarks the absence of the salads which are in the oldest tradition of English cookery, as also of those sauces "keen" and "poynaunt" and "sly" which delighted pre-Puritan England. Chaucer's "Frankéleyn" would be as crestfallen as de Grammont, were he to dine with Charles II. Puritanism is revealed in simplicity of style; the revolt *against* Puritanism is shown by excess. The Elizabethan gentleman, *teste* Harrison, ate and drank with moderation. The Caroline consumes his food with Rabelaisian gusto, and swallows rather than sips his wine. In all this Mr. Pepys is of his day. "January 13th, [1662]. So my poor wife rose by five o'clock in the morning before day, and went to market and bought fowls and many other things for dinner, with which I was highly pleased." So the diarist repairs to the office, whence in due course he returns home, "whither by and by comes Dr. Clarke and his lady, his sister and she-cozen, and Mr. Pierce and his wife, which was all my guests. I had for them after oysters, at first course, a hash of rabbits, a lamb, and a rare chine of beef. Next a great dish of roasted fowl, cost me about 30s.; and a tart, and then fruit and cheese. My dinner was noble and enough. . . . At night to supper; had a good sack posset and cold meat, and sent my guests away about ten o'clock, both them and myself highly pleased. . . ." And all this supply, sitting down but eight to dinner! Were they anticipating a *siege*? When due allowance has been made for the breakfasts being but draughts of ale, having regard also to the lightness of the suppers, here is still an Homeric repast! It possesses quantity and quality, since we need not doubt that the food is the best of its kind that money can buy. It is not for nothing that Mrs. Pepys rises before daylight. She wishes to outdistance neighbours and secure the pick of the market. What then *is* lacking? I should say, imagination. We English produce the most imaginative of poets, and the least imaginative of cooks. At least, we have done since Cromwell's day. From King Charles to the Regent, from Mr. Pepys to Beau Brummel, we are to witness the *British oak* of cookery; the "square meal" *par excellence*; the "pub dinner" *in excelsis*. "Taste?" To the devil with taste! Hunger is the *enemy*, and we advance in tanks.

"Even in the best houses, when I was a young man, the dinners were wonderfully solid, hot, and stimulating." So writes Captain Gronow, a rich, well-born, vivacious Welsh Guardsman, who fought at Waterloo, and knew everybody of note in Regency London. "The *menu* of a grand dinner was thus composed: Mulligatawny and turtle soups were the first dishes placed before you; a little lower, the eye met with the familiar salmon at one end of the table, and the turbot surrounded by smelts, at the other. The first course was sure to be followed by a saddle of mutton or a piece of roast beef; and then you could take your oath that fowls, tongue, and ham, would as assuredly succeed as darkness after day. While these never-ending pièces de résistance were occupying the table, what were called French dishes were, for custom's sake, added to the solid abundance. The French, or side dishes, consisted of very mild but very abortive attempts at Continental cooking; and I have always observed that they met with the neglect and contempt that they merited. The universally adored and ever-popular potato, produced at the very earliest period of the dinner, was eaten with everything, up to the moment when sweets appeared. Our vegetables, the best in the world, were never honoured by an accompanying sauce, and generally came to the table cold." I should infuriate neo-Puritans were I to derive from Puritanism the conception of a dinner outlined above. I should be justified, however. Where are the salads, where are the sauces of older days? Where is the moderation, where the balance? "A prime difficulty," says Gronow, "was the placing upon your fork, and finally in your mouth, some half-dozen different eatables which occupied your plate at the same time. For example, your plate would contain, say, a slice of turkey, a piece of stuffing, a sausage, pickles, a slice of tongue, cauliflower, and potatoes. According to habit and custom, a judicious selection from this little bazaar of good things was to be made, with an endeavour to place a portion of each in your mouth at the same moment. In fact, it appeared to me, that we used to do all our compound cookery between our jaws." Then, of course, there would be dessert. "The wines were chiefly port, sherry, and hock; claret, and even Burgundy, being then designated 'poor, thin, washy stuff.' A perpetual thirst seemed to come over people, both men and women, so soon as they had tasted their soup; as from that moment everybody was taking wine with everybody else till the close of dinner; and such wine as produced that class of cordiality which frequently wanders away into stupefaction."

This—shall I call it the "Caroline" tradition, since the meals of Pepys and of Beau Brummel differed but little in their main essentials—survived into modern Edwardian times. In my boyhood, except at Christmas, when beef *must* supplement turkey, a dinner in the course of which a saddle of mutton did not figure, and fowls, was unthinkable. But that other tradition, with its Elizabethan salads and sauces, had been broken by the Puritans.

What then shall I say of contemporary cooking? From chance remarks, here and there, in the course of this article, it may be assumed that I regard it with contempt. Such an assumption would be unjust to myself. I see both good and bad in it. Let me give an example of what I think bad. A few weeks ago a friend visited me from the Continent. His father had been an ambassador in a Paris embassy, and he himself was familiar with well-nigh every famous restaurant of every Continental capital. He spoke of English cooks as though they were witches, and of ourselves as effete for suffering them to poison us. We met in the country, and thinking this attitude exaggerated, I surreptitiously telephoned a provincial hotel which possesses a local reputation for good cooking, explaining that I was bringing a connoisseur, that I hoped they would not let me down, and adding that I would give them two hours before we should call, in order not to rush them. When dinner-time drew near, I suggested that we should "take pot-luck" at the Blank Hotel. The first course consisted of tinned soup, with tinned peas in it—and that at a season when vegetables were to be had for the picking. The second course consisted of "bottled chicken breasts," although throughout the meal one heard the cluck of poultry scratching outside in the yard. Last of all came tinned fruit. We drank beer and spirits, since I dared not face the wine. The meal was expensive! But let us discard the superstition that every Frenchman is a born cook, and every Englishman a bungler. I have eaten atrocious meals in France, upon rare occasions, and excellent English-cooked meals, sometimes. There is a theory which underlies this Caroline cooking. It may be thus stated. If the flavour of anything be disagreeable, why eat it? If it be agreeable, why disguise it? I understand this philosophy, but I do not hold with it. Even with our own admirable materials, Scotch beef, Welsh mutton, Severn salmon, home-grown vegetables, rendered succulent with showers, and never dried of their juices by too fierce a sun, one *must* avoid monotony. Plain boiled and roast did well for Robin Hood. He took more exercise than we! Our culinary shortcomings are due to sheer laziness. All arts require time, and to this rule that of the cook offers no exception. Loose the dog on those delusive commercial gentlemen who assure your cook that the dinner will prepare *itself* while she reads a novelette, if only she will induce you to purchase the "Cooker with a Million Gadgets." Distrust the pseudo-scientific jargon of industrialism. Never be persuaded that "Churno" contains more "nutrition value" than butter, or that the strength of ox-carrying Milo is contained in every box of the latest substitute for a substitute. The last gentleman whom I heard promulgate the theory that two bananas contained more "nutrition value than roast beef", is now in a nursing-home, if it be not, indeed, as I rather suspect, a mental home; for he took me aside and whispered that "the spirits" had "inspired every word" of the depressing address upon "What Progress Means to Me," with which he regaled us in the draughty Town Hall. Encouraging signs which seem to point to a renaissance of cookery are the increasing demand for practical manuals upon the art, and for articles upon it in the Press, by outstanding exponents. Wine licences are being sought for, and sound wine is now obtainable, at not prohibitive prices, at restaurants and taverns where, but a dozen years back, one might ask in vain for anything but beer or spirits. Those side-dishes beloved of the Elizabethans, and tolerated, at least, by the Regency men, are again in favour, and the *menu à prix fixe* tempts wandering eyes in London no less than in Paris. A better balanced diet, in which lighter viands are washed down by generous and witty, but yet lighter wines, has rendered gout a thing of the past, and when statesmen gibber we no longer blame the port. No longer do we eschew the freshly picked vegetable—crisp raddish, tender lettuce, or succulent kale; and spring onions are welcome, though not to lovers. Dead is the day when the "First Gentleman of Europe" inscribed himself member of "The Sublime Society of Beefsteaks," and when Beau Brummel recalled having "once eaten a pea". The future promises well, if we will but take trouble. But let us never take from a tin what may be had from the ground. Let Nature speak; give vitamins a rest.

PAINTING

BY

T. W. EARP

PAINTING

I

THE manifestation of the English genius in art is hardly two centuries old. Some of the works produced before then by painters of this country have merits which depend on more than rarity, yet, excepting in subject, they express nothing particularly native. Their spirit and manner are the same as those of other Europeans.

We may be well satisfied with the two hundred years' achievement. But sentiment, turning enviously to the early masterpieces of the continental schools, regrets that England can offer them no rivals. Lulled by insufficiency of data, it has sought refuge in a delightful dream. The vision has been evoked of a host of artists arising in the land to share with mason and craftsman in the splendour of English Gothic, and add to it a brightness of colourful imagery. Scraps of marred fresco in a few churches endow this fancy with but faint substance, and record does not support it, though the iconoclasm of Reformation and Roundhead prevents its positive denial.

The scarcity of secular pictures remaining from pre-Reformation days also tells against the probability that painting flourished either within the churches or elsewhere during our Middle Ages. In regard to what might have been, giving all indulgence to imagination, the question of native or continental workmanship would still arise. That most of the pictures painted under the Tudors and Stuarts are by foreign masters increases the conviction that no distinct English impulse to art existed up to the end of the seventeenth century.

Holbein, Rubens, Van Dyck, Lely and Kneller were in practice the begetters of our painting; it is their genius which flickers in the output of their pupils. The growth of a school more directly national was hampered by this late budding. The home-made artist had to meet comparison drawn from the skill of his Netherlands masters, matured by tradition. Beyond that, as the peak of an excellence he might not hope to attain, was the example of the great Italians in the galleries of noble collectors. It was no encouragement that patrons took his inferiority for granted.

At the same time, popular taste did not stimulate him to explore the niceties of his art, and was unaware of them. It simply demanded, through the medium of the print, an imitation of reality, which it most enjoyed when flavoured with anecdote or caricature. More than the sponsorship of connoisseurs, however, it was in sympathy with the development of an English school.

II

Hogarth, who turned from engraving to painting in 1728, rebelled against fashionable criticism which demanded the imitation of old masters. His taste was the people's, though he brought exceptional gifts of his own to its satisfaction. They make him the first representative of the English genius in art.

That he was an Englishman and a genius would not of necessity earn him that title. He might have been both, but with an accomplishment not different from that of contemporary foreign or earlier painters. An Englishman, his work might have been steeped in national feeling, yet worthless. It is the painters of this country who added something new to the world's great art with whom we are concerned. Their chronicle begins with Hogarth.

To the end of his career many of his canvases show a pronounced Dutch influence; he made disastrous attempts at the grand manner in the style of the later Italians. But there is an individual Hogarth in "The Painter's Servants," "The Stay-maker" and, above all, "The Shrimp Girl," which, reaching back to Hals and forward to Manet, is among the great masterpieces. With these, the perception is instantaneous, the actual painting a natural gesture.

Yet it is where the artist is revealed in his more everyday quality, careful of detail and with the reminiscence of a stage scene in his composition, that the Hogarthian spirit is especially evident. In the various sets of pictures methodically following the progress of an industrious and an idle apprentice, a rake, a harlot, a marriage *à la mode*, or an election, is seen the pictorial novelist and social critic.

Swinging from pure genre to caricature, he drives on through his "Comédie Humaine," which is in large part a sermon. A Protestant, he dwells with fervid realism on the sordid element of his theme, in which moral intensity mingles with love of a dramatic situation. Though he had passed beyond the medium, and was one of its more skilled practitioners, it is still the popular print that he has exalted to art. A pure artist at the peak of his achievement, in the bulk of his work the story dominates the admirable painting. He is the ancestor of that peculiar horror, the problem-picture, which is the ultimate development of graphic melodrama. But more immediately in his own day, the current at whose head he stands wears a finer aspect.

The conversation-piece, at its best, and as he sometimes painted it, a direct, unprejudiced reflection of national manners, ranges from the portrait group in a domestic setting to illustration of social incident. It is by no means an exclusively native product, as Watteau, Chardin and Longhi demonstrate. But English artists like Devis, Highmore or Philips give it a strong tinge of middle-class sentiment which becomes a characteristic of its version here.

Zoffany's scenes from plays are a specialisation of this branch of painting, while Morland extends its range to the borders of landscape. Not confined to human representation, from the hands of Stubbs and Ben Marshall it flows into a long line of sporting pictures and animal portraiture and anecdote, to whose establishment in European art this country may lay claim. It returns close to Hogarth in the case of Landseer, many of whose canvases adapt essentially Hogarthian themes.

Much of Hogarth's work is caricature, though it deals

with passions and types rather than with politics and individuals. He raised it to the level of great painting, and there again led a particularly English strain of treatment, where consummate draughtsmanship, and often an exquisite feeling for colour, are lavished on satiric or humorous subjects. Not until Goya and Daumier was so much artistry to be devoted to them abroad. There more usually they were conveyed in scarifying terms of physical distortion.

These were freely indulged in the English handling too, and by the artist who in this field comes nearest to Hogarth in genius. But with Rowlandson the art continually over-runs the caricature. Without Hogarth's moral seriousness, he is apt to let the satire ebb, by way of playful description, till the result joins his conversation-pieces, or even his landscapes. He is nearer to Rabelais than to Swift, exuberantly expressing a boundless interest in the English scene through an instinctive sense of design and the harmonies of colour.

III

Hogarth's painting is as natural as a signature, and if individuality makes style, he is a stylist. Yet when a picture is called Hogarthian, the term applies rather to its satiric realism than its craftsmanship. It is not given to those few greatest achievements in which, possibly by accident, he reveals himself most purely a creator in form and colour. Habitually, he did not use these in order to produce an effect on their own account, so much as by the subject at whose service they were placed, and its general human implication. His career was overlapped by that of a painter who was conscious throughout in style, and whose work is altogether English in spirit as in content.

So conscious, indeed, was Gainsborough in his manner, that his range of social description is frequently disregarded in admiration of the artist alone. Yet in the production of his early Suffolk period, which is now beginning justly to win appreciation at the expense of the later fashionable portraiture, he fixes an aspect of English life with a perception only equalled, in a different medium, by "The Vicar of Wakefield."

It is easy to compare details in these pictures with others in the Dutch masters of his apprenticeship studies, or to note a convention in the arrangement of figure, tree and landscape. What is of importance, in such things as "Mr. and Mrs. Robert Andrewes" or "The Artist with his Wife and Child," is the marvellous truth of their placid humanity and their East Anglian setting. Provincial England, with particularity of place and time, springs to life in these works where art and truth of record are radically mingled. And their workmanship, despite the influences contained within it, has a lucidity, a peculiar intimation of temperament, which gives them their own independent place in the great European tradition.

With the ensuing Bath period, landscape and portraiture part company in Gainsborough's painting, the latter turning, as in the case of so many English artists after him, to a task well-nigh mechanically carried out, in which the painter's genius flickers with extreme variability. But the landscapes remain fresh and potent. That Gainsborough never entirely abandoned this side of his art, in spite of the lack of appreciative patrons, cultivating it in the final London days with a kind of desperate truancy from the portraits, proves how intensely necessary it was to him as a means of expression.

The compactness of the Suffolk scenes is loosened. Rubens, seen in the collections in the great houses near Bath, replaces the Dutch influence, though with his tawny emphasis transmuted to a softer, golden grace. The features of nature become generalised, but as identity of place dissolves and portrait-figures give place to peasant-types engaged in gentle pastoral drama, a new strain of nature-poetry enters English painting. "The Watering-Place," "The Harvest Waggon" or "The Cottage Door," their vitality glowing through an Augustan mould of style, reach in sentiment from Gray's "Elegy" towards Wordsworth.

The real Gainsborough stands revealed in a passage from a late letter—"I'm sick of Portraits and wish very much to take my Viol-da-gam and walk off to some sweet village, where I can paint landskips and enjoy the fag end of life in quietness and ease."—But the portraits are a part of the world's art, and that of his daughters, painted obviously for pleasure, and without need to satisfy the tyrannical demands of "finish," is, like "The Shrimp Girl," a masterpiece in the most exclusive sense. Unlike the landscapes, however, they are not a part of the original English contribution to the development of the European artistic tradition, as we are examining it. They have individuality, they are often enchanting, but in basic method and idea they are not distinct from the contemporary production elsewhere.

This applies also to the other portraitists of the period. Their names must bulk large in the catalogue of English art, but, on the plane of European values, they have too long obscured our painters of conversation-pieces and landscapes —branches of art in which the country's genius can claim definite merits of invention. The reputation of Reynolds, for instance, has been greatly heightened by historical associations. He was a charming painter of children; his talent flowered in a gift for careful characterisation when he was portraying his many friends among the great of the time; with its other outstanding figures he rarely falls below a high standard of likeness. But his work is singularly lacking in the imaginative qualities which gave Romney grace, and Lawrence or Raeburn vigour. His doctrines were an attempt to keep in check the free development of our native art, taking practical form in his slighting of Gainsborough, Wilson and Constable, and he survives in his exalted position mainly by the interest of his sitters.

The spirit of Reynolds and his followers was still that of the eighteenth century and classicism, for portraiture is eminently a social art, in which supply is conditioned by demand. And the demand comes almost entirely from those ranks of society which favour stability rather than innovation in ideas. Gainsborough's landscapes are in spirit more modern than his portraits, and it is with his contemporaries in landscape that we find English painting keeping abreast of the Continental achievement, though hardly preceding it with his force of personality. If only to make the bridge between him and Constable, three of these artists deserve mention.

Richard Wilson, just before him both in birth and death, can with difficulty bear the weight of the title, "the father of British landscape," bestowed chronologically rather than critically. He was bound by many influences, which crystallised into an adaptation of Guardi and Canaletto; he did not so much originate landscape in England as transplant there a foreign product. But he had a profound appreciation of nature, and his sensitiveness to calm atmospheric effect was expressed in luminous tones of rare clarity. Tentatively he prefigures the romantic attitude.

Crome of Norwich, aware of him and of the early Gainsborough, and drawing on them both to break a Dutch stiffness, is still more consciously romantic. He deepens with a drama of cloud and changing light his limpid presentations of East Anglian scenery. His simplification in design, aiming at unity of mood and pattern, was followed with less force but fine rhythmic quality by his fellow-townsman, Cotman. While Wilson had painted Wales exquisitely, but as though it were Italy, the two Norwich artists found a poetry of nature without any transferred picturesque.

IV

With Constable, English painting is both at its greatest and most native. Hardly a century old, through him it was to give laws to a century to come. Imbued with a sense of past accomplishment, he, like Crome, saw that Wilson and Gainsborough, though still unacknowledged by the authority of connoisseurship in their landscape work, had contributed to the interpretation of nature equally with the acclaimed examples of Claude and Hobbema. But he felt that more remained to do, and quietly insisted that "there was room for a natural painter."

The odds that he had to meet may be judged by the

remark of Sir George Beaumont, himself an artist of accomplishment and a friend of Wordsworth, who exclaimed, on seeing one of Constable's pictures, "But where is your brown tree?" For even to enlightened eyes, the painting of nature was ruled by the conventions of established masters, instead of by its actual appearance. Hobbema dictated the trees, Poussin the sky, Claude and Cuyp the light, and Salvator the emotion.

Constable's great discovery was that time could be as great an element in landscape-painting as form; that it was just the aspects which change in a scene that give its rendering a final truth. Until his arrival, nature, though in every essential alive, had been portrayed as motionless. Constable saw that light in space was the element that his predecessors had ignored, and on which the ultimate verisimilitude depended.

It was not a picturesque that he sought, but a reality. He was a naturalist and not a romantic. While deeply admiring the poetry of Wordsworth, it was the descriptions of nature and the affirmation of orthodox religion that he appreciated, rather than any implications of a movement. "I hold the genuine pastoral feeling of landscape," he said, "to be very rare and difficult of attainment. It is by far the most lovely department of painting, as well as of poetry," and, "I never saw an ugly thing in my life, for let the form of an object be what it may—light, shade and perspective will always make it beautiful."

Thus it was an art of minutiæ that he pursued. Subject he narrowed down to a small area of his native Suffolk, with but occasional excursions to Brighton or Salisbury. In appearance, he concentrated on a moment of atmospheric effect; yet the work wins from its very particularity, from its pinning of the local and the momentary, an abiding grandeur.

The passion of his feeling for nature, though something new as he expressed it in his art, is an English quality that he gave to the world. In painting, it was a revelation to his own country also, receiving no recognition except from a small band. His fellow-Academicians insisted on his deadening with glaze just the liquidity of light in which his greatness of innovation consisted; his best work lay stacked and unsold in his studio at his death.

Appreciation, and the start of his influence which was to flow in an unbroken current not yet exhausted, came in France, when his "Hay-Wain" and a small sketch were exhibited in the Paris Salon of 1824. Stendhal praised them. Delacroix painted out, and repainted within three days, his "Massacre of Scio," after seeing them.

By way of Daubigny and the Barbizon School, Constable became an ancestor of Impressionism. His emphasis on atmosphere as a principle, and his use of divided colour as a means, were eagerly seized on by its theorists. Then, through the channel of the French impressionist masters, he at last became a force in his own country, one of the most apt examples in art of a prophet without honour, and yet the most absolute manifestation of the English genius.

Much the same fate was Turner's. Though of broader range, and generalising in effect where Constable sought the particular, he was a romantic instead of a naturalist. His was a concentration in painting of the English romanticism founded on an emotional reading of nature, not mystical and dream-swathed as in Germany, or an historical revival as in France. It was, however, the French Impressionists and not his fellow-countrymen who appreciated his oil-paintings, and Monet and Pissarro, when they came to London in 1870, absorbed him into their system of technique. His imitations of Claude, and his water-colours, met favour here, but the Turner of iridescent mist and tempest, of "The Evening Star" and "Norham Castle," was swept into European tradition before becoming a native influence.

In the medium of water-colour, however, his originality at once imprinted itself. For when the practice of water-colour, which for purposes other than the mere sketch was almost confined to this country, ceased to be directed to purely topographical ends, the especial picturesque of Turner was closely imitated. But the early English water-colourists included also many artists of individuality, who worked on parallel lines to the English romantics in poetry, such as Sandby and his followers, with their Gothic predilections; Cozens and Towne, who gave their own version of Childe Harold in landscape; and Girtin, who came near to Wordsworth in spirit, and to whom both Constable and Turner paid homage.

But the water-colour was most closely allied to English romantic poetry at the hands of Blake, whose appreciation as a pure artist has even suffered from the difficulty of dissociating his painting from his verse. In organisation of pattern, salience of form, and vital rhythm, he was to no small extent a precursor of Cézanne. The illustrations to the Book of Job, Dante, and Blair's "Grave," are easily susceptible to the reduction of their component parts of design to the figures of solid geometry, proclaimed by Cézanne the bases of formal construction.

The power of imagination, however, which is so completely interwoven with Blake's dynamic design, has that startling intensity which, on the lower level of moral illustration, pulses also in the works of Hogarth. This emotional content, ultimately religious in feeling, is a characteristic of the English subject-picture at the service of ideas. The Pre-Raphaelites were to evolve from it a kind of painting which foreign critics still consider our special product in art, and it is worth remembering that the study of Blake, both as poet and painter, was eagerly pursued by Rossetti and his school.

v

The formation of the Pre-Raphaelite Brotherhood, and the subsequent development of its various members, stand out as the most important phase of English art between the close of Romanticism and the start of Impressionism. Like so much of English painting, the movement owed its rise as much to the impulse of contemporary events as to purely artistic inception.

For the English school, except for its work in water-colour, which seems never to have deviated from a consistently high standard of technique, fell into a feeble phase of genre-painting after Constable and Turner. Those men of genius produced no immediate followers here. The current of effort flowed back to the outworn historical picture, or contemporary description, presumably founded on Hogarth without Hogarth's passion.

A certain vitality in his familiar reduction of the beau-ideal on the part of Etty, and Wilkie's domestication of Rubens, leading on the overcrowded detail of Egg's or Frith's scenes of contemporary life, are among the few achievements that stand out in a catalogue of decadence. The happening upon a set of reproductions of the Campo Santo frescoes at Pisa, by Rossetti and a group of students at the Academy Schools, was hardly in itself sufficient to start the glow of reaction that became the Pre-Raphaelite movement.

It was part of a wider stir, in which the growth of the High Church, Chartism, and the poetry of Tennyson and Browning, all had a share. The revolt against an effete and ineffective kind of painting linked up with a more general kind of dissatisfaction over industrialism and materialism. Along with a vague liking for the Italian masters before Raphael, on whom the Brotherhood possessed but little information, went a real effort towards a more spiritualised kind of invention, and a study of nature in close detail, undisturbed by academic rules.

The remarkable gifts of Rossetti were the most powerful influence in keeping the fellowship together, and here again, it may be noted, a movement in English painting progresses simultaneously with contemporary poetry. For some time the unity of effort was preserved. A splendid youthful enthusiasm fired the band, and even now communicates something attractive to work whose æsthetic hold has lost much of its force. A too self-conscious *naïveté*, and lack of coherent design, are the chief flaws that time no longer disguises. The Pre-Raphaelite picture seems built up of unrelated particles, though each by itself is often an inspiriting flame of colour or a little gem of faithful representation. Rossetti's "Ecce Ancilla Domini," Millais's "Ophelia," and Holman Hunt's "Lorenzo and Isabella," show the strength of the group while it was held together by a common purpose.

Even after they dissolved company, the work accomplished by the various artists of the P.R.B. is at its best when it retains most of its early fervour. Rossetti's "Lucrezia Borgia," Millais's "Autumn Leaves," and Holman Hunt's "Hireling Shepherd," make serious claims for attention; and Ford Madox Brown, though never actually of the Brotherhood, adapted its technical canon to studies of contemporary life, with success in feeling and execution, in "The Last of England" and "Work."

When the original founders had taken other directions in maturity, the force which they had concentrated for a few brilliant years still had the energy to attract others to follow in their way. Along with the less prominent members of the group, who remained stalwart Pre-Raphaelites to the end, like Hughes and Stephens, came Burne-Jones, whose power as a decorative painter cannot be denied, Fred Walker and Albert Moore. The fount has never since run entirely dry. Gustave Moreau and Maurice Denis have drawn from it the incentive to found a school that continues to-day in France. An exhibition of the New English Art Club is rarely without its Pre-Raphaelite reminiscence, as a rule most ably presented by Stanley Spencer.

In its duration, and because the English temperament does not run naturally to the group-movements so frequent in continental painting, Pre-Raphaelitism is unique in the annals of our art. We may condemn it, or try to disown it, but its very tenacity of survival points to its being an expression of something deep-rooted in the national spirit.

VI

After Pre-Raphaelitism, James McNeill Whistler for some time held the stage of English art almost alone. Since he passed most of his working life here, was inextricably involved in our art-controversies, and was the master of several of our more important painters, he can but be included as a member of the English School. He began his career, too, as a disciple of Rossetti, though a Rossetti who had passed beyond Pre-Raphaelitism. At the risk of overstressing the connexion between our painters and our poets, it may be remarked that a poem by Swinburne was appended to "The Little White Girl," one of his finest early works.

Whistler brought Impressionism to England, but it was not of Constable's brand. An extremely individual artist, he invented a perfect instrument for his own purposes, in which are mingled echoes of Velasquez, Courbet, Manet and the Japanese colour-print. In his figure-work an harmonious fusion of detail, in his landscapes chiefly confined to the effect of a "Nocturne," it is decorative and limited. It seeks generalisation, a vagueness which suggests instead of stating precisely. Yet it is true creation, and in the pictures of the misty, twilight Thames has imperishably netted a final nuance of London.

At present, Whistler's manner seems curiously isolated from contemporary endeavour, though for long it made a lively battle-ground for criticism, while its influence on the early Wilson Steer and Sickert cannot be forgotten. The disconcerting way in which Walter Greaves, Whistler's studio-assistant, caught to a nicety the mode of the Nocturnes should not be allowed to hide the more personal achievement of that delightful Victorian primitive.

To Wilson Steer belongs the honour of having brought back the doctrine of Constable to his own country. Steer's studies in Paris loosened the link with Whistler and attached him to the more scientific Impressionism of Manet and Sisley. But a strong susceptibility to the inherent characteristics of the English country scene, and an appreciation of Constable's genius in conveying them, drew him much nearer to the native source of the movement. His portraits and interiors are often invested with a deliberate eighteenth-century air of the grand manner, and for all their quivering atmosphere, there is a certain formality in his landscapes, a balance of design and a plasticity, which is his own addition to the impressionist treatment. In many exquisite notes of the subtler shades of light and weather, he has renewed the art of English water-colour.

The two other painters of this century whose gifts have projected an element of the English genius into the mainstream of European painting are Augustus John and Richard Sickert. With Gainsborough as the likeliest rival, John is the greatest of English portrait-painters. Keeping its freshness, with him that branch of his art has never become mechanical. An exalted view of character, which bespeaks a genuine romantic attitude, and a brave directness of approach, add a personal distinction to the authority of tradition that imbues the portraiture. The pictures of gipsy life and the landscapes are brimmed with a vital intensity of poetic feeling.

Sickert shows an affinity with Degas in manner, but it is translated into a very real English idiom. His scenes of Camden Town possess an unmistakable metropolitan flavour, a sense of drama illuminated by a penetrating humanity. The many studies of popular theatres and music-halls display an aspect of the city's life with superb gusto. The vivid portraits and the views of Bath, Dieppe and Venice form important sections of a great master's work, but it is unique in its attachment of the subject-picture to certain phases of the London spectacle.

Masterpieces are not in the majority in any country's output. Here, as everywhere else, a vast amount of the production is either parochial or anonymously international. Yet it may reasonably be claimed that, within its comparatively brief span, the English genius has formed a tradition of its own in art, and has made a valuable contribution to the main current of European achievement.

What that consists in is better described by citing the artists themselves than by general summary. For the great English masters are individuals rather than personifications of painterly attributes. With the exception of the Pre-Raphaelites, they have not reached fame in groups, and the strict code of Pre-Raphaelitism was swiftly loosened.

It can be said, though, that our examples of the English genius are essentially English. The country, in one aspect or another, expresses itself through them in direct fashion. For their ardour is devoted to representation rather than experiment in form or colour. With them, technique is farther from being an end in itself than with the Italian or French artist.

So the style with which the representation is tinged depends not so much on matters of craftsmanship as on their attitude to their subject, naturally shaded by the national cast of mind. This brings an element of literature into the work. An association of spirit can be traced continually between these artists and the writers interpreting what is most vital in the thought of the period, its poets especially. For the English painter at his best is a poet also, his picture distinguished, above all, by its qualities of imagination.

E3